THE TREASON OF THE SENATE

GEORGE E. MOWRY was born in Washington, D.C., and studied at Miami University (Ohio) and the University of Wisconsin. He is the author of *Theodore Roosevelt and the Progressive Movement, The Era of Theodore Roosevelt,* and *The California Progressives.* He is at present Professor of American History at the University of California, Los Angeles.

JUDSON A. GRENIER was born in Indianapolis and studied at the University of Minnesota and the University of California, Berkeley and Los Angeles. He has been a reporter for small newspapers in Minnesota and California and for the *Los Angeles Mirror-News,* and has taught and written about journalism, and about muckraking particularly. He is at present Professor of History at El Camino College in California.

DAVID GRAHAM PHILLIPS

THE TREASON

OF THE SENATE

by David Graham Phillips

EDITED WITH AN INTRODUCTION BY

GEORGE E. MOWRY AND JUDSON A. GRENIER

QUADRANGLE BOOKS / *Chicago* / 1964

E
75 6
. P 45
1964

CONTENTS

INTRODUCTION

PUBLICATION of David Graham Phillips's "The Treason of the Senate" by the *Cosmopolitan Magazine* in 1906 was, in many respects, the climax of the muckraking movement in American journalism. The bold, outspoken, often intemperate language of an author dedicated to "the search for truth" captures the essence of both the best and worst aspects of muckraking. In addition, the political dialogue stirred by publication of these articles constitutes a chapter in the history of the progressive movement and provides insight into the careers of two major public figures, Theodore Roosevelt and William Randolph Hearst.

The "era of the muckrakers" is generally assumed by historians to have begun with the publication by *McClure's Magazine* of Lincoln Steffens' "Tweed Days in St. Louis" in October, 1902, and to have ended in the Progressive party's Götterdämmerung with the election of Woodrow Wilson in 1912. The muckraking movement thus coincides in time with progressive domination of the Republican party, rising to fame with Roosevelt and, though castigated by him, supporting the Colonel as history swept by at Armageddon. Progressivism as a social force received its impetus from the journalistic technique of exposing to public view the malpractices of nineteenth-century society. Like journalism, progressivism relied upon the moral and ethical efficacy of democracy to correct social evils once they were exposed. In most social upheavals, a vanguard usually brings old institutions into disrepute, paving the way for new ones. The muckrakers played this role. From 1902 to 1912, they led the nation in the systematic uncovering of the strands of a giant web of control, linking politics, education, the press, religion, health, and high finance. Their names—Lincoln Steffens, Ida M. Tarbell, Ray Stannard Baker, Charles Edward Russell, Thomas W. Lawson, Samuel Hopkins Adams, Upton Sinclair, David Graham Phillips—were household words. The magazines that published their articles—*McClure's, Collier's, Everybody's,* the *American,* and the *Cosmopolitan*—achieved circulations in the hundreds of thousands and won an unprecedented mass readership across America for the "literature of exposure." Trained in the Christian ethic and devoted to the people's right to know, the muckrakers revealed the corruption of public men and corporations in the name of morality, a heightened public awareness, and the common good. Their crusade was consecrated to the precept of St. John viii:32: "And ye shall know the truth and the truth shall make you free."

Many muckrakers conformed almost to a pattern. They were born in the 1860's to middle-class parents and grew up in Midwestern towns which their families had, a generation or two earlier, helped to establish. Their fathers, landowners or editors, ministers or bankers, but seldom factory-owners, were influential in the business-professional society of the town. Usually thoroughly Protestant oriented, these young men were trained in the public schools to have deep reverence for American historical tradition, particularly the individualistic and equalitarian romance of the frontier, and an intimate knowledge of the forms and moral messages of English literature and classic parable. Small Midwest colleges sharpened their talents for expression and stimulated their desire to give their lives meaning by becoming creative writers. The necessity of earning

a living, however, diverted their talents into journalistic channels, and they became newspaper reporters in some nearby city.
Within a few years, they migrated to New York or Chicago and
were caught up in the glamor and excitement of the golden
age of American journalism, with reporter Richard Harding
Davis its symbol and Park Row his throne.

Steadily, these newsmen became conscious of the changes
in American society produced by the industrial revolution, particularly "our serious public corruption . . . of a kind unknown
to the people of two generations ago." Images were seared into
their minds—extremes of wealth and poverty shattering their
comfortable illusion that America was composed of commu-
nities of neighborly homesteaders who uplifted the community
by uplifting themselves. Sometimes their eyes were opened by
reading Henry George's *Progress and Poverty*, but more often
by what they observed: in Chicago a dynamic World's Fair providing a glittering backdrop for a dirty slum; in New York a
fashionable Fifth Avenue within walking distance of long rows
of tenements stuffed with penniless immigrants and owned by
a wealthy Wall Street church. They pondered ethical questions:
What has happened to American morality? How have we gone
astray? Who has betrayed us? And, as reporters exploring the
labyrinth of debased city politics, they came to pin responsibility on the businessman ("predatory wealth"), because the
money used by the corrupters originated with him.

Yet it was their writing ability, not their social philosophy,
that won them the respect of the metropolitan press, and when
the new mass-circulation magazines in the late 1890's infused
interviews and investigative articles into the potpourri of verse,
essay, and short fiction which was the nineteenth-century for-
mula, it was natural that they should tap Park Row for original
and responsible talent. The reporters, still harboring a desire
to be creative artists, but far wiser in their knowledge of how
both halves of society lived, became magazine writers and,
eventually, "muckrakers." Their articles and stories were peo-
pled with wise Ohio mothers, old-timers with salty speech, farm

boys and cow hands, kindly preachers and public school teachers, ethical corner grocers and blacksmiths, villainous Eastern
lawyers, crooked politicians, crude and self-centered factory
owners with hopelessly spoiled children. They would speak
wistfully of the country and the old home town and sometimes
pay hurried trips to the Midwest, to return (they said) reju-
venated. But the city was their "beat" now, and it gave them
comfort and doubt, stimulation and shame. So long as readership was high and fame opened most doors, New York remained their home.

The life of David Graham Phillips essentially corresponds
to this pattern. He was born on October 31, 1867, in Madison,
Indiana, a town of ten thousand population lying fifty miles
above Louisville on the Ohio river. Madison was founded in
1806, and its days of commercial glory were the two decades
prior to the Civil War, when for a time it was the largest and
wealthiest city in Indiana, a port for steamboat traffic. By the
1870's, however, the railroad had replaced the river as a carrier
of commerce; Madison's prosperity had begun to wane, its
shipyards to decline, its meatpacking industry to lose business
to Chicago and St. Louis. Stately homes, a fixed society, and
patterns of living established in the time of Jackson were the
heritage of the town's pre-war business vitality. Phillips's father,
an Indiana farm boy, lived in Madison from the time he was
sixteen years of age, attended Indiana Asbury University, served
as sheriff and clerk of court, and for thirty-one years was
cashier of the National Branch Bank of Madison. Phillips grew
up in an atmosphere compounded of banking, Republican politics, Bible-reading, Methodist morality, and love of learning.
His father owned one of the best private libraries in southern
Indiana, and Phillips was encouraged to read widely, particularly in American history. In later years he attributed his
omnivorous reading and tenacious writing habits to that
encouragement.

Graham, as he was called at home, gained his early education in the Madison public schools, which, according to

Arena editor B. O. Flower, were staffed in the seventies by enthusiastic New England teachers who created a thoroughly democratic environment and were famous for efficiency and a high standard of ethical conduct. Phillips told Flower, "I went to the public-schools . . . and I do not know of anything I am more thankful for. If I had my way, there should not be any other kind of schools, high or low." Although his principal interests were history, politics, and government, Phillips was an avid reader of novels and verse; his biographer, Issac F. Marcosson, reported that Graham had read all of Dickens, Hugo, and Scott before he was twelve and knew thousands of lines of poetry, including the whole of Gray's "Elegy." In 1882, at the age of fifteen, he enrolled at Asbury, his father's college, a Methodist institution in the rural atmosphere of Greencastle, Indiana (which changed its name to DePauw University about the time Phillips departed). Among his college interests were languages, French realistic literature, debate, football, and the Delta Kappa Epsilon fraternity, where he met the man who would become his closest and life-long friend, Albert Beveridge. Beveridge, a self-made man, impressed Phillips with his integrity, magnetism, and commanding voice. He was Phillips's roommate, and the writer in later years used him as model for his politician-hero, Hampden Scarborough, in a series of novels. Phillips admired Beveridge's determination to be a success, and the experience may have altered his own ambitions. By 1885, when Phillips left Indiana for Princeton University, he had decided not to follow his father's banking profession. At Princeton for two years, he won reputation as a brilliant conversationalist and a fastidious dresser, and there he resolved to become a writer.

Phillips graduated from Princeton in 1887 and began his journalistic career in Cincinnati, Ohio, ninety miles upriver from Madison. A college friend, Marshal Halstead, helped him get a position as reporter for the *Times-Star,* and, after Phillips had demonstrated his ability, offered him a similar job with the Halstead family's *Commercial-Gazette.* His three years in

Cincinnati were an apprenticeship spent reporting disaster, crime, politics, government, and recreation—the standard city assignments—and were spiced with frequent feature articles and a gossip column. In 1890, he left Cincinnati for New York City, where he joined the staff of Charles A. Dana's *Sun,* the best written and edited newspaper of its day. Dana insisted that reporters be able to recognize truth when they saw it, and then to express that truth in pungent, concise English. Phillips could have attended no better school of journalism. Many of his social ideas were shaped by the three years he covered the streets, homes, and offices of New York for the *Sun.* His mode of living was established during these years: he dressed well, in high fashion and high collar; he dined well, at Mouquin's, Delmonico's, and, after 1899, at Rector's; he roomed in tasteful bachelor quarters at, for example, The Players, a private club for actors and writers on Gramercy Park. Phillips never married, perhaps because his intense dedication to work allowed little time for feminine companionship. He usually left the *Sun* office at midnight and returned to his rooms to write until dawn. He wrote standing at a high, portable drafting desk, smoking cigarettes continuously, covering reams of lined copypaper with pencil in a fine, cramped script. For the rest of his life, the major part of Phillips's writing would be done while the city slept, a habit originating in his years with a morning newspaper.

While he was in college, Phillips determined that his newspaper career would be but a stepping stone to becoming a novelist. As a reporter he would be at school in society; he would learn the truth about the American people and their institutions, and then he would tell them that truth. Not newspapers, but magazines and books would be his outlet. In 1891, *Harper's Weekly* published the first of a stream of his articles, all written in off-duty time. But the nature of the goals Phillips had set for himself demanded that his experience be broad and varied, and after three years on the *Sun,* he joined the staff of the *World,* largest and most energetic newspaper in

New York. From 1893 to 1902, he served the *World* as reporter, foreign correspondent, editorial writer, and sometime traveling companion for Joseph Pulitzer, its publisher.

For the United States, these years were crucial in preparing the way for the Progressive Era. They were years of violence and change: bloody strikes at Homestead, Pennsylvania, and Chicago; financial panic and depression; the march on Washington of Coxey's army; President Cleveland's desperate attempts to borrow gold from Wall Street; increasing concentration of corporate wealth and the growth of trusts; drought, bankruptcy, and tenancy on the farms of the West and South, culminating in the Populist revolt; the revelations of poverty and squalor in tenement and tenderloin by Jacob Riis and Rev. Charles Parkhurst; Bryan's emotion-charged campaign for free silver and the Presidency; the rise of the American navy, jingoism, and delusions of imperialist grandeur; yellow journalism and its war with Spain in the Caribbean; sanguinary fighting with Philippino insurrectionists; anarchism and the collective national shock at the assassination of William McKinley; the accession to the Presidency of a younger, vigorous generation in the person of Theodore Roosevelt. Such were the raw materials of Phillips's *World* years. Some he gathered first hand, on assignment from city editor Charles Edward Russell; much he analyzed editorially under the guidance of Pulitzer himself, high in the *World* tower.

Late in 1896, Phillips became an editorial writer, and his promotion to this position coincided with the start of the intense rivalry between Pulitzer and Hearst's *New York Journal,* the so-called "war of the yellows." To express Pulitzer attitudes toward politics, imperialism, civic corruption, and monopoly became second nature to Phillips during these years. As Russell recalled: "At Mr. Pulitzer's direction David Graham Phillips wrote a series of articles reciting the misdeeds of trust after trust, sternly demanding thereto the immediate attention of . . . [Cleveland's Attorney General] Richard Olney, and notifying the citizenry that it had been betrayed." The Presidency and both houses of Congress came in for their share of Phillips's attention, and the *World* frequently scolded the Senate and Senator Chauncey M. Depew in particular. It may be that "The Treason of the Senate" was born in the editorial offices of the *World;* surely Phillips's antipathy for Congressional spokesmen for corporate wealth was an attitude shared by Pulitzer and his editors in the crusading nineties. The aging, nearly blind publisher frequently requested the companionship of the tall, handsome Hoosier, and in long conversations attempted to shape his outlook much as a father would advise a son.

But Phillips's days as a newspaperman were numbered. His output of magazine articles increased; his first novel, *The Great God Success,* was published in 1901 under the pseudonym John Graham (because its rather bitter depiction of newspaper life was thinly disguised). The book was read by the young editor of the *Saturday Evening Post,* George Horace Lorimer, who convinced Phillips to resign from the *World* in 1902 to become a free-lance writer. His old friend, Beveridge, now Senator from Indiana, was a frequent *Post* contributor. In the ensuing three years, Phillips wrote some fifty signed articles and numerous editorials for Lorimer, and perhaps conditioned himself for the "Treason" articles by penning political portraits of Roosevelt, Cleveland, Root, Rockefeller, and J. P. Morgan. He also contributed articles and short stories to *Everybody's,* the *Cosmopolitan, Harper's, McClure's,* the *Arena,* and *Collier's,* and published one or two successful novels each year.

David Graham Phillips's reputation as a muckraker rests largely upon his "Treason" series, but he probably contributed more to the seedbed of progressivism as a novelist than as a writer of nonfiction. Hundreds of thousands of middle-class Americans shared Phillips's attitudes and prejudices and found them reflected in his novels: *The Master-Rogue* (1903) and *The Cost* (1904), scathing critiques of Wall Street; *The Deluge* (1905), a fictional version of the financial revelations of Thomas

W. Lawson; *The Social Secretary* (1905), a depiction of the deterioration of Washington, D.C., and the Federal government because of the self-promoting standards of the rich; *The Plum Tree* (1905), a description of the rise to power of a United States Senator whose standards and convictions were a blend of those held by Marcus Hanna and Boies Penrose; and *The Second Generation* (1907), a portrayal of the idle, degenerate children of the wealthy. These novels and others, many published by the Indiana firm of Bobbs-Merrill, constituted an effective counterpoint to the exposés of Baker, Steffens, Tarbell, and Russell, and, together with Upton Sinclair's *The Jungle,* remain the standard examples of muckraking fiction.

In his *Post* articles and novels, Phillips examined the problems of industrialization and urbanization from a nostalgic, Jeffersonian perspective. His heroes display small-town virtues: they are honest, neighborly, independent, moral, observe the Golden Rule, respect their wives, take their mothers' advice, have "a Covenanter fiber tough as ironwood," and resist temptation. His villains are Easterners, city-bred or exhibiting acquired city manners: they are money-crazed and power-seeking; they practice bribery and fraud to pervert the democratic process and destroy honest government; their worship of luxury and wanton display increases the cleavages between classes; their marriages fail, and often their own conniving brings about their doom. They are essentially weak men, and their intelligence is "of the kind that goes with weakness—shrewd and sly, preferring to slink along the byways of craft even when the highway of courage lies straight and easy." The villains constitute "Privilege," the heroes are "the People," and Phillips's novels are essentially a dialogue between these forces of good and evil, with "the People" triumphant only after constant vigilance and a long struggle. Phillips's plea was for a return to the old moral standards, for the hard-headed integrity of the frontier farmer, for the revival of democratic methods of selecting public officials in place of the boss-ridden, money-dominated political practices of his day.

Phillips's greatest weakness, shared by most of his fellow muckrakers, was the inadequacy of his specific proposals for ending the corruption. For example, the fictional Senator Scarborough, upon winning the Presidential nomination, promised only to obey the Constitution and enforce the laws, leaving his intent to the reader's imagination. Phillips was vague and uncertain as to the methods by which corporate skullduggery might be restrained. Some of his contemporaries turned to socialism, but for Phillips socialism, like charity, was an aristocratic scheme to destroy self-reliance and individuality; it meant "withering and denuding paternalism" which would coddle incompetents. Phillips's solutions, being ethical, nostalgic, and deficient, enhanced his dilemma, but, insofar as they reflected the insecurity of an industrialized society nurtured upon Jeffersonian ideals, probably contributed to his popularity. It may be that his success as a writer was due, as critic Kenneth S. Lynn charges, to his ability to pander to the private hopes and dreams of the middle class. Though hopelessly anachronistic, Lynn writes, what makes Phillips important is that he ". . . actually did for a time become the secretary of American society."

When the *Cosmopolitan Magazine* selected Phillips to write the series of articles collectively entitled "The Treason of the Senate," its editors must have anticipated both the nature of his material and the manner of his presentation. Phillips had made his predispositions abundantly clear in his novels. In *The Cost*, monopolies managed the state legislatures which chose Senators. In *The Social Secretary*, rich men bought their way into the Senate. *The Plum Tree* muckraked the Senate itself. Its chief figure, Senator Harvey Sayler, custodian of "the plum tree" (an allusion to a telegram attributed to Senator Matthew Quay, political boss of Pennsylvania), manipulated both parties and controlled legislation in league with a syndicate of wealthy businessmen. Sayler's career as a political boss began when he realized

. . . that graft was the backbone, the whole skeleton of legislative business, and that its fleshly cover of pretended public service could be seen only by the blind. I saw, also, that no one in the machine of either party had any real power. The state boss of our party, United States Senator Dunkirk, was a creature and servant of corporations. Silliman, the state boss of the opposition party, was the same, but got less for his services because his party was hopelessly in the minority and its machine could be useful only as a sort of supplement and scapegoat.

This characterization is suggestive of the Aldrich-Gorman relationship depicted by Phillips in "Treason." Six months prior to the commencement of the "Treason" articles, Phillips published a book of essays, *The Reign of Gilt,* in which he bitterly castigated the political spokesmen for the rich. He predicted their ultimate doom. Representatives of a financial aristocracy, they would not exist beyond the time that "the People" became educated. Nothing could prevent the ultimate triumph of democracy—"the inevitable sequence of widespread intelligence"— and that, in turn, would rid America of the rascals. Democracy, for Phillips, was "not a theory that may someday be discovered false"; its progress was human history itself, with "a force as irresistible as that which keeps stars swinging" to sustain it. The role of the writer in the cause of democracy, be he essayist or novelist, was that of educator. The literature of exposure (even "yellow journalism") played a part in the process, for, as Phillips wrote in *The Cost,* "There is an abysmal difference between everybody knowing a thing privately and everybody knowing precisely the same thing publicly . . . the tremendous blare of publicity act[s] like Joshua's horns at Jericho." The image of himself as a latter-day Joshua, supported by historical inevitability and challenging a citadel of entrenched privilege, would have appealed to Phillips.

Though David Graham Phillips was the author of "The Treason of the Senate," he was not accountable for its genesis nor for its ultimate publication. That was the responsibility of Publisher William Randolph Hearst and his editors, Charles

Edward Russell and Bailey Millard. Perhaps the publication of
the "Treason" series was just a calculated step in Hearst's
political ambitions. From February 5, 1899, a major editorial
policy of the Hearst newspapers was the direct election of
United States Senators. Attacks upon the Senate were a standard feature of Hearst's political campaigns. For example, when
accepting the Democratic party nomination for Congress from
New York on October 6, 1902, he noted that "the people will
never be protected against the trusts by a Senate in which the
trusts occupy many seats and control a majority," and vowed
to support direct election as "a first step." Elected to Congress,
Hearst introduced such a resolution into the House and continued to agitate for the reform in his press. During his unsuccessful 1904 campaign for the Democratic Presidential nomination, he repeatedly supported direct election. Then, in the
spring of 1905, Hearst purchased his first magazine, the *Cosmopolitan,* founded in 1886 and owned since 1888 by John Brisben
Walker. Under Walker, *Cosmopolitan* was a general family
magazine, nonpartisan and not inclined toward muckraking,
though it published six articles by Phillips. Under Hearst, the
magazine was sensationalized, long-time *Examiner* editor-re-
porter Bailey Millard was made editor, and such standard
Hearst writers as Arthur Brisbane, Russell, Alfred Henry
Lewis, Edwin Markham, and Ambrose Bierce became regular
contributors.

Russell claimed at a later date to have originated the
"Treason" series. As he recalled, the idea came to him in 1905
while he was in the press gallery of the Senate listening to a
debate in which the great majority of "well-fed and portly
gentlemen" below represented not the people but an array of
predatory interests. Upon returning to New York, Russell suggested to Hearst a series of articles for *Cosmopolitan* "on the
fact that strictly speaking we had no Senate; we had only a
chamber of butlers for industrialists and financiers." According
to Russell, Hearst approved the idea; "I had begun to accumulate the facts when I received an assignment from *Everybody's*

. . . My task for Mr. Hearst was passed along to David Graham Phillips."

When Editor Millard first suggested to Phillips that he undertake the Senate series, the writer pleaded that he was occupied with his novels and proposed that William Allen White be given the job. But White was busy, and Millard again turned to Phillips, offering to pay any price named by the author. He also promised Phillips research assistance in amassing the facts and statistics upon which the articles would be based. A final appeal to the author's social conscience brought consent, and Graham's brother, Harrison, a Colorado newsman, and Gustavus Myers, a brilliant and dogged researcher, were hired as assistants. Myers had written *The History of Tammany Hall* in 1901; his socialist inclinations gave him an almost instinctive sense of the pitfalls and temptations in the path of businessmen, and with the determination of a detective, he pored over old books, newspapers, and magazines, on the trail of corruption. Myers used some of this data in his classic *History of the Great American Fortunes* (1909). His research gave him a sense of the continuity of the American past which eluded Phillips; he did not share the Indianan's reverence for pre-Civil War days and believed that the roots of political corruption lay in the landed wealth of colonial times. Aware of the methods by which companies gained real estate in the eighteenth century and bank charters and railroad land grants in the nineteenth century, Myers concluded that graft always had been prevalent, that the level of politics in the 1900's was better, not worse, than it had been in the past, and that progressive "reformers" were simply members of a self-satisfied class that wished to maintain its traditional social dominance. Myers believed himself to be more objective, more historical-minded than the muckrakers; yet, to the extent that his class consciousness determined the nature of the information he furnished Phillips, the "Treason" may have been given, as President Roosevelt charged, socialistic overtones.

Phillips prepared himself for his assignment by traveling

to Washington, where newspapermen and Congressmen gave
him confidential tips and leads which he used in the series. He
then returned to New York and, white-hot with enthusiasm,
indignation, and prejudice, began to turn out copy at his usual
pace. Staff members and lawyers pored over his articles for
libelous material. It was a painstaking task. Though the series
at one time was scheduled to begin in the February, 1906, issue
of *Cosmopolitan,* it was delayed until the March number. A
Hearst biographer reports that the publisher took a personal
interest in the series, stopping the press run of the first article
in order to insert more facts and rewrite the conclusion.

The process of selection to the Senate in 1906 was what it
had been in the early days of the republic, when state legislatures were designated by the Constitutional Convention to
select United States Senators. Thus was election made indirect,
less democratic, and supposedly less subject to political wran-
gling. And as Madison's *Journal* clearly indicates, many members of the Constitutional Convention hoped that a Senate so
fashioned would represent wealth as well as the individual
states. At the convention, only James Wilson of Pennsylvania
suggested direct election of Senators by vote of the people;
selection of legislatures to do the job eventually was adopted
unanimously. Congress was given the right to regulate the time
and manner of holding elections, but it did not exercise this
right until July 25, 1866, and many states were not represented
in the Senate at times for lack of agreement upon a candidate.
In 1866, a law was enacted providing that each house of a
state legislature would choose its Senatorial candidate on the
second Tuesday following organization. The next day a joint
session would be held. If both houses selected the same man he
would be declared elected; if not, a joint ballot would be taken
on that and every day the legislature remained in session until
a Senator was chosen. Yet this 1866 law did little to prevent
Senate vacancies. For example, Delaware failed, after daily

balloting, to elect a Senator in 1895, 1899, 1901, and 1905. Even when one man gained a clear majority, delaying tactics—such as preventing a quorum—could be employed by the opposition. From 1890 to 1906, eight states had Senate vacancies for portions of a term.

Moreover, in the post-Civil War period, state legislatures seemed increasingly subject to bribery and intimidation in their selection of Senators. Though only one case of alleged bribery came before the Senate prior to 1866, nine such cases were tried from 1866 to 1906. As early as the 1870's, charges were made in the press that the Senatorial selection process was colored by corruption and subservience to corporate interests seeking such privileges as franchises, land grants, and protective tariffs. That some politicians sold their favors was evident, as was the late nineteenth-century tendency of lawyers representing corporations and, later, wealthy businessmen themselves, to seek election to the Senate. Gustavus Myers suggested that the movement of millionaires toward the Senate was "led by the mine magnates of the far West"—William Sharon and James G. Fair of Nevada (1875, 1881), and Leland Stanford and George Hearst of California (1885, 1886). The *World Almanac* of 1902 listed eighteen Senators as millionaires, including Aldrich, Depew, Elkins, Fairbanks, Kean, Lodge, and Hanna. In 1906, Phillips listed twenty-five, though Senator George Perkins considered this number to be an exaggeration. A moot question sometimes debated in the press, prior to the appearance of "Treason," was whether it was less harmful to have millionaires elected to the Senate than to have Senators use their office to make millions. In either case, the Senate was known in the popular vernacular as the "Millionaires' club."

In 1906, the political scientist George H. Haynes summarized the public standing of the body:

Judged by the fruits which it has produced in recent years, in the estimation of the public, the Senate has fallen from its high estate . . . Never before in its history has the Senate been the target of such scathing criticism as during the past fifteen years. On all sides is heard the charge that the Senate . . . is now the stronghold of the trusts and of corporate interests.

In examining the 58th Congress (1903-1905), Haynes was appalled to discover that one-tenth of the Senators had had serious charges of dereliction from duty brought against them. Other statistics compiled by Haynes showed that Republicans comprised 64.4 percent of Senate membership, that the average age of members was 59.8 years, that about two-thirds of the Senators were lawyers by profession, and that only two members of the present Senate had "written a book in stiff covers." (That is, men of letters were not well represented.) He then submitted a list of the Senators in the 58th Congress to "five impartial observers of the Washington scene" (including two Washington correspondents and one magazine writer), and asked that the Senators be classified according to what or whom each represented in Congress. One out of three Senators owed his election to "wealth" or "manipulation"—qualities which "make their usefulness as members of the dominant branch of Congress decidedly open to question." Yet, many of the Senators attacked by Phillips were given a clean bill of health by Haynes's panel. Its classifications included:

I. "Statesmanship": Allison, Bailey, Fairbanks, Foraker, Frye, Hale, Hoar, Spooner
II. "Rank and File": Nelson
Either I or II: Cullom
III. "Wealth": Kean, Depew, Elkins
IV. "Political Manipulation": Gorman, Penrose, Platt, Stone
Either III or IV: Aldrich
V. Unclassified: Burton

Following this introduction are capsule biographies of twenty-one Senators muckraked by Phillips in his "Treason" articles. These men had certain characteristics in common: eighteen were Republicans, half of whom were committee chairmen; sixteen were lawyers by profession, a higher percentage than the Senate average; seniority was characteristic even of North-

ern senators—eight of the twenty-one established longevity
records for serving their states in the Senate. Eleven won
election to the House of Representatives prior to their selection
as Senators (for a higher average than the Senate's overall 35.9
percent), and all had won some popular election, suggesting
that their success and influence were partially due to prelim-
inary political experience. Sixteen represented states lying east
of the Mississippi and north of the Potomac and, with the
exception of Bailey of Texas, none was from the deep South
or far West, indicating that political control of the Senate in
1906 differed from that of today.

Although criticism of the Senate antedated the muckraking
movement, investigation of that body increased noticeably after
the turn of the century. Articles analyzing the Senate, some
critically, appeared in the *North American Review* in 1902; the
Atlantic Monthly and *Century* in 1903; the *Nation,* the *Independent,* and *World's Work* in 1905, to name a few. The press
abounded in statements linking Senators and trusts. For example, the *New York Post* in March, 1904, caustically com-
menting upon the investigation of Senator Reed Smoot of Utah,
wondered if it wouldn't be as proper to expel a Senator who
took orders from the beef or sugar trust as one who took orders
from the Mormon church. Or the *Chicago Record Herald* of
one year later: "Caesar had a listening senate at his chariot
wheels. He must have been the forerunner of the railroad
magnate." In *McClure's,* Ray Stannard Baker branded the Elkins
committee railroad investigations a farce, charging Elkins, Kean,
Aldrich, and Foraker with collusion to whitewash the railroads.
In 1905, a public uproar resulted over the arrests and trials of
Senator John H. Mitchell (Oregon) and Joseph Burton (Kansas) on charges of land and postal frauds; both men were fined
and sentenced to prison. Under the heading, "The Senate's Roll
of Dishonor," the *Nation,* on December 7, 1905, claimed that
the Senate's prestige "has suffered a terrible blow" because
of the convictions. Included in the *Nation's* roll of "disgraced
Senators" were Thomas C. Platt and Chauncey Depew of New

York and Boies Penrose of Pennsylvania, largely because of their implication in New York insurance scandals. The Armstrong investigating committee, led by its chief counsel, Charles Evans Hughes, clearly indicated the privileges accorded insurance companies because of political pressures brought by these men, and produced a clamor for their resignations. Even so business-minded a paper as *The Journal of Commerce* suggested that neither Platt nor Depew "has been, is or can be a good and faithful servant of this great State, and their presence in the Senate covers it with confusion and humiliation."

Probably the most significant muckraking series to reflect upon the dignity of the Senate prior to "Treason" was Thomas W. Lawson's "Frenzied Finance" published in *Everybody's*. Financier Lawson's exposés of the operating methods of insurance companies helped trigger the Armstrong investigation. Then, in the November, 1905, issue of *Everybody's*, Lawson charged that Senator Clark of Montana purchased his election. After the election, according to Lawson, Henry Rogers of the Standard Oil Company requested a Senatorial investigation because Clark was an industrial competitor. When Clark resigned his seat and was then re-elected to the Senate, again under questionable circumstances, Rogers warned him he would be expelled unless he co-operated with Standard Oil. To back up his threat, Rogers supposedly produced a list containing the names of two more Senators than the majority needed for expulsion. Popular reaction to the Lawson charges was widespread; the *Arena*, in its January, 1906, issue, specifically asked the following men if their names were on the Rogers list: Lodge, Aldrich, Depew, Platt, Gorman, Bailey, Penrose, Spooner, and Elkins. It also demanded a Senate investigation of the Lawson exposures and suggested that the Senate ". . . is becoming more and more a machine for registering the will of Wall-street campaign contributors and the puppet of privileged wealth."

Lincoln Steffens' series of articles on statewide corruption for *McClure's* in 1904-1905, titled "Enemies of the Republic," may be considered a forerunner of "Treason." Steffens' investigations led him repeatedly to the Senate, and though his language was more restrained than that of Phillips, his conclusions were similar. For example, in "New Jersey: A Traitor State" (April, 1905), Steffens wrote: ". . . it has seemed that the United States Senate must be made up of the representatives from each state, not of the people, not even of the state, but of the corrupt system of each state. This would account for much that happens in the Senate." He added, "We have been in at the birth of several United States Senators, so we can begin, if we are honest, to realize that that august chamber is the earthly heaven of traitors." Steffens' article on Rhode Island centered upon Nelson Aldrich, "the arch-representative of protected, privileged business," who had become the "boss of the United States." Steffens believed Senator Spooner to be representing the railroad interests of Wisconsin, and Senator Stone the baking powder interests of Missouri. Finally, Steffens visited Washington itself and, in a series of articles for a newspaper syndicate in 1906, charged that "the chamber of bosses" had sabotaged the President's legislative program.

The immediate political background for the "Treason" series lay in the 59th Congress, which opened in December, 1905, in an atmosphere of criticism, scandal, and doubt. Public and newspaper attention was focused on the President's request for railroad rate reform; cartoonists depicted Aldrich, Elkins, and Foraker as a trio of determined opponents of Roosevelt's proposals. *Current Literature* told its readers that the fate of the railroad measure, as well as other legislation, treaties, and appointments, rested in the hands of an unofficial " 'steering committee' chosen at a caucus of the dominant party." This steering committee consisted of Senators Allison (chairman), Hale, Aldrich, Cullom, Lodge, Perkins, Clark (Wyoming), Elkins, Spooner, Kean, and Beveridge; eight of the eleven would be attacked by Phillips. A prolonged debate at the outset of the session indicated Senatorial sensitivity to rising public

criticism. On December 18, Senator Bailey remarked that ". . .we
have fallen to the point that even when in the common play-
houses of the country where cheap playwriters stage cheap
plays, the audience applauds when Senators are described as
grafters." His remark was immediately challenged, and a debate
raged as to whether the Senate ought to expel a Senator accused of graft while the courts were in the process of trying
him. Theodore Roosevelt characterized the mood of Washington on January 10, 1906: "Just at the moment the people at
large, and therefore Congress too, seem to be Lawson-ized, so
to speak. They are so jumpy, even about reform, that it is
difficult to get coherent—that is, effective—action from them."

Within days after Roosevelt's edgy letter on the emotional
state of Congress, street-corner placards appeared throughout
Washington, proclaiming in giant type the coming publication
of "The Treason of the Senate!" The promotional campaign for
the major muckraking series of 1906 was intense, thorough,
and highly sensational—a page out of Hearst canon. The Hearst
metropolitan press and small-town newspapers throughout the
nation printed anticipatory news releases supplied by the magazine's circulation department. Reaching the news stands on
January 15, the February issue of *Cosmopolitan,* with its editorial introduction to the series, promised stirring revelations
and hinted that Chauncey M. Depew, target of the March
issue, would resign. He did not, but the March number of the
magazine sold out. So did the April *Cosmopolitan* containing the
article on Senator Nelson W. Aldrich. Subscriptions poured in
and, if publisher's figures are to be trusted, circulation in May
stood at 450,000, or about 50 percent higher than the magazine's
1905 average. Measured in terms of profit, circulation, letters
to the editor, and by the extent to which the articles were
reprinted in the country's smaller dailies and weeklies, "Treason"
was a smashing success.

The nine articles comprising "Treason" appeared monthly
from March through November and dealt at length with the
private and public careers of twenty-one Senators, selected ap-

parently because of their private wealth and their power in the Senate and party organizations. Stone of Missouri, Gorman of Maryland, and Bailey of Texas were Democrats, the remainder Republicans. All were either immensely wealthy, like Depew of New York, or like Spooner of Wisconsin and Lodge of Massachusetts were influential because of their Senatorial committee assignments. Some, such as Aldrich of Rhode Island and Elkins of West Virginia, were both multi-millionaires and wielders of power in the Senate. They by no means represented a typical cross-section of that body; on the other hand, their political sins were apparently no greater than those of most of their colleagues. Phillips probably could have written double the number of articles had he and Hearst cared to continue muckraking the lesser lights of the Senate in a similar vein.

Phillips's technique was to present a short biography of his subject that stressed a triangulation between his public success, his willingness to serve private business interests, and his accumulation of a sizable fortune. The remainder of the article was devoted to his subject's political career, with emphasis upon a number of legislative incidents in which the Senator had invariably cast his influence and vote in a way befriending his corporate allies at the expense of the general public. The articles usually concluded with a short homily on the man and his public ethics.

The "Treason" articles presented very little factual information about the Senators and the Senate that had not appeared previously on the public record in one form or another. How then is one to explain the series' impact upon the public, the indignation it caused in conservative circles, and the wrath it stirred in the President? Part of the answer lies in its aggregate weight—the accumulated effect of piling charge upon charge, article after article—which, in totality, implied that most Senators were guilty of great public wrongdoing. Part lies in the fact that the articles appeared in a supposedly reputable national magazine owned indeed by a member of Congress. Additionally, the effect of Phillips's articles was heightened by his use of sentences which implied more than they actually said, a technique which his contemporary, Norman Hapgood, termed "adroit insinuation."

For example, in his article on Lodge, Phillips claimed that the Massachusetts legislature was characterized by public plunder and betrayal, and then concluded that "this is notoriously typical of the body which has three times elected Lodge. A stream can rise no higher than its source—that is not an axiom of physics only." As an axiom applied to Lodge, it was nonsense. The articles were replete with such outlandish suggestions—that John Spooner's seat in the Senate chamber was designed to give him a "coigne of vantage as the mouthpiece of special privilege," or that because Hemenway of Indiana and Brandegee of Connecticut favored Fairbanks's Presidential ambitions, that "is, of itself, enough to locate them." The reader was to use his imagination.

But perhaps the major reason for "Treason's" impact is to be found in the unrestrained language Phillips used to describe his subjects, in the intensity of his adjectives and adverbs rather than in the gravity of his rather well-known facts. Bailey, for example, was compared unfavorably to Judas Iscariot, Gorman described as "a grafter," Elkins accused of "sneak thievery," and Aldrich of "three acts of treason" that had brought him wealth and rank. Collectively, the Senate was depicted as "stealthy," "treacherous," and "traitorous," made up of "bribers" and "perjurers" and "change-pocket thieves." During heated political campaigns, especially in Populist days, personal charges of such intensity had not been unknown. But rarely outside of campaigns had such blunt words been used so coolly about august public servants by a respected journalist writing for a reputable national magazine. Little wonder that Theodore Roosevelt feared a general public discrediting of his party, the national legislature, and indeed the administration if the effects of such charges were not somehow dissipated.

son" series. In them his personal friend Lodge was characterized
Roosevelt had reasons for being indignant about the "Trea-

as a "product of petty grafters" and his former cabinet member Knox described as a man who had made his millions through fees "from armor-plate and rebate rascals." Roosevelt also feared that his legislative program for the regulation of railroads, stockyards, and food manufactures would be endangered by the controversy, and possibly as a result his party might lose the Congressional elections of 1906 and thus mar his incredibly popular record with a sign of public displeasure.

Even before the articles appeared in print, the President was apprehensive about them; he had good reason to be. The writer had linked him with plutocracy and ridiculed his ostentatious "ceremonial of a king" in *The Reign of Gilt*. The publisher was perhaps his major political enemy. It seems probable, therefore, that the President had made up his mind about the series before he read it. At any rate, he had been growing disenchanted with the "literature of exposure" for nearly a year. Lawson's articles, followed by Boss Platt's subsequent testimony that he recognized a moral obligation to care for the interests of corporations that contributed to campaigns, upset Roosevelt because he was, by implication, involved. The investigations by Ray Stannard Baker of railroad corruption and by Lincoln Steffens of state politics for *McClure's* in 1905 had troubled him in their cumulative effect. As McClure's biographer suggests, ". . . these articles constituted a devastating report on the State of the Union, so graphic and so telling that they had wrested from the President his political leadership. He was no longer summoning, he was being dragged." Roosevelt wrote McClure on October 4, 1905:

I think Steffens ought to put more sky in his landscape. I do not have to say to you that a man may say what is absolutely true and yet give an impression so one-sided as not to represent the whole truth. It is an unfortunate thing to encourage people to believe that all crimes are connected with business, and that the crime of graft is the only crime.

He warned writer Ray Stannard Baker on November 28, 1905: "In social and economic, as in political, reforms, the violent

revolutionary extremist is the worst friend of liberty, just as
the arrogant and intense reactionary is the worst friend of
order." To his friend, editor Lyman Abbott of the *Outlook,* he
wrote on October 14, 1905, that an author who lies by over-
exaggerating graft ". . . occupies a position in my judgment
not one whit better than the real grafter, and infinitely below
the very worst of the men whom he accuses; for most of
the latter are not guilty of any shortcomings whatever."

But of all the sensational writers and publishers, Hearst
had annoyed him most. A potential political rival since Span-
ish-American War days (when TR refused to give "a certificate
of character to the New York *Journal*"), Hearst had long
borne the brunt of his invective. In his first speech to Congress, for example, the President spoke of his predecessor's
assassin as probably having been inflamed ". . . by the reckless utterances of those who, on the stump and in the public
press, appeal to the dark and evil spirits of malice and greed,
envy and sullen hate. The wind is sowed by the men who
preach such doctrines, and they cannot escape their share of
responsibility for the whirlwind that is reaped." He was by
implication blaming Hearst for the death of McKinley, and
when Hearst ran for governor of New York in 1906, Roosevelt
authorized his Secretary of State, Elihu Root, to state publicly that when uttering those words he "had Mr. Hearst
specifically in mind. And . . . what he thought of Mr. Hearst
then he thinks of Mr. Hearst now."

Roosevelt's apprehensions about exposé increased when
Poultney Bigelow muckraked the Panama canal situation in
the *Independent* and the charges were repeated in other magazines. The President and his Secretary of War were incensed
and called in the press in January, 1906, to answer each
charge with facts and figures. (Later in the year Bigelow was
after Panama again, for the *Cosmopolitan.*) Shortly thereafter,
the provocative billboards advertising "Treason" appeared,
followed by the February number of *Cosmopolitan* with its
announcement that Chauncey M. Depew would be the first

target. The attack on Depew was a final straw for the President. Depew, though a front man for the railroads, was considered by Roosevelt to be a harmless good-fellow, and at the state Republican convention of 1898 he had made the speech nominating TR for governor of New York, reciting his accomplishments in glowing terms. Roosevelt's reaction to the "Treason" announcement was, at first, indirect. His close associate, Postmaster General George B. Cortelyou, dispenser of all-important mailing privileges, warned in a Lincoln's Birthday speech at Grand Rapids, Michigan:

Of late years there has developed a style of journalism, happily as yet limited in its scope, whose teachings are a curse and whose influence is a blight upon the land. Pandering to unholy passions, making the commonplace to appear sensational, fanning the fires of sectionalism and class hatred, invading the privacy of our firesides, it presents one of the most important of our present-day problems.

When the March *Cosmopolitan* containing the Depew article reached him on February 17, the President wrote an associate, "I need hardly tell you what I feel about Hearst and about the papers and magazines he controls and their influence for evil upon the public and social life of this country . . ." That same day he suggested that Alfred Henry Lewis, head of the Washington bureau of the *New York Journal,* and himself a *Cosmopolitan* contributor, drop in for conversation:

I have just been reading the Cosmopolitan. There is no need for me to say that so far as in one article or another corruption and fraud are attacked, the attack has my heartiest sympathy and commendation; but hysteria and sensationalism never do any permanent good, and in addition I firmly believe that to the public, as well as to private individuals, the liar is in the long run as noxious as the thief.

In a letter written to William Howard Taft on March 15, two days before he addressed the Gridiron Club, Roosevelt named Phillips, Lawson, and Upton Sinclair as a trio of lurid

sensationalists who were building up a revolutionary feeling
in the country.

The meetings of the Gridiron Club of Washington newsmen and correspondents were a capital tradition, attended
by most important government officials, including the President. Sessions were informal and off the record, and reporters
felt as free to lampoon the politicians as they to ridicule the
press. Chauncey Depew had addressed the first dinner of the
Gridiron Club—its organizational meeting—and often since
had been its guest. Roosevelt could expect a sympathetic
audience there for a defense of Depew, and his opportunity
arose when House Speaker Joseph Cannon gave a dinner for
the club on March 17, 1906. The President spoke off-the-cuff
and without notes of "the man with the muckrake" who
makes slanderous assaults on public officials. Although he
had originally intended to mention Phillips by name, he was
dissuaded by Senator Root from giving the author further
notoriety. The "muckrake" allusion, though not original with
Roosevelt, immediately caught on, and, if the speech was
meant to be a trial balloon, it was a success. The following
day, Roosevelt told Steffens that he had spoken "to comfort
Depew," but, ever sensitive to wider political potentialities,
the President determined to expand his remarks for a national
audience at the laying of the cornerstone of the House Office
Building on April 14, 1906. Steffens thought Roosevelt "felt
the satiety of the public with muckraking." Ray Stannard
Baker attempted to deter him from making the speech, on
the grounds it would encourage indiscriminate attack upon
exposures "which may prevent the careful study of modern
conditions and the presentation of the facts in a popular
form," but the President insisted that he wanted to make the
speech to prevent such a misunderstanding—he would dis-
tinguish between the "light and air" of responsible publications and the "sewer gas" of Hearst's papers and magazines.
When the speech was delivered, no such distinction was made.

Roosevelt's muckrake speech is reprinted in the Appendix. In it he combined "the man with the muckrake" with suggestions for federal inheritance taxes and controls over corporations. It indicates the familiar Roosevelt technique of balancing attacks on the left with attacks on the right. It is said that when he reached the phrase, "Under altered external form we war with the same tendencies toward evil that were evident in Washington's time . . . ," he waved his hand over the heads of the Senators gathered around him, and the crowd laughed merrily. Actually, the President misused the "muckrake" allegory he borrowed from John Bunyan's *Pilgrim's Progress*. Traditionally, the muck of the barnyard symbolized worldly riches; the muckraker image would better represent the money-seeker than the truth-seeker. But the name stuck, permanently affixed not only to Phillips and Hearst but to a generation of magazine reporters.

The President's speech did not end his concern over the "Treason" series. Each new article seemed to rekindle his indignation. On May 23, he suggested to Lorimer, the *Post* editor, that Phillips had accepted Hearst money in order "to achieve notoriety." Most of the Senators Phillips attacked, rather than being "all black" and concerned only with their own pecuniary interests, were simply normal men. Roosevelt added:

Phillips takes certain facts that are true in themselves, and by ignoring utterly a very much larger mass of facts that are just as true and just as important, and by downright perversion of truth both in the way of misstatement and of omission, succeeds in giving a totally false picture . . . [The articles] give no accurate guide for those who are really anxious to war against corruption, and they do excite a hysterical and ignorant feeling against everything existing, good or bad; the kind of hysteria which led to the 'red fool fury of the Seine' . . ."

On June 18, the President wrote Lyman Abbott that the *Cosmopolitan*, thanks to Hearst and Phillips, "is the friend of disorder, less from principle than from the hope of getting profit out of troubled waters." On August 17, he told Taft and Cortelyou that "the fact that a thing appears in the *Cosmopolitan* is presumptive evidence of its falsehood." On October 25, he wrote the Englishman John St. Loe Strachey that Hearst "is the most potent single influence for evil we have in our life."

Although the President seemed to grow angrier as he pondered Phillips's articles, the suspicion remained that Roosevelt had encouraged attacks on Congress by using outspoken language about his Senatorial adversaries in private conversation. After his muckrake speech, some newspapers—such as the *New York World* and the *New York Post*—suggested not only that the President was a muckraker himself but that some of the very anecdotes about various Senators originated at his table. A personal experience of Upton Sinclair confirms this impression; Sinclair, who lunched with Roosevelt in the spring of 1906, recalls that the President characterized Eugene Hale as "the Senator from the Shipbuilding Trust . . . The most innately and essentially malevolent scoundrel that God Almighty ever put on earth." On another occasion, Roosevelt wrote Steffens that Senator Bailey's leadership showed ". . . an eagerness to sacrifice the interests of the public to the favored interests of a faction . . ." This sort of language was not far removed from that used by Phillips.

The United States Senate, loath to dignify the "Treason" series by direct defense of itself, generally maintained an attitude of silence toward it. That the Senators were increasingly sensitive, however, was indicated when Senator Foraker, assuming that a fellow Senator was questioning his motives, announced March 14:

> I do not want any Senator to insinuate again that I have any interest in any railroad, or that I am an advocate of any special interest, or that I am influenced here in my conduct and in my arguments and in my votes by anything whatever except only a sense of duty.

(Yet he was accepting payment from the Standard Oil Company, as Hearst revealed in 1908 by publishing the so-called

"Archbold letters.") On March 22, after publication of the Aldrich article, Senator Lodge rose in the Senate to denounce reckless attacks upon public men. Lodge said, "Concocting slanders and heaping together falsehoods for the purpose of selling them is not a pleasing trade, and when carried on in the name of virtue and reform it is a peculiarly repulsive one." Such articles, Lodge continued, sought to gratify envy and were "morally on a very low level." Their real evil lay not in the extent to which they affect the man attacked, but in the creation of distrust in our institutions. But virulent attacks on the Senate had occurred before—"checks and balances are rarely popular"—and sober second thought would vindicate us, Lodge concluded.

No further comments were heard on the floor of the Senate until Senator Bailey of Texas rose, on June 27, to criticize Hearst and Phillips and to defend himself against the *Cosmopolitan* charges. He would not normally answer such an attack, he said, "But the fact that the publication which contains the false and offensive matter to which I object is owned by a Member of Congress seems to take this case out of the general rule and to demand the answer which I am about to make." His answer was a strange one, compounded of indignation, self-righteousness, and the realization that he was speaking for a large number of his listeners who did not attempt (or could not attempt) to controvert the charges of "Treason." Bailey's speech was not so much a challenge to the facts contained in the Phillips articles as it was to the conclusions the author drew from the facts. He claimed that it was fantasy to believe that "Democratic and Republican Senators are acting together in a secret agreement . . . carried out behind closed doors and in committee rooms." He also defended his commercial dealings, saying:

I despise those public men who think they must remain poor in order to be considered honest. I am not one of them. If my constituents want a man who is willing to go to the poorhouse in his old age in order to stay in the Senate during his middle age, they will have to find another Senator. I intend to make every dollar that I can honestly make, without neglecting or interfering with my public duty . . .

In essence, therefore, Bailey's disagreement with Phillips was moral—what should constitute the proper standards for public officials—and his indignation with the "Treason," in addition to the threat it posed to his political career, resulted from the extent to which it challenged contemporary political standards in the Senate. (Bailey's arguments are reprinted in the Appendix.)

No further direct answer to Phillips was made on the floor of the Senate, although Senator George C. Perkins of California defended the Senate in an article in the *Independent* of April 12, 1906. Perkins's attestation was vague and inconclusive. He wrote that the Senate was fair, impartial, and truth-seeking, and indicated that he did not believe any Senator sought his seat for a reward other than the honor of belonging to the "most distinguished legislative body in the world."

Reaction of the nation's press to "The Treason of the Senate" was mixed, but on the whole, unfavorable. Conservative newspapers and magazines considered the articles inflammatory, even revolutionary. Phillips's old paper, the *Sun,* editorialized, "Those who seek to undermine that confidence and to destroy respect are playing with matches in dangerous proximity to a powder magazine." In *The Critic,* F. Hopkinson Smith charged Phillips indirectly with "sowing the seeds of anarchy." *Century* called periodicals like *Cosmopolitan* "the parents of all the vulgarities . . . a danger to American democracy." Some of the moderate New York newspapers, such as the *World* and the *Post,* treated both "Treason" *and* the Senate with amusement. Other publications, such as the Hearst metropolitan press and smaller newspapers further West, came to the defense of the series, insisting: "The Senate has become an appendix to the trusts and the protected interests. It represents the people no longer."

"Treason" troubled most of the other muckraking magazines; they feared that the series would discredit the entire movement. Hearst publications had a reputation for leaping aboard reform bandwagons, only to derail them by insensitivity, sensationalism, and commercialization. One did not uplift politics, as Ellery Sedgwick moaned in the *American,* by ". . . two weeks in Washington and then a general onslaught on the Senators, good, bad, indifferent." Of all the criticisms of Phillips, that which depressed him most was the judgment of *Collier's* editor Norman Hapgood, which appeared on November 17, 1906:

"The Treason of the Senate" has come to a close. These articles made reform odious. They represented sensational and money-making preying on the vogue of the literature of exposure, which had been built up by truthful and conscientious work . . . Mr. Phillips's articles were one shriek of accusation based on the distortion of such facts as were printed, and on the suppression of facts which were essential.

Throughout the appearance of 'Treason," David Graham Phillips bore the brunt of criticism. The author expected Washington to react sharply and at first paid little attention to attacks upon himself. His fame and *Cosmopolitan's* circulation reached new heights, and he basked in both. Compliments from his friend, Senator Beveridge, assured him that the articles were not without effect. Yet Phillips was hurt by Roosevelt's Gridiron Club speech and, particularly, by the censure from his former colleagues in the press. He began to receive threatening letters. Some of his judgments were blue-penciled by the editors. In August, as pressures built up against "Treason," Phillips wrote Beveridge, "I don't mind telling you that I would even make sacrifices in order to carry the thing to some sort of decent finish. However, I don't think sacrifices will be necessary, as Mr. Hearst has shown every disposition to leave me entirely alone." The conclusion of the series, when it came in November, was abrupt. No summary paragraph of consequence, no prognostications for the future, standard Phillips devices, were included, beyond the simple suggestion that until the people woke up to what was going on, things would be as they were. No novel Phillips wrote ended on such a flat, anti-climactic note. It is probable that he had grown discouraged; Charles Edward Russell later wrote that ". . . Phillips could never see the good that he had wrought and to the end regarded his series as the one failure of his career." The editorial attack by Hapgood caught him in a pessimistic mood. The Sunday after it appeared, Russell walked Phillips around the streets of New York. Russell recalled:

> I had an anxious time . . . tr[ying] to comfort and console him under the blow. He was terribly cut up, but need not have been . . . All reformers are rascals. Good men are always perfectly content with things as they are. . . . Then the good men, having vindicated their superior virtue and the perfect state of everything in general, presently proceed in a quiet way to remedy the evil complained of and to that extent straighten their walk.

Phillips had no worries about libel; he was not sued. Phillips's biographer assumed that the lack of libel suits attested to the validity of the author's sources, the truth of his facts, and the strength of his conclusions. But public figures who were muckraked during the progressive years generally did not sue. If a story was ignored, people might forget about it, whereas at a libel hearing a great deal more unfavorable publicity might be brought out. Most of the muckrakers, to protect themselves against suit, withheld some of the most damaging information about their subjects. This may have been true in the case of "Treason"; certainly Hearst had facts in his possession which he did not turn over to Phillips. In late 1904, he began buying a series of letters stolen from the papers of John D. Archbold, executive vice president of the Standard Oil Company, which indicated that Archbold had manipulated legislation with the aid of Senators Foraker, Hanna, Penrose, Quay, and Bailey, among others. These letters would have provided documentary evidence of Phillips's charges, but they were not revealed by Hearst until the 1908 election campaign.

Many muckraking articles resulted in the passage of reform legislation during the progressive years. To what extent did "The Treason of the Senate" series influence the passage of the Seventeenth Amendment, which provided for direct election of Senators by the people? The answer is probably little and much. Though Congress did not act for six years to pass the amendment, "Treason" did excite wide public discussion and made the issue a dominant one for most reformers. The editors of *Cosmopolitan* accompanied Phillips's articles with editorials and letters to the editor pleading for direct election, probably to indicate that the magazine was not simply "raking the muck" but had a definite "uplifting" purpose in mind. In June and August, 1906, editorial introductions by Ernest Crosby suggested that Senators naturally represented those who chose them. The muckrake had revealed the dirt, Crosby said; now must come the man with the hose to wash it away—"Let the people elect their Senate!"

The first resolution providing for direct election was introduced into the House in 1826, and, in the eighty-five years prior to 1912, was followed by 197 similar resolutions. Of these, six came to a vote in the House; they were passed by the necessary two-thirds majority in 1893, 1894, 1898, 1900, 1902, and 1911. The Senate ignored this mandate. Not until February, 1911, was the matter brought to a vote in the upper house; then it was narrowly defeated. However, political pressures for Senate action were strong for several years prior to the appearance of "Treason." Among the parties to advocate such a measure were the Peoples party, in its platforms of 1892, 1896, 1900, and 1904; the Democratic party, in 1900 and 1904; and the Prohibition party in 1904. Referendums urging direct election were passed by the voters of California by a 14 to 1 margin in 1892, of Nevada by 7 to 1 in 1893, and of Illinois by 6 to 1 in 1902. By 1906, thirty-one state legislatures had proposed that Congress initiate steps necessary to secure the amendment.

In June, 1896, the Senate committee on privileges and elections strongly recommended adoption of such an amendment, deploring the fact that ". . . the tendency of public opinion is to disparage and depreciate its [the Senate's] usefulness, its integrity, its power," and suggested that the amendent would revivify its reputation. But the committee's report was ignored and the resolution pigeonholed. Similar measures were blocked in succeeding years by the opposition of such Senators as Depew and Penrose. On February 23 and March 12, 1906, just after the first issue of "Treason" appeared, the Iowa legislature instructed Governor Cummins to call a national convention on the matter.

On December 4, 1905, early in the first session of the 59th Congress, Hearst introduced into the House a joint resolution (H.J. Res. 22) providing for direct election of Senators. Nine similar resolutions were introduced and, as the publicity for "Treason" mounted, so did pressures upon Congress for passage of the amendment. The Hearst press, the *Arena,* and the *Independent* were among the publications to link the Phillips series with a call for direct election. On June 30, 1906, midway through the series, Senator Gallinger told the Senate that copies of a Senate committee report on direct election, published by the 57th Congress, had been exhausted in recent months, and that demand for reprints was heavy. The Senate authorized the printing of another five thousand.

Though the "Treason" articles may have stimulated public interest in direct election, the Senate took no action during the 59th Congress. It may well be that the immediate impact of the articles was negative, for the Senate's chief concern in public debate seems to have been defensive. Some progressive Senators, like some progressive editors, assumed that the intemperate nature of the series gave the enemies of direct election a further weapon in their formidable arsenal of delay.

Because one-third of the Senate is elected every two years, three elections are necessary to accomplish a complete turnover. Precisely three Congresses following the publication of

"Treason," the Seventeenth Amendment was passed. In a special session of Congress convened in April, 1911, the resolution was introduced into the House by William W. Rucker of Missouri, and into the Senate by Senators Bristow of Kansas, Culberson of Texas, and Borah of Idaho. The character of debate in both houses was profoundly different from that of 1906. Many of the speeches rang with phrases out of Phillips:

Senator Owen (Oklahoma), June 1, 1911: "The American people have been very patient and long-suffering, but the limit of their patience has been reached by the subservience of the United States Senate to the selfish commercial interests of this country and the indifference of the Senate to public opinion . . ."

Senator La Follette (Wisconsin), May 23, 1911: "We complain sometimes here because we think that the so-called muck-raking magazines . . . present to the public a distorted and imperfect characterization of the Senate of the United States. But . . . taken as a whole, this collective editorial judgment of the Senate . . . is generally in accord with what they deserve."

Representative Adair (Indiana), April 13, 1911: "Wealth, plutocracy and subserviency to the interests . . . [are] the qualifications necessary for a Senator . . ."

Similar sentiments were offered by Congressmen Rucker, Underwood (Alabama), and Kindred (New York), and Senator Chamberlain (Oregon). That the Senate concurrently was investigating charges that corruption and bribery marred the election of Senator William Lorimer (Illinois) enlivened the debate and probably aided adoption of the resolution.

The Rucker resolution passed the House on April 13, 1911, by a vote of 296 to 16, and was reported favorably to the Senate by its Committee on Judiciary. On June 12, the Senate added an amendment which, in effect, retained Congress's power to supervise elections, and then passed the resolution by a vote of 64 to 24. Of the Senators attacked in "Treason" who remained in the Senate in 1911, Bailey, Cullom, Stone, and Nelson voted in favor of the resolution, Lodge, Penrose, and Crane against. For nearly a year, the Senate-House conference wrangled over a compromise between the two versions; finally on May 13, 1912, the House agreed to the Senate version. Three days later the amendment was proposed to the states; it was declared ratified on May 31, 1913. Phillips's series was only one of a number of factors influencing ratification, but it was certain that his articles dramatically focused attention on the problems of the Senate and stimulated popular discussion of their solution.

A more immediate result of "Treason" may have been the passage of progressive legislation stalled in committee. The Pure Food bill, passed by the Senate 63 to 4, became the first Roosevelt proposal "to run the gauntlet of the upper house to safety," reported *Current Literature* in April, 1906, after pointing out that "for a 'treasonable body' . . . the United States Senate has been behaving very well of late," under the "tonic influence" of the critics. The Oklahoma statehood bill, the Hepburn bill providing railroad regulation, the Beveridge meat inspection amendment, a consular reform law, and an employers' liability act were all passed by the Senate while the heat of public attention was focused upon it.

It is difficult to evaluate the effect of the series upon the political careers of the Senators criticized by Phillips, because the exposures of investigating committees and other muckraking publications also influenced public estimation of candidates for office. Some Senators involved died in office, some simply retired. Nevertheless, a considerable turnover resulted, which contrasts strikingly with the length of time these men had been in office prior to publication of "Treason." Of the twenty-one Senators analyzed by Phillips, among those who refused to seek re-election or who were defeated following the *Cosmopolitan* articles (for one reason or another) were Aldrich, Burton, Depew, Foraker, Hale, Kean, Platt, and Spooner. Only four of the twenty-one were present when Congress convened in 1913.

Phillips's career as a successful novelist was abruptly ended by an assassin's bullet on January 24, 1911, prior to the passage of the Seventeenth Amendment. He was killed by a member of an old Washington family, Fitzhugh C. Goldsborough, who mistakenly believed that Phillips had been persecuting Goldsborough's sister in his novels. For more than a day, with Beveridge, Lorimer, Lewis, and Brisbane among the callers at his bedside, Phillips fought for life, but eventually he succumbed. Shortly before losing consciousness, he said, "I could have won out against two bullets, but it is pretty hard against six." The author's gravestone, in Kensico cemetery in New York, bears the inscription, "Father forgive them, for they know not what they do."

Phillips's best-known novel, *Susan Lenox, Her Fall and Rise*, was published posthumously in *Hearst's Magazine* from 1915 to 1917. His papers were dispersed to his family, and eventually, some of the original manuscripts of his novels passed into the special collections department of the library of his alma mater, Princeton University. The manuscript of "Treason" was not publicly acknowledged, but Judson Grenier located a major part of it in an uncatalogued folder labeled "Special Articles" among the Phillips papers at Princeton. Like many of his novels, "Treason" was written on a tablet of yellow copy paper, torn in half; the manuscript is faded and decaying but clearly displays Phillips's small, scratchy, but neat handwriting. It bears little evidence of correction; its revisions are largely additions, some provided by Phillips and some by his editors. The manuscript cannot outlive the century unless it is in some way preserved.

Professor Louis Filler, probably the most astute observer of the muckrakers and their times, has written that "Treason" did not receive a contemporary reprint in book form like many lesser exposés because "It was too desperate a work, and too dangerous." Phillips's gallery of Senators was therefore unavailable to history, buried away in *Cosmopolitan*, and forgotten. Phillips's intemperate idiom is no longer considered good journalistic style, but the questions of public morality he raised remain. Direct election altered but did not purify the Senate.

Although the Senate is no longer as sensitive to the rich man's point of view, it still is subject to the enticements of those who seek to use public power for private profit. Charges by contemporary critics that the Senate suffers from "influence-peddling" and "conflict of interest" are not far removed from Phillips's complaints about "vested interests" and "entrenched privilege." When Senators plead for a code of ethics—to prohibit members from acting as counsel for firms seeking legislation, accepting commissions from another branch of government, or refusing to make public their sources of income—they are agitating in the reformist tradition of LaFollette and Beveridge.

Throughout its history, the Senate has continued to play the role for which it originally was conceived—to represent the states in the federal system, and, by expressing the attitudes of the wealthy and influential, to provide checks and balances in the government. Much of the criticism of the Senate, then as now, stems from the character of its representation. Whenever things move fast, as they did in the Progressive era and as they do today, the Senate comes under attack; it is accused of inelasticity, of inability to respond to rapid social change, of representing a minority of the citizens, of becoming enmeshed in the rigidity of its own procedures. Yet the Seventeenth Amendment, combined with modern communication procedures, has considerably broadened the electorate to which Senators must justify themselves. Although their ethical standards need be no greater than those of their constituents, we may hope that Senators resolve that their position demands exemplary behavior and maintain the highest possible personal integrity. To aid them and the voting populace in developing increased political morality, continuing examination of the origins and roots of political corruption seems justified. If renewed acquaintance with Phillips's "The Treason of the Senate" strengthens our ability to recognize the sources of corruption, it should help mitigate their effect.

A Political Directory of the Senators
Named in "The Treason of the Senate"

The following capsule biographies of the men criticized by David Graham Phillips in "The Treason of the Senate" are provided for reference purposes. They include each Senator's political affiliation, home state, life span, years in the Senate, profession, number of terms in Congress, and committee chairmanships held in 1906. If an individual had no experience in the House of Representatives, the biography contains his major elective office at the state level, if any, in order to indicate his political appeal. Much of the data is excerpted from *Biographical Directory of the American Congress, 1774-1949* (Washington, 1950).

NELSON WILMARTH ALDRICH (R, RI), 1841-1915; Senate 1881-1911, not a candidate for re-election. Merchant. Two terms in House, five in Senate. Chairman, finance committee.

WILLIAM BOYD ALLISON (R, Ia), 1829-1908; Senate 1873-1908, nominated in Senatorial preferential primary for re-election in 1908, but died. Lawyer. Four terms in House, six in Senate. Chairman, appropriations committee, steering committee (unofficial).

JOSEPH WELDON BAILEY (D, Tex), 1862-1929; Senate 1901-January 3, 1913, when he resigned. Lawyer. Five terms

47

in House, two in Senate. Unsuccessful candidate for governor of Texas in 1920. Acting minority leader.

JOSEPH RALPH BURTON (R, Kans), 1850-1923; Senate 1901-June 4, 1906, when he resigned. Lawyer. No terms in House, four years in state house of representatives, one term in Senate.

WINTHROP MURRAY CRANE (R, Mass), 1853-1920; Senate 1904-1913, declined to be candidate for re-election in 1913. Paper manufacturer. No terms in House, but terms (two years each) as lieutenant governor and governor of Massachusetts; one and one-half terms in Senate (appointed after death of Sen. Hoar).

SHELBY MOORE CULLOM (R, Ill), 1829-1914; Senate 1883-1913. Lawyer. Three terms in House, two terms as governor of Illinois, five terms in Senate. Chairman, foreign relations committee.

CHAUNCEY MITCHELL DEPEW (R, NY), 1834-1928; Senate 1899-1911, unsuccessful candidate for re-election in 1910. Lawyer. No terms in House, two years in state assembly, two terms in Senate.

STEPHEN BENTON ELKINS (R, WVa), 1841-1911; Senate 1895-January 4, 1911, when he died. Lawyer. Two terms as delegate to Congress from territory of New Mexico, three terms in Senate. Chairman, interstate commerce committee.

CHARLES WARREN FAIRBANKS (R, Ind), 1852-1918; Senate 1897-1905, when he resigned, having been elected Vice President of the U.S. (1905-1909). Lawyer. No terms in House, one and one-half in Senate. Presiding officer of Senate at time of "Treason." Unsuccessful candidate for Vice President (R) in 1916.

JOSEPH BENSON FORAKER (R, Ohio), 1846-1917; Senate 1897-1909, unsuccessful candidate for re-election in 1909. Lawyer. No terms in House, four years as governor of Ohio, two terms in Senate.

WILLIAM PIERCE FRYE (R, Me), 1830-1911; Senate 1881-August 8, 1911, when he died. Lawyer. Six terms in House, six in Senate, though first term only two years (replaced Blaine) and last shortened by death. President pro tempore of the Senate. Chairman, commerce committee.

ARTHUR PUE GORMAN (D, Md), 1839-1906; Senate 1881-1899, unsuccessful candidate for re-election; re-elected 1903-June 4, 1906, when he died. Businessman. No terms in House, six years in state senate, four terms in Senate. Minority leader.

EUGENE HALE (R, Me), 1836-1918; Senate 1881-1911, not a candidate for renomination. Lawyer. Five terms in House, five in Senate (at time of retirement, Senator with longest continuous service). Chairman, naval affairs committee.

JOHN KEAN (R, NJ), 1852-1914; Senate, 1899-1911. Banker. Two terms in House, two in Senate. Chairman, contingent expenses committee.

PHILANDER CHASE KNOX (R, Penn), 1853-1921; Senate 1904-1909, resigned to become Secretary of State; Senate 1917-October 12, 1921, when he died. Lawyer. No terms in House, U.S. Attorney General 1901-1904, two terms in Senate.

HENRY CABOT LODGE (R, Mass), 1850-1924; Senate 1893-November 9, 1924, when he died. Lawyer, author, and scholar. Three terms in House, six in Senate.

KNUTE NELSON (R, Minn), 1843-1923; Senate 1895-April 28, 1923, when he died. Lawyer. Born in Norway, three terms in House, two years as governor of Minnesota, five terms in Senate.

BOIES PENROSE (R, Penn), 1860-1921; Senate 1897-December 31, 1921, when he died. Lawyer. No terms in House, eleven years in state senate, five terms in Senate. Chairman, post offices and post roads committee.

THOMAS COLLIER PLATT (R, NY), 1833-1910; Senate 1881,

1897-1909. Businessman. Two terms in House, three in Senate, though resigned after two months of first term in disagreement over patronage.

JOHN COIT SPOONER (R, Wisc), 1843-1919; Senate 1885-1891, 1897-April 30, 1907, when he resigned. Lawyer. No terms in House, one term in state assembly, three terms in Senate. Chairman, rules committee.

WILLIAM JOEL STONE (D, Mo), 1848-1918; Senate 1903-April 14, 1918, when he died. Lawyer. Three terms in House, four years as governor of Missouri, three terms in Senate.

THE TREASON OF THE SENATE

AN EDITORIAL FOREWORD

A PLAIN, honest Californian lived on an island in the mouth of the San Joaquin river. He was a good citizen, a man of family, a hard-working rancher, not without ideas of his own, and excessively proud of the fact that he was a member of the Grand Army of the Republic. He was also proud of his Americanism—so proud, in fact, that when he read in the papers of the corrupt doings of legislators who betrayed their country by assisting the ignoble money power in its predatory plans, he would wince and shake his head and set his teeth. These things preyed upon the mind of the islander. He could hardly talk of anything else.

One day, only a few years ago, the telegraph flashed the news across the continent that a notoriously corrupt politician —a tool of the trusts—had bought a seat in the United States Senate. Our simple-minded ranchman immediately arose in his wrath, went and took pen and paper and laboriously wrote a declaration of independence in which he withdrew himself, his family and his island from the jurisdiction and the protection of the United States. He sent a copy of his declaration to Congress.

Of course, the crude document created a smile at Washington. No reply was ever made to it. The sum total of practical result was that the Grand Army post to which our righteous islander belonged gravely adopted a set of resolutions chiding and deriding him.

The sum total? Well, hardly the sum total, for, as the sturdy rancher still persisted in the idea that his island was no longer under the control of the United States, although he still paid tribute in the form of taxes, the notion went around among his neighbors, up and down the river—men who had always respected him as a good citizen—that in some way his act really did reflect upon the government, or at least, upon the corrupt element in it. So the declaration of one man's independence made an impression. Queer and quixotical as it was, it was still an "object lesson."

Now, of course, we cannot all secede from the Union because of the corruption of our national Senate. It would be obviously visionary and foolish for us to do so on that or any other account. Besides, there are not enough islands to go around. Our part as citizens of the republic is plain enough. We must stand our ground. We must fight the good fight. Heartsick and depressed as we may be at times because of the spread of graft in high places and its frightfully contaminating influence, we must still hold up our heads.

We must never lose an opportunity to show that as private citizens we are opposed to public plunderers. We should interest ourselves in every scrap of information as to official treason that comes our way. We must be as patient in the study of corruption as we are impatient of its creatures and their punishment.

For example, it should be the duty of every citizen of this republic—every man, woman, schoolboy and schoolgirl—every person who can understand facts as presented in print—to read "The Treason of the Senate" by David Graham Phillips, a series of tremendously important articles to be commenced in the March number of the COSMOPOLITAN.

A searching and unsparing spot-light, directed by the masterly hand of Mr. Phillips, will be turned upon each of the iniquitous figures that walk the Senate stage at the national

Capitol. This convincing story of revelation, to be told in several chapters, and to run well through the magazine year, has been called "The Treason of the Senate" for the reason that that is a fit and logical title for this terrible arraignment of those who, sitting in the seats of the mighty at Washington, have betrayed the public to that cruel and vicious Spirit of Mammon which has come to dominate the nation.

The truth told in the courts and in public print about the senators now under indictment, as well as the facts collected by Mr. Phillips against many of their corrupt colleagues, proves beyond a doubt that these men of the toga, selected by their state legislatures to represent the people, are really the retainers of the money power. What American is there so simple-minded, so innocent in his patriotic faith, who does not believe that a petition signed by a million of the common people would not have half as much influence in the Senate as the mere nod of a Havemeyer, an Armour or a Morgan?

Who, then, do these public misrepresentatives really represent?

From exhaustive statistics made by the late Charles B. Spahr, the conclusion is reached by Robert Hunter in his "Poverty" that one per cent. of the families living in the United States hold more property than the remaining ninety-nine per cent. If we grant the truth of these deductions it is easy to see, by observation of the known policy and settled attitude of the Senate, that it is not the ninety-nine, but merely the one per cent. that is really represented by that sedate and decorous body, so often referred to as the "Rich Man's Club," and which Mr. Ernest Crosby has dubbed "The House of Dollars."

Obstructive though it has been toward nearly all corrective legislation aimed at the further usurpation of power by the lawless plutocrats, the Senate has always cheerfully voted money for the building of warships, for coast-defense works and heavy armament for the protection of the people of the nation against foreign aggression. But the question now arises: Who is to protect us from the Senate? This question comes with peculiar force while five senators are under indictment, others are publicly charged with betraying their trusts and at least one has been permitted to draw a regular salary from the government while under conviction for flagrant violation of the federal laws.

Who, then, is to protect the people but the press?

The COSMOPOLITAN is ready to do its share, and by the presentation of Mr. Phillips' "Treason of the Senate," it will probably do a more conspicuous act of exposure of corruption than has ever before been attempted. For in all the literature of exposure no such series of articles has ever been presented to the public. Well-meaning and amazingly industrious persons, writing without inspiration and without that gift of selection which is half the art of the great author have been able to pile before magazine readers indiscriminate masses of arid facts, of little interest save to the technical mind. Some of them are, indeed, so dry as almost to cause one to embrace the flagon. But Mr. Phillips, from the wealth of material at hand, and to be dug up out of the dark, will be able to select such picturesque, arrestive and interest-compelling matter as will make this series the most vascular and virile, as well as the most notable of all thus far printed.

When, four months ago, our intention of engaging the author of "The Cost," "The Plum Tree" and "The Deluge" to write this series was made known to a famous modern thinker and writer, he said with enthusiasm:

"No better selection could have been made. Mr. Phillips writes in a most interesting and convincing manner. His subject is far bigger than Lawson's. It is, in fact, the biggest of any before the public to-day. His work will be a tremendous reform stroke.

The COSMOPOLITAN had hoped to present Mr. Phillips' opening chapter in this February number, but the work of preparation and revision of this exhaustive series has been such that, at the last moment, it has been found impossible to do so. It was also necessary, in order to make an elaborate and convincing presentation, that the first chapter should be illustrated in a striking manner, with whatever of facsimiles of letters and public documents might be secured. This has also occasioned delay.

The editor trusts that the impatience of the COSMOPOLITAN's readers—evidenced by the letters of inquiry sent in from day to day—will not lessen in any degree the ultimate gratification of the outraged public in seeing its misrepresentatives scotched by the hand of that artist in exposure who has undertaken the worthy task of writing this, the most remarkable story of political corruption ever told in print.

Our readers may rest assured that Mr. Phillips' widely announced opening chapter, on Chauncey M. Depew, will be well worth waiting for. Senator Depew's possible resignation before February 15th, the date of the publication of the March COSMOPOLITAN; will not affect our determination of printing this slashing review of the misdeeds of one of the most conspicuous of our undesirable statesmen. For though Mr. Depew may leave the Senate Chamber forever, his odor will remain.

> Treason against the United States shall consist
> only in levying war against them, or in *adhering
> to their enemies, giving them aid and comfort.*
> —THE CONSTITUTION OF THE UNITED STATES,
> Article III, Section 3.

I

NEW YORK'S

MISREPRESENTATIVES

ONE morning, during this session of the Congress, the Senate
blundered into a discussion of two of its minor disreputables,
Burton and Mitchell, who had been caught with their fingers
sliding about in the change pocket of the people. The discussion on these change-pocket thieves was a fine exhibition of
"senatorial dignity and courtesy," which means, nowadays, regard for the honor and dignity of the American people smugly
sacrificed to the Senate's craftily convenient worship of the
Mumbo-Jumbo mask and mantle of its own high respectability.
In closing the brief debate over his fellow-senators who had
been so unluckily caught, Senator Lodge said,

"There is too much tendency to remember the senators,
and to forget the Senate."

A profound criticism—profounder far than was intended,
or realized, by the senator from the "interests" that center in
Massachusetts.

Let us take Mr. Lodge's hint. Let us disregard the senators
as individuals; let us for the moment "remember the Senate."

The treason of the Senate!

Politics does not determine prosperity. But in this day of
concentrations, politics does determine *the distribution of prosperity.* Because the people have neglected politics, have not

educated themselves out of credulity to flimsily plausible political lies and liars, because they will not realize that *it is not enough to work, it is also necessary to think,* they remain poor, or deprived of their fair share of the products, though they have produced an incredible prosperity. The people have been careless and unwise enough in electing every kind of public administrator. When it comes to the election of the Senate, how describe their stupidity, how measure its melancholy consequences? The Senate is the most powerful part of our public administration. It has vast power in the making of laws. It has still vaster power through its ability to forbid the making of laws and in its control over the appointment of the judges who say what the laws mean. It is, in fact, *the final arbiter of the sharing of prosperity.* The laws it permits or compels, the laws it refuses to permit, the interpreters of laws it permits to be appointed—these factors determine whether the great forces which modern concentration has produced shall operate to distribute prosperity equally or with shameful inequality and cruel and destructive injustice. The United States Senate is a larger factor than your labor or your intelligence, you average American, in determining your income. And the Senate is a traitor to you!

The treason of the Senate! Treason is a strong word, but not too strong, rather too weak, to characterize the situation in which the Senate is the eager, resourceful, indefatigable agent of interests as hostile to the American people as any invading army could be, and vastly more dangerous; interests that manipulate the prosperity produced by all, so that it heaps up riches for the few; interests whose growth and power can only mean the degradation of the people, of the educated into sycophants, of the masses toward serfdom.

A man cannot serve two masters. The senators are not elected by the people; they are elected by the "interests." A servant obeys him who can punish and dismiss. Except in extreme and rare and negligible instances, can the people either elect or dismiss a senator? The senator, in the dilemma which the careless ignorance of the people thrusts upon him, chooses to be comfortable, placed and honored, and a traitor to oath and people rather than to be true to his oath and poor and ejected into private life.

Let us begin with the state which is first in population, in wealth, in organization of industries. As we shall presently see, the nine states that contain more than half the whole American people send to the Senate eighteen men, no less than ten of whom are notorious characters, frankly the servants of the interests the American people have decided must be destroyed, unless they themselves are to be crushed down. And of these servants of the plutocracy none is more candid in obsequiousness, in treachery to the people, than are the two senators from the state which contains one-tenth of our population and the strong financial citadel-capital of the plutocracy.

Thomas Collier Platt! Chauncey Mitchell Depew!

Probably Platt's last conspicuous appearance will have been that on the witness stand in the insurance investigation, where he testified that he had knowingly received thousands of dollars of the stolen goods of the insurance thieves. He confessed this with obvious unconsciousness of his own shame. We shall come across this phenomenon frequently in our course through the Senate—this shamelessness that has lost all sense of moral distinctions. Our Platts and Burtons have no more moral sense than an ossified man has feeling. Then, there are those of our public men who, through fear or lack of opportunity or some instinct of personal self-respect, sit inactive, silent or only vaguely murmurous spectators, while the treasons are plotted and executed. These men have been corrupted by association. The public man meets the people only in masses, at political gatherings. His associations are altogether with other public men and with the class that is either fattening on the people or quite cynical about corruption of that kind. Hence, his sense of shame becomes paralyzed, atrophied. The very "interests" that are ruining the people come to stand in his mind for the people themselves, and in his confused mind prostitution becomes a sort of patriotism.

Platt cannot live long. His mind is already a mere shadow. The other day a friend found him crying like a child because Roosevelt was unable to appoint for him to a federal district attorneyship a man who had been caught stealing trust funds, and insisted that he must select some henchman wearing the brand less conspicuously. "Platt was like an unreasonable child," said his friend.

Just before the holidays, Platt called Chauncey Depew, his junior, over to his seat, and said, "Chauncey, I hear you are thinking of resigning." Depew began to shift and fumble and hem and haw—to act as he has been acting ever since he was publicly disgraced. Platt looked him coldly in the eye. "Chauncey," he said, "whenever are you going to grow up and stop being a —— fool?"

It was one of those rare moments of "supreme courage" when Platt gives way to profanity. His colleague's shame excited the contempt of his brass-plated soul. And well it might; for, Depew's shame was not shame for his dishonorable and dishonest acts; nor was it even so little erect a feeling as the shame that follows the shock of being found out; it was that basest of all the base kinds of shame—the shrinking fear of the steady, pointing finger of public scorn and contempt. And from that finger Depew is not secure anywhere but in the Senate itself—when the galleries are cleared and only his colleagues are there.

But let us not linger upon Platt—Platt, with his long, his unbroken record of treachery to the people in legislation of privilege and plunder promoted and in decent legislation prevented. Let us leave him, not because he is sick and feeble; for death itself without repentance or restitution deserves no consideration; but because he needs no extended examination to be understood and entered under his proper heading in the record. Wherever Platt is known, to speak of him as a patriot would cause wonder if not open derision. The most that could be said of him is that, wherever the interests of the people do not conflict with the interests of the "interests" or with his own pocket, which includes that of his family, Platt has been either inactive or not positively in opposition.

DEPEW, THE COURTIER

Let us turn to the other of the two representatives whom the people of New York suffer to sit and cast the other of their two votes in the body that arbitrates the division of the prosperity of the country, the wages and the prices. At this writing Depew has just given out a flat refusal to resign. "Why should I resign?" he cried out hysterically. "Has anybody put forward any good reason why I should resign?" And he added, "As soon as I have completed my resignation from certain companies, I shall give all my time to my senatorial duties."

What are his senatorial duties? What does he do in the body that is now as much an official part of the plutocracy as the executive council of a Rockefeller or a Ryan? No one would pretend for an instant that he sits in the Senate for the people. Indeed, why should he, except because he took an oath to do so—and among such eminent respectabilities as he an oath is a mere formality, a mere technicality. Did the people send him to the Senate? No! The Vanderbilt interests ordered Platt to send him the first time; and when he came up for a second term the Vanderbilt-Morgan interests got, not without difficulty, Harriman's O.K. on an order to Odell to give it to him. Since he became a large public figure, the only time he has presented himself to the people, he was overwhelmingly beaten. In no part of the state of New York, these thirty-five years, would the people have elected him to any office of trust, great or small. Except, then, for the negligible reason of his oath, he has no reason to represent the people. His "senatorial duties" are like the duties of more than two-thirds of his colleagues— to serve his master, the plutocracy, in his old age as he has served it from his earliest youth. He has or has borrowed

enough of the "statesman's supreme courage" to act upon the
theory that, if he should resign from the Senate, he would be
ejected from his seventy and odd directorships which bring
him in upward of fifty thousand dollars a year in attendance
fees alone; whereas if he resigns the directorships and clings
to his senatorial seat, his plutocratic associates, needing his
vote there, will treat him with what he regards as consideration.

To show what he represents in the Senate, in whose service
his vote and his talents are entirely enlisted, we must look at
his past. For, a man is his past—not its pretenses and palaver-
ings but its performances.

In January, 1862—forty-four years ago—there appeared at
Albany among the new members of the Assembly a young man
of unusual opportunities, gifts and promise. His name was C.
M. Depew, and soon everybody was calling him Chauncey,
and was liking him. He was twenty-seven years old, was a
graduate of Yale—and in that day a degree from a college,
while it perhaps meant less as to attainments, certainly meant
more in the ears and imaginations of men. He was a young
lawyer from Peekskill, good as a lawyer, better as a mixer,
best of all as a jollier; for nature had given him that dangerous
flexibility which tempts a man to seek success by the sideling,
cringing, crawling way of the courtier.

It was the day of big enthusiasm for country, and so the
politicians were even more offensive with their shallow shout-
ings of patriotism than now. The Depew youth developed a
fine talent for "tall talk," for "making the proud bird soar."
And he laid well the foundations of the public reputation behind which he has so industriously plied his cowardly trade
these forty years. In those days the big "interests" had not yet
appeared, and graft was not consolidated and glozed slimy
with respectability, as now. But the politicians were for the
most part grafters, as now; and very bold and coarse they were
about it. Graft wasn't "campaign contributions" and "retainers"
and such smooth and delicate evasions; it was plain bribery,
plain passing of money from briber to bribed. The legislative

bodies of to-day are no more corrupt than then; the corruption is simply more subtle, more "gentlemanly," more respectable. The vast difference, the vast excess of peril in the now over the then, lies in the fact that the corrupting force is to-day the national dispenser of the sharings in prosperity where then it was simply small corporations and individuals stealing a relatively small part of the people's abundance.

DEPEW FINDS A MASTER

Young Depew was looking about for a master. Nature has made him the kind of man who, whether good or bad, cannot be self-owned. Soon his glib tongue and fertile brain had ingratiated him into favor with Thurlow Weed, the boss of the Republican party in that day and a corruptionist who will never get his dues in history because so many men so much more skilled at his specialty, rotten politics, have lived since and have eclipsed his fame. Depew, at twenty-nine, was nominated for secretary of state by a trick: the boss was beaten in convention; but the nominated candidate declined to run and Depew, whom the convention had rejected, was put on the ticket by the boss' state committee. Depew was elected, and proceeded publicly to parade his branding-mark.

He took a boss' census of the state and, to cut down New York city's Democratic representation, gave it a population smaller than the federal census of five years before, 1860, had given it. "Depopulator Depew" was denounced by the Democrats and despised by the Republicans; for, while the rank and file of as partisan a party as was the Republican in those war times will accept the fruits of the shameful acts of the politicians, it will not thereafter respect or trust them. Thus, when Depew became a conspicuous public figure, his characteristics were fully developed. His first distinct public appearance was as a traitor to the people; for, his treachery of procuring fraudulent representation is of that same kind of fundamental and unmitigated treason as the ballot box stuffer's or the vote buyer's. At twenty-nine Depew was definitely launched upon his career of treason. Round and round the press in the mid-sixties went this "suggestion for the next edition of the dictionary:"

"Depewism—any inexplicable depopulation of a town or village; sudden desertion of a neighborhood; falling off in the inhabitants of any locality."

Depew was not renominated. The Republican organization had to drop him from its list of figureheads available for submission to the people. Several attempts otherwise to "take care of him" miscarried. He finished his term as secretary of state at the end of 1865 and became a "lawyer" for corporate and other seekers of favors from the legislatures. His acquaintance, his knowledge of the wheels of political machinery, his intimacy with the leaders, gave him peculiar fitness for the work of a lobbyist. At that time the Vanderbilt fortune was being stolen from the people of the state. The "old commodore" had discovered that millions could be made by bribing legislatures where scant thousands would be the reward of honest industry; and he was acting upon the discovery with all the energy of a cutpurse at a county fair, and no police about. His son and chief "pal," William H., first employed Depew; Depew's successes, combined with his personal qualities which seemed capable of great development, attracted the commodore to him. Depew, in his "Retrospect of Twenty-five Years with the New York Central," has given his version of how he got the bit and saddle he was to wear proudly and docilely for forty years:

"William H. Vanderbilt said to me, 'We want your services,' and the commodore remarked, 'Chauncey, politics don't pay. The business of the future in this country is railroading.'"

It is impossible to say whether the commodore indulged in that bit of persiflage, or whether Depew's memory, as flexible as his tongue, his knees, his brain and his conscience, has here bent for him. The commodore never was and hardly professed to be a railroad man, any more than Ryan is an insurance man or Morgan a steel man; he was, almost frankly, a purchaser of stolen franchises, a procurer of profitable legislation, a bond and stockjobber and swindler, a parasite upon production; he founded and entailed the policy which has made the New York Central about the most corrupt and about the least progressive railroad in the world in proportion to its opportunities. So, he must have meant by that remark to Depew if he made it, "railroading legislation"; must have meant that while politics as an honorable pursuit did not "pay," politics as a criminal industry was the future business of the country; for, not out of business but out of politics have the vast fortunes been made, except the few real estate and mining accumulations.

A RAILROAD LAWYER

Depew became a "lawyer" for the New York Central, with headquarters at Albany, of course. In view of the true nature of old Commodore Vanderbilt's "business" activities, Depew's fairly accurate description of his own position becomes interesting. "My duties," says he, "covered everything official or personal in which the commodore was interested. For the last eleven years of his life I was in daily consultation with this remarkable man." Further: "Vanderbilt cared little for details and speedily wearied of them. He stated in general terms the results he desired, and then expected the officers of the companies to work them out. It was impossible to explain to him a failure."

Read aright, this last is a wonderful picture of the first typical plutocrat—ignorant of business, indifferent to it, rich and growing ever richer by hoarding the property of the people which his agents stole for him, and treating those agents as a Fagin treats the clever boys he sends out to pick pockets. Depew's picture of old Vanderbilt belongs beside Rockefeller's self-painted portrait in his famous sentence, "I don't know anything about those matters; I am a clamorer for dividends."

But, incidentally, Depew presents a picture of himself—the sly courtier-agent, with the greasy conscience and the greasy tongue and the greasy backbone and the greasy hinges of the knees.

It would be a mistake to suppose that Depew had not a good brain. On the contrary, his brain was, and perhaps still is, far superior to the first Vanderbilt's, or to any of the first Vanderbilt's successors as chief custodian of the millions he got by robbing the people and by "milking" the New York Central system. Why, then, should superior serve inferior? For the same reason that the great lawyers of to-day, with their splendid brains, are yet mere fetchers and carriers to the pluto-crats who are like huge, soft grubs—mere feeders. Depew lacked that courage which never goes with such adaptability, such timidity of soul as his. He would do anything, and do it thoroughly, as a lieutenant; but as an initiator, he was always worthless. He had to have a man behind him, some one to stiffen him to the execution of the clevernesses his brain de-vised. His nature was essentially servile, parasitic, typical of the truckler and the procurer. Brains without courage will serve, to the further extremity of sycophancy, courage, even though it has no brains.

It was, therefore, when Depew was but thirty-two years old that he took "personal and official" service with the Vander-bilt family. And ever since then they have owned him, mentally and morally; they have used him, or rather, he, in his eager-ness to please them, has made himself useful to them to an extent which he does not realize nor do they. So great is his reverence for wealth and the possessors of wealth, so humble is he before them, that he probably does not appreciate how much of the Vanderbilt fortune his brain got for that family. The successive heads of the family have been, like the old commodore, typical plutocrats. The plutocrat sees something he wants; he has not the brains to get it, only the appetite for it and the determination to gratify that appetite. He hires a brain, a lawyer, to tell him how to get what he wants.

DELIVERING HOMILIES TO YOUNG MEN

AS AN AFTER-DINNER SPEAKER

AS A FAMILIAR PARK FIGURE

Drawn by Homer Davenport

"Chauncey Depew? Oh you mean the man that Vanderbilt sends to Albany every winter to say 'haw' and 'gee' to his cattle up there."—*Roscoe Conkling*

Depew's public front of light-hearted, superficial jester and buffoon, and his private reputation, and character, of spineless sycophant have combined to make him mentally underestimated both by others and by himself. Probably the old commodore, and perhaps William H., did dimly realize that without their Chauncey to think for them and to cloak them, they would have been unable to steal so largely or with so little outcry. But even they, shrewder though they were than the later heads of the family, must have been prejudiced by Depew's utter lack of self-assertiveness, and by his extreme and sordid parsimony, a quality to which we must return later, as it was the immediate cause of his final downfall.

THE VANDERBILT LOBBYIST

The Vanderbilts, when he entered their service, were engaged in stealing a series of franchises and existing railroads, and in getting upon the statute books laws legalizing the thefts and other laws making them absolute masters of the railway situation in the richest territory between New York and Buffalo. Their object was two-fold—to rob the people and to rob the capitalists whom they had induced to invest in the stolen railways. It may be said in passing that while the investors whom they cheated may possibly deserve a little sympathy—not much, as investors all knew the whole enterprise was a swindle and went in because they thought they were on the "ground floor"—the people deserve no sympathy. Year after year they sent back the same old thieves to the legislature. Indeed, are they not still sending notorious rascals there by the score? However, Depew became an ideal lieutenant for a plutocrat, incomparably the best, take him all round, this country has yet been foozled by. A few years after he had hired out to the Vanderbilts, Roscoe Conkling, being asked one day what he thought of him, said, "Depew? You mean the fellow Vanderbilt sends to Albany every winter to say 'gee' and 'haw' to his cattle there." Depew understood the "cattle business"; Vanderbilt did not; but he did not need to understand it, as he owned Depew.

Before Vanderbilt got control of the New York and Harlem and New York Central, the New York Central had been one of the most industrious and extensive corruptors of the legislature. In the fourteen years up to 1867, it had spent upward of half a million dollars, a big sum for those Spartan days, in buying laws at Albany and to "protect its stockholders against injurious legislation"—which phrase always means to prevent just laws from being enacted, since an unjust law would be unconstitutional and would be upset by the courts. Not long after Depew became "junior counsel," there was put through the first of the series of stupendous swindles that netted the Vanderbilts the cash, the franchises, the vested rights to levy upon the people in perpetuity which have enabled them to reach out and out until now they control twenty-two thousand miles of railway and have in the total a wholly owned fortune of nearly half a thousand millions. On May 20, 1869, the Vanderbilts got, in one bill, the right to consolidate several railways, and a free grant of franchises worth hundreds of millions, and the right to water stocks and bonds practically as freely as they might choose. Of the immediate plunder—the watered stocks—the Vanderbilts put in their pockets no less than forty million dollars which cost them nothing whatsoever and to which they had no title and as to which they could never give any pretense of explanation. According to Charles Francis Adams, the distinguished railway man, the first douche of water into the stock was about fifty thousand dollars per mile for every mile between New York and Buffalo.

Here is just one instance of the effrontery of the Vanderbilt lobby in those days: An innocent looking bill, which freed the railroad from payment of heavy judgments in suits pending against it and gave it the right to raise the passenger fare from two to three cents a mile, was introduced in the closing days of the session of 1872. The bill's true nature was exposed and it was defeated.

Immediately, it was hidden away in the depths of another bill and was passed. "During that hour," said the Buffalo "Express," "Depew was the busiest man in the lobby."

Another Buffalo newspaper, the "Commercial," said, "Depew stands convicted of being a corrupter of the lawmakers of the commonwealth," and that he "had the audacity to cajole or bribe the chief magistrate of the state into endorsing one of the greatest frauds ever perpetrated."

In that same year when the press was describing Depew as a "regular attendant" at the sessions of the "third house," the lobby of the legislature, the bill was put through that presented Fourth Avenue, New York city, to the New York Central, and compelled the city to spend millions of dollars in improving the railway!

A POLITICAL CHANGE OF HEART

Depew left the Republican party with the Greeley movement which looked very promising until election day. He took, with his owner's hearty consent, the nomination for lieutenant governor. In those days the lieutenant governor was ex-officio the chief power in control of the Erie Canal. It has been a fixed part of the Vanderbilt policy to inflict upon the canal, the one restraint upon its monopoly, all possible damage. If Depew had been elected, he would have had the chance to "depopulate" it. But he was overwhelmingly beaten. His reputation at that time would alone have been enough to wreck the ticket.

In no one of Depew's own accounts of his career will you find mention that he was a commissioner of the state capitol from 1871 to 1875. It was during this period that the plans were adopted and the works undertaken which have made the capitol the most expensive building for its size in the world. It ought to have cost about four million dollars. It has cost more than twenty-five million and is not yet finished. The scandal over the doings of Depew and his colleagues was

so great that the legislature was forced to appoint a committee
to "whitewash" them. The commission in its report complied
to the extent of saying that it had "found nothing involving
the personal integrity of the commissioners." But it went on
to say of one part of the work that "if it had been *honestly*
done, the commission would have saved at least a million dollars." It cited one building "made entirely of brick, stone and
iron," yet against which bills of $59,129.64 were charged for
lumber and $110,215.25 for carpenter work! Depew and his
colleagues were kicked out of office.

THE VANDERBILTS' CREATURE

Now followed a quarter of a century of arduous and most
adroit lobbying, as counsel and then as figurehead president
of the Vanderbilt road, and finally as "honorary" chairman of
it. He got for the Vanderbilts, with ever increasing facility
and ever decreasing public clamor, free franchises large and
small, large free grants of land, immensely valuable shore
rights and rights to land under water, authorizations of more
consolidations and of more issues of watered stock, exemptions
from taxation, etc., etc., etc. Also he was always on hand to
cover the operations of the bribe-brigade with speeches full of
catching sophistries against any and all legislation seeking to
lessen the oppressive burdens imposed by the Vanderbilts upon
the people. He managed it all most ably. He grew more and
more respected. By generous, even wholesale, distribution of
passes, by cultivating editors and reporters, by ingratiating himself with small politicians and the influential men of little towns
and villages, by making popular addresses and after-dinner
speeches, by the thousand and one devices which his ingenious
mind and his expansive temperament and his passion for public
applause suggested, he made himself a popular figure. Every-
one knew he was the Vanderbilts' creature. Those who saw
him in the presence of the members of the family to which he
was soul-vassal, whether the elder members or the little children, half-pityingly despised him for his truckling, despised

him the more that he was beyond question a man of unusual ability and mentality. The wife of one of the younger Vanderbilts refused to have him at her table.

"I do not let my butler sit down with me," said she to the head of the house; "Why should I let yours?"

But in general he was liked. The contempt for him was tolerant. He was regarded as a "good fellow, for the kind." And so he got what he sought. His persistent and good-humored and clever pushing of himself in public produced valuable results to him and invaluable results to the Vanderbilts.

It would be a moderate statement that the geniality of Depew has cost the people of New York State a thousand million dollars, besides the infamous grants of the rights to tax the public in perpetuity. The Vanderbilts and their clique kept much; but it is characteristic of plutocracy that it damages and destroys much more than it carries away, like a bear in a beehive. "Our Chauncey's" geniality is responsible, to cite one of a graver kind of instances, for the tunnel exit from New York city, a criminal nuisance which the Vanderbilts have maintained all these years in brutish disregard of the comfort of the people, and at an appalling sacrifice of human lives.

Depew's popularity with the public so loth to believe that "one may smile and smile, and be a villain," his "pull" with the too good-natured editors and reporters throughout the state have gracefully cloaked the ignorant and greedy and criminal policy which the Vanderbilts have always pursued, and which, by the way, has cost them many more millions than they put in the bag. Our history offers no more striking instance of one-man power than the wide paralyzing effect and the vast and sinister economic results of the studied and shallow geniality of this sycophant to a plutocratic family.

And, for reward, the Vanderbilts have given him scant and contemptuous crumbs. After forty years of industrious, faithful, and, to his masters, enormously profitable self-degradation he has not more than five millions, avaricious and saving though he has been. And they tossed him the senatorship as if it had been a charity. Of all the creatures of the Vanderbilts, none has been more versatile, more willing or more profitable to his users than Depew. Yet he has only five million dollars and a blasted name to console his old age, while his users are in honor and count their millions by the score.

THE INSURANCE INIQUITY

Besides the Vanderbilts, he has served one other member of the plutocracy—the famous, the curious, the posthumously exposed and disgraced Henry B. Hyde. Hyde discovered Depew's genius for giving "good" advice away back in the late seventies—in 1877. Depew, on the witness stand last December, told the shameful story. He said,

I came in close touch with Mr. Hyde because a revolution was taking place in life insurance largely through the instrumentality of Mr. Hyde."

This revolution was, he went on to explain, the "deferred dividend plan," which means, though he did not admit it, a scheme by which the managers of a life insurance company accumulate in their own hands an enormous sum to be used in gambling and stockjobbing and in a variety of ingenious ways for adding vastly to their own personal fortunes, while the owners of the risked wealth get only the meagerest, if any, interest on their money.

Depew, without shame or consciousness of the necessity for it, testified that Hyde and he and their associates in the insurance (!) company roped in the public by the familiar device of the "get-rich-quick" jail birds. Revolution, indeed!

It was this "revolution" that made Hyde rich, and also the heads of such of the Equitable's rivals as adopted Hyde's methods, which, by the way, he did not invent but imported from abroad, where they had been practiced until the law forbade.

Depew testified that he advised with Hyde only about investing the huge sums; for, to use Depew's own language, "from the moment when the Equitable entered into that plan of Mr. Hyde's, their business began to grow by leaps and bounds, and money came in with great rapidity." Depew swore he advised only as to the storage of those huge masses of loot for Hyde and his gang, including Director and Trustee Depew, to graft upon. He denied on oath all knowledge of the infamous laws which Hyde bought—laws to make the policy holders defenseless. He denied on oath that he knew anything whatever as to the Equitable's traffic with the lobby and the legislature. Later, this following letter was shown him by Mr. Hughes:

"NEW YORK, Dec. 19, 1896.

"MY DEAR DEPEW:

"My friend who usually gets around at this time of the year has written me several letters to which I have not replied. He now writes that he will be here Monday or Tuesday, and desires to have me help him as usual. What shall I do?

"Faithfully yours,

"JOHN A. NICHOLS."

To show Depew's notion of the obligation of his oath, he, after admitting that he received the letter, gave this testimony:

"Do you know to whom the letter refers?" asked Mr. Hughes.

"I do not," replied Depew on oath.

"Reference is made to some one who 'usually gets around at this time of the year.' Does that refresh your recollection?"

And Depew swore, "It does not refresh my recollection as to his name."

Mr. Hughes then handed him this second letter:

"NEW YORK, December 24th, 1900..

"MY DEAR SENATOR:

"Our friend up the River has been very rantankerous of late and wants to know, you know. Don't care a hang, etc., and etc. As soon as you can conveniently say, will you kindly do so?

"Wishing you all the good things of life in this holiday season, I am,

"As ever yours,

"JOHN A. NICHOLS."

"*To Honorable Chauncey M. Depew,*
"*New York City.*"

Again Depew admitted having received a letter he dared not repudiate. Then came this astounding "lapse of memory":

"To what does that refer?" inquired Mr. Hughes.
"It refers to the same person," replied Depew.
"Do you now recall who he is?"
"I do not recall his name, no."
"Do you recall the subject-matter?"
"It was some claim he had against the company, which I never understood, and why I should have been written to on the subject I do not know."
"Was it anyone connected with the New York legislature?"
"No, not at all," was Depew's hasty and eager and significantly positive reply.
"Or connected with New York politics?"
"I think not."
"Or with the legislature or politics of any jurisdiction?"
"I think not."

This testimony on oath! It is explainable only on one of three theories—that Depew has had dealings with so many queer fish that he could not remember this one; or that he perjured himself; or that he both perjured himself and has had dealings with a multitude of queer fish.

Depew was a director of the Equitable from 1877, and an enthusiastic and even noisy public advocate of insurance. Yet he had no insurance himself, seeker of safe, conservative investments though he was. From 1888 he drew twenty thousands dollars a year as counsel—to give the Hydes and Alexanders advice on the "vast and intricate problems" which the Hyde "revolution" of life insurance, from an honorable and even public-spirited business to a swindling scheme, had created. And he took this salary graft—though the law forbids life-insurance directors to make money for themselves out of their trust funds. He did more and worse. As a member of the executive committee he voted to authorize a loan of two hundred and fifty thousand dollars to the Depew Improvement Company, an enterprise in which he was interested to the extent of one hundred thousand dollars of stock and whose total properties were appraised by the insurance department at one hundred and fifty thousand dollars. He went still further and did still worse. When the enterprise went smash, he promised— but let us quote the exact words of the testimony of Gerald H. Brown, the superintendent of the Equitable's bond and mortgage department:

Q. "What did you say to him (Depew) on that subject?"

A. "At that time he led me to believe that he was going to see the Equitable through without any losses."

Q. "What did he say in substance?"

A. "He said in substance that he had been dragged into this matter by Walter Webb, who is now deceased, I believe a brother of Dr. Seward Webb; that the place had been named after him without his consent, and that he had sunk one hundred and twenty-five to one hundred and fifty thousand dollars of his own money in it, which he was willing to lose if necessary or put in more to help the Equitable out and get it out without loss."

Q. *"Did he say in substance that he would save the Equitable harmless for the delay?"*

A. *"Yes, he did."*

Q. "Do you know if Mr. Depew made the same statement to any other person in your presence?"

A. "He made the statement to the comptroller of the society in my presence."

Q. "To Mr. Jordan?"

A. "Yes, sir."

HIS PREDOMINANT TRAIT

Last spring, before the quarrel which is still raging in Wall Street over the great life insurance bone, Depew was urged to "pay up" by friends of his, who knew what was coming. He was warned that disgrace was imminent for him. But he has one further characteristic which his mask of geniality has hid. He is stingy. To quote one of his intimates, "Chauncey is as stingy as Russell Sage. The only difference between them in that respect is that Chauncey keeps up his personal appearance." It is his stinginess that has prevented him from getting enormously rich, despite the niggardliness of the Vanderbilts

—his stinginess and that utter lack of courage to act for himself
which is best revealed in his adoring admiration of very rich
men who have the courage to risk real money. This admiration
seems the quainter when it is considered that no one knows
better than he that those "bold captains of industry" put their
money down only when they have marked the cards and loaded
the dice; and that, if by some strange chance they should lose
in an enterprise, they make the people, as passengers or freight
shippers or policy holders, bear the loss. Depew's stinginess
made it impossible for him to settle up his Equitable "loan"
loot, which, as he was forced to admit on the stand, he had, as
a member of the executive committee, voted to himself and his
associates. He went away to Europe—and the blow fell. And
now he is back where he was thirty years ago in the matter of
reputation. With this difference—the world judges youth le-
niently, but not maturity, especially not such experienced maturity as Depew's.

As the financial result of Depew's shortsighted stinginess
in failing to get himself off the black list of the insurance investigating committee, suits for seven hundred and fifty thousand dollars are now pending against him—seven hundred and
fifty thousand dollars of the money of the Equitable policy
holders whose trustee he was for twenty-eight years.

II

ALDRICH,

THE HEAD OF IT ALL

BUT Platt and Depew are significant only as showing how New York, foremost state of our forty-five, is represented in the Senate, in the body that is the final arbiter of the distribution of the enormous prosperity annually created by the American people. Long before Platt and Depew were sent to the Senate by and for "the interests," treason had been organized and established there; they simply joined the senatorial rank and file of diligent, faithful servants of the enemies of their country. For the organizer of this treason we must look at Nelson W. Aldrich, senior senator from Rhode Island.

Rhode Island is the smallest of our states in area and thirty-fourth in population—twelve hundred and fifty square miles, less than half a million people, barely seventy thousand voters with the rolls padded by the Aldrich machine. But size and numbers are nothing; it contains as many sturdy Americans proportionately as any other state. Its bad distinction of supplying the enemy with a bold leader is due to its ancient and aristocratic constitution, changed once, away back before the middle of the last century, but still an archaic document for class rule. The apportionment of legislators is such that one-eleventh of the population, and they the most ignorant and most venal, elect a majority of the legislature—which means that they elect the two United States senators. Each city and township counts as a political unit; thus, the five cities that together have two-thirds of the population are in an over-whelming minority before twenty almost vacant rural town-ships—their total population is not thirty-seven thousand—where the ignorance is even illiterate, where the superstition is mediaeval, where tradition and custom have made the vote an article of legitimate merchandising.

The combination of bribery and party prejudice is potent everywhere; but there come crises when these fail "the in-terests" for the moment. No storm of popular rage, however, could unseat the senators from Rhode Island. The people of Rhode Island might, as a people and voting almost unani-mously, elect a governor; but not a legislature. Bribery is a weapon forbidden those who stand for right and justice—who "fights the devil with fire" gives him choice of weapons, and must lose to him, though seeming to win. A few thousand dol-lars put in the experienced hands of the heelers, and the sen-atorial general agent of "the interests" is secure for another six years.

The Aldrich machine controls the legislature, the election boards, the courts—the entire machinery of the "republican form of government." In 1904, when Aldrich needed a legis-lature to reëlect him for his fifth consecutive term, it is esti-mated that carrying the state cost about two hundred thousand dollars—a small sum, easily to be got back by a few minutes of industrious pocket-picking in Wall Street; but a very large sum for Rhode Island politics, and a happy augury of a future day, remote, perhaps, but inevitable, when the people shall rule in Rhode Island. Despite the bribery, despite the swindling on registration lists and all the chicane which the statute book of the state makes easy for "the interests," Aldrich elected his governor by a scant eight hundred on the face of the returns. His legislature was, of course, got without the least difficulty—the majority for "the interests" is on joint ballot seventy-five out of a total of one hundred and seventeen. The only reason Aldrich disturbed himself about the governorship was that, through the anger of the people and the carelessness of the machine, a people's governor had been elected in 1903 and was up for reëlection; this people's governor, while without any power whatever under the Constitution, still could make disagreeable demands on the legislature, demands which did not sound well in the ears of the country and roused the people everywhere to just what was the source of the most respectable politician's security. So, Aldrich, contrary to his habit in recent years, took personal charge of the campaign and tried to show the people of Rhode Island that they were helpless and might as well quiet down, accept their destiny and spare his henchmen the expense and labor of wholesale bribery and fraud.

But, as a rule, Aldrich no longer concerns himself with Rhode Island's petty local affairs. "Not until about a year or so before it comes time for him to be elected again, does he get active," says his chief henchman, Gen. Charles R. Brayton, the state's boss. "He doesn't pay much attention to details." Why should he? Politically, the state is securely "the interests'" and his; financially, "the interests" and he have incorporated and assured to themselves in perpetuity about all the graft—the Rhode Island Securities Company, capitalized at and paying excellent dividends upon thirty-nine million dollars, representing an actual value of less than nine million dollars, owns, thanks to the munificence of the legislature, the state's street and trolley lines, gas and electric franchises, etc., etc. It began in a street railway company of Providence in which Aldrich, president of the Providence council and afterwards member of the legislature, acquired an interest. The sugar trust's Searles put in a million and a half shortly after the sugar trust got its license to loot through Aldrich at Washington; the legislature passed the necessary laws and gave the necessary franchises; Senator Steve Elkins and his crowd were invited in; more legislation; more franchises, more stocks and bonds, the right to loot the people of the state in perpetuity. Yes, Aldrich is rich, enormously rich, and his mind is wholly free for the schemes he plots and executes at Washington. And, like all the other senators who own large blocks of stocks and bonds in the great drainage companies fastened upon America's prosperity, his service is not the less diligent or adroit because he himself draws huge dividends from the people.

EARLY TRAINING OF ALDRICH

He was born in 1841, is only sixty-four years old, good for another fifteen years, at least, in his present rugged health, before "the interests" will have to select another for his safe seat and treacherous task. He began as a grocery boy, got the beginning of one kind of education in the public schools and in an academy at East Greenwich, Rhode Island. He became clerk in a fish store in Providence, then clerk in a grocery, then book-keeper, partner, and is still a wholesale grocer. He was elected to the legislature, applied himself so diligently to the work of getting his real education that he soon won the confidence of the boss, then Senator Anthony, and was sent to Congress, where he was Anthony's successor as boss and chief agent of the Rhode Island interests. He entered the United States Senate in 1881.

In 1901 his daughter married the only son and destined successor of John D. Rockefeller. Thus, the chief exploiter of the American people is closely allied by marriage with the chief schemer in the service of their exploiters. This fact no American should ever lose sight of. It is a political fact; it is an economic fact. It places the final and strongest seal upon the bonds uniting Aldrich and "the interests."

When Aldrich entered the Senate, twenty-five years ago, at the splendid full age of forty, the world was just beginning to feel the effects of the principles of concentration and combination, which were inexorably and permanently established with the discoveries in steam and electricity that make the whole human race more and more like one community of interdependent neighbors. It was a moment of opportunity, an unprecedented chance for Congress, especially its deliberate and supposedly sagacious senators, to "promote the general welfare" by giving those principles free and just play in securing the benefits of expanding prosperity to all, by seeing that the profits from the coöperation of all the people went *to* the people. Aldrich and the traitor Senate saw the opportunity. But they saw in it only a chance to enable a class to despoil the masses.

Before he reached the Senate, Aldrich had had fifteen years of training in how to legislate the proceeds of the labor of the many into the pockets of the few. He entered it as the representative of local interests engaged in robbing by means of slyly worded tariff schedules that changed protection against the foreigner into plunder of the native. His demonstrated excellent talents for sly, slippery work in legislative chambers and committee rooms and his security in his seat against popular revulsions and outbursts together marked him for the position of chief agent of the predatory band which was rapidly forming to take care of the prosperity of the American people.

Various senators represent various divisions and subdivisions of this colossus. But Aldrich, rich through franchise grabbing, the intimate of Wall Street's great robber barons, the father-in-law of the only son of *the* Rockefeller—Aldrich represents the colossus. Your first impression of many and conflicting interests has disappeared. You now see a single interest, with a single agent-in-chief to execute its single purpose—getting rich at the expense of the labor and the independence of the American people. And the largest head among the many heads of this monster is that of Rockefeller, father of the only son-in-law of Aldrich and his intimate in all the relations of life!

There are many passages in the Constitution in which a Senate, true to its oath and mindful of the welfare of the people and of the nation, could find mandates to stop wholesale robbery, and similar practices.

And yet, what has the Senate done—the Senate, with its high-flown pretenses of reverence for the Constitution? It has so legislated and so refrained from legislating that more than half of all the wealth created by the American people belongs to less than one per cent of them; that the income of the average American family has sunk to less than six hundred dollars a year; that of our more than twenty-seven million children of school age, less than twelve millions go to school, and more than two millions work in mines, shops and factories.

And the leader, the boss of the Senate for the past twenty years has been—Aldrich!

In vain would "the interests" have stolen franchises, in vain would they have corrupted the public officials of states and cities, if they had not got absolute and unshakable control of the Senate. But, with the Senate theirs, how secure, how easy and how rich the loot!

SOURCE OF HIS POWER

The sole source of Aldrich's power over the senators is "the interests"—the sole source, but quite sufficient to make him permanent and undisputed boss. Many of the senators, as we shall in due time and in detail note, are, like Depew and Platt, the direct agents of the various state or sectional subdivisions of "the interests," and these senators constitute about two-thirds of the entire Senate. Of the remainder several know that if they should oppose "the interests" they would lose their seats; several others are silent because they feel that to speak out would be useless; a few do speak out, but are careful not to infringe upon the rigid rule of "senatorial courtesy," which thus effectually protects the unblushing corruptionists, the obsequious servants of corruption, and likewise the many traitors to party as well as the people, from having disagreeable truths dinged into their ears. Tillman will "pitchfork" a president, but not a senator, and not the Senate in any but the most useless, futile way—this, though none knows better than he how the rights and the property of the people are trafficked in by his colleagues of both parties, with a few exceptions. There are a few other honest men from the South and from the West, as many of the few honest Republicans as honest Democrats. Yet party allegiance and "senatorial courtesy" make them abettors of treason, allies of Aldrich and Gorman.

"Senatorial courtesy!" We shall have to return to it, as it is the hypocritical mask behind which the few senators who pose as real representatives of the people hide in silence and inaction.

The greatest single hold of "the interests" is the fact that they are the "campaign contributors"—the men who supply the money for "keeping the party together," and for "getting out the vote." Did you ever think where the millions for watchers, spellbinders, halls, processions, posters, pamphlets, that are spent in national, state and local campaigns come from? Who pays the big election expenses of your congressman, of the men you send to the legislature to elect senators? Do you imagine those who foot those huge bills are fools? Don't you know that they make sure of getting their money back, with interest, compound upon compound? Your candidates get most of the money for their campaigns from the party committees; and the central party committee is the national committee with which congressional and state and local committees are affiliated. The bulk of the money for the "political trust" comes from "the interests." "The interests" will give only to the "political trust." And that means Aldrich and his Democratic (!) lieutenant, Gorman of Maryland, leader of the minority in the Senate. Aldrich, then, is the head of the "political trust" and Gorman is his right-hand man. When you speak of the Republican party, of the Democratic party, of the "good of the party," of the "best interests of the party," of "wise party policy," you mean what Aldrich and Gorman, acting for their clients, deem wise and proper and "Republican" or "Democratic."

To relate the treason in detail would mean taking up bill after bill and going through it, line by line, word by word, and showing how this interpolation there or that excision yonder meant millions on millions more to this or that interest, millions on millions less for the people as merchants, wage or salary earners, consumers; how the killing of this measure meant immunity to looters all along the line; how the alteration of the wording of that other "trifling" resolution gave a quarter of a cent a pound on every one of hundreds of millions of pounds of some necessary of life to a certain small group of men; how this innocent looking little measure safeguarded the railway barons in looting the whole American people by excessive charges and rebates. Few among the masses have the patience to listen to these dull matters—and, so, "the interests" and their agents have prosperity and honor instead of justice and jail.

No railway legislation that was not either helpful to or harmless against "the interests"; no legislation on the subject of corporations that would interfere with "the interests," which use the corporate form to simplify and systematize their stealing; no legislation on the tariff question unless it secured to "the interests" full and free license to loot; no investigations of wholesale robbery or of any of the evils resulting from it— there you have in a few words the whole story of the Senate's treason under Aldrich's leadership, and of why property is concentrating in the hands of the few and the little children of the masses are being sent to toil in the darkness of mines, in the dreariness and unhealthfulness of factories instead of being sent to school; and why the great middle class—the old-fashioned Americans, the people with the incomes of from two thousand to fifteen thousand a year—is being swiftly crushed into dependence and the repulsive miseries of "genteel poverty." The heavy and ever heavier taxes of "the interests" are swelling rents, swelling the prices of food, clothing, fuel, all the necessities and all the necessary comforts. And the Senate both forbids the lifting of those taxes and levies fresh taxes for its master.

Drawn by James Montgomery Flagg

THE CHIEF OBSTRUCTIONIST AT WORK

"Various senators represent various divisions and subdivisions of this colossus. But Aldrich, rich through franchise grabbing, the intimate of Wall Street's great robber barons, the father-in-law of the only son of *the* Rockefeller—Aldrich represents the colossus. Your first impression of many and conflicting interests has disappeared. You now see a single interest, with a single agent-in-chief to execute its single purpose—getting rich at the expense of the labor and the independence of the American people."—*The Treason of the Senate*

THREE ACTS OF TREASON

Let us concentrate on three signal acts of treachery which Aldrich had to perpetrate publicly and which are typical and all-embracing in effect.

There are, of course, two honestly tenable views of the tariff question. But both the honest advocates of high tariff and the honest advocates of low tariff are agreed in opposition to tariff for plunder only. And we are noting there only that last kind of tariff, which is as hateful to protectionist as to free trader because it is in truth a treason.

Two years after Aldrich came to the Senate there was a revision of the tariff law enacted during the Civil War. In that revision Aldrich took an active part, and laid the foundations of his power with "the interests," then in their early formative period. But it was not until 1890 that he had an opportunity to make his first large contribution toward the firm establishment of conditions of unequal division of prosperity which have now resulted in expropriating the American people from the ownership of their own country. In 1890 the House of Representatives passed the so-called McKinley bill. As it left the House it was, on the whole, a fairly honest protective-tariff measure, extreme, in the opinion of some Republicans and of many Democrats, but on the whole an attempt to raise revenue and to protect all American industries. "The interests" had their representatives in the House by the score; but the House is so directly responsible to the people that it dared not originate and utter a measure of frank treason. The bill went to the Senate, was there handed to Aldrich and his committee for examination in the secrecy of the committee room. When Aldrich reported the bill, there was a wild outcry from the House—largely for political effect upon the astonished people, who almost awakened to the enormity of the treason. The McKinley bill had been killed; for it Aldrich had substituted a bill to enrich "the interests" with the earnings and savings of the masses. The sugar trust's schedule, for example, was so scandalous that even the mild and devotedly partisan McKinley exclaimed publicly that it was far too high. It gave the trust a loot of sixty cents the hundred pounds, of three million dollars a year over and above the high protection it already had, when sugar can be refined more cheaply in this country than anywhere else in the world, the labor cost being insignificant.

But the traitor Senate stood firm for its masters; and the House, in terror of Aldrich and his "campaign contributors" accepted what it knew meant temporary political ruin—better offend the short-memoried people than "the interests" that forgive and forget nothing and never. The Aldrich bill was passed and was signed by the President. The party and the President, and Congressman McKinley and all who had had anything to do with the bill went down in defeat—but not Aldrich, secure in his Rhode Island seat, and not any of the senators who were needed by "the interests." And "the interests" got their loot— literally, hundreds of millions a year, every penny of it coming out of the pockets of the people.

The Democrats came in, and in 1894 the Wilson bill passed the House—a fairly honest and really moderate expression of the low-tariff view of the tariff question. The Senate had a small Democratic majority, nominally. So, Aldrich was pretending to take a back seat; and his right bower, Gorman, was posing as leader of the Senate, that is, of its traitorous band of servants of "the interests"—more than half of all the senators. The Wilson bill reappeared from the secrecy of the Aldrich-Gorman committee so absolutely transformed from a thing of decency to a thing of shame that the whole country was convulsed. Again "the interests" had been looked after; there had been injected into the bill provisions for loot for each and every one of Aldrich's powerful clients, the electors of senators, Democratic and Republican, the suppliers of campaign funds and tips on stocks and shares in "good things," and of funds to be lost at poker to congressmen too "honest" and too "proud" to accept a direct bribe. The scandal was enormous—

so enormous that there had to be a farcical investigation at which Havemeyer, the sugar king, and Chapman, the agent of the brokers through whom the senators and representatives gambled in stocks, refused to tell what they knew of the utter rottenness of the leaders of Senate and House. Chapman got a few days in jail for contempt; Havemeyer, tried for the same offense, and whistling softly all through this farcical trial, was acquitted. But the scandal did not stagger Aldrich and Gorman and their band. They, more than a majority of the Senate, most of them traitors to the people wearing the Republican disguise, enough of them from among the Democrats—Gorman, Jim Smith of New Jersey, Brice of Ohio, Ed Murphy of New York—formed a solid, brazen phalanx and forced the House— again in terror of the "campaign contributors"—to accept the Aldrich bill or nothing. The President denounced it, refused to sign it—he almost took the advice of Tom Johnson to veto it. But the "Aldrich-Gorman political trust" had been shrewd enough to leave in the bill some features popularly attractive that happened not to injure any of the interests, some features that made it *seem* less predatory than the Aldrich bill of 1890; and the President let it become a law without his signature. In action, it soon demonstrated that as a whole it was quite as effective as the Aldrich bill of 1890 in doing all that a tariff law could to accelerate the expropriation of the people from ownership of any property whatever.

Poor Wilson! Had he been a "practical" tariff expert like Aldrich, how he would have cried out against that law which bore his name as a cover for Aldrich's treachery!

Aldrich's next great positive tariff opportunity came in 1897. The Dingley tariff bill left the House more satisfactory to "the interests" than any that had preceded it. The House had been gradually passing into the control of "the interests" and the doctrine that to serve "the interests" which financed the party and acted as fatherly guardians of the poor, helpless and so mysteriously impoverishing American people was to serve God and country, had gained ground, had become almost as axiomatic as it now is. Still, the leaders of the House had not dared wholly to lose their point of view—or, rather, to pretend to lose it. The Dingley bill entered the Senate, almost perfect from the standpoint of the agents of the enemies of the people there enthroned. But not quite perfect. The defects were all speedily remedied, however, in the secrecy of Aldrich's committee room. And the third Aldrich tariff bill became a law. Like the Aldrich-emasculated anti-trust legislation, like the Aldrich-manipulated laws for the regulation of railways, this law is, in its main schedules—those dealing with the fundamental necessaries of civilized life used by all the people, a stupendous robbery, taking cognizance of the huge developments of American resources to arrange that all but a scanty share of them shall become profit for the plunderers. And since 1897 the uppiling of huge fortunes, the reduction of the American people toward wage and salary slavery has gone forward with amazing rapidity. The thieves use each year's rich haul to make larger nets for larger hauls the next.

The abounding prosperity, the immense amount of work to do, has caused the paying of salaries and wages that, as the reports of the commercial agencies show, are *in money* almost as high as they were fifteen years ago and about where they were *in purchasing power* thirty years ago. But the cost of living is going up, up, faster than incomes; and the number of tenant farmers, of renters, of paupers, of unemployed has increased as never before, even in straightened times. In place of the old proportion in the lot of the American people, there is gross disproportion. How Aldrich must laugh as he watches the American people meekly submitting to this plundering through tariff and railway rates and hugely overcapitalized corporations! And what, think you, must be his opinion of the man who in all seriousness attributes the astounding contrasts between the mountainous fortunes of the few and the ant-hill hoardings of the many to the superior intelligence of the few? Yet, Aldrich's contempt for the mentality of the masses is not unjustified, is it?

A JUGGLER OF LEGISLATION

How does Aldrich work? Obviously, not much steering is necessary, when the time comes to vote. "The interests" have a majority and to spare. The only questions are such as permitting a senator to vote and at times to speak against "the interests" when the particular measure is mortally offensive to the people of his particular state or section. Those daily sham battles in the Senate! Those paradings of sham virtue! Is it not strange that the other senators, instead of merely busying themselves at writing letters or combing their whiskers, do not break into shouts of laughter?

Aldrich's real work—getting the wishes of his principals, directly or through their lawyers, and putting these wishes into proper form if they are orders for legislation or into the proper channels if they are orders to kill or emasculate legislation—this work is all done, of course, behind the scenes. When Aldrich is getting orders, there is of course never any witness. The second part of his task—execution—is in part a matter of whispering with his chief lieutenants, in part a matter of consultation in the secure secrecy of the Senate committee rooms. Aldrich is in person chairman of the chief Senate committee—finance. There he labors, assisted by Gorman, his right bower, who takes his place as chairman when the Democrats are in power; by Spooner, his left bower and public mouthpiece; by Allison, that Nestor of craft; by the Pennsylvania Railroad's Penrose; by Tom Platt of New York, corruptionist and lifelong agent of corruptionists; by Joe Bailey of Texas, and several other sympathetic or silent spirits. Together they concoct and sugar-coat the bitter doses for the people—the loot measures and the suffocating of the measures in restraint of loot. In the unofficial but powerful steering committee—which receives from him the will of "the interests" and translates it into "party policy"—he works through Allison as chairman—but Allison's position is recognized as purely honorary.

And, also, Aldrich sits in the powerful interstate-commerce committee; there, he has his "pal," the brazen Elkins of West Virginia, as chairman. He is not on the committee on appropriations; but Allison is, is its chairman, and Cullom of Illinois is there—and in due time we shall endeavor to get better acquainted with both of them. In the commerce committee, he has Frye of Maine, to look after such matters as the projected, often postponed, but never abandoned, loot through ship subsidy; in the Pacific Railroad committee he has the valiant soldier, the honest lumber and railway multi-millionaire, the embalmed-beef hero, Alger, as chairman; in the post-office and post-roads committee, which looks after the railways' postal graft, a clean steal from the Treasury of upward of ten millions a year—some put it as high as thirty millions—he has Penrose as chairman. In that highly important committee, the one on rules, he himself sits; but mouthpiece Spooner is naturally chairman. Their associates are Elkins and Lodge—another pair that need to be better known to the American people. Bailey is the chief "Democratic" member. What a sardonic jest to speak of these men as Republicans and Democrats!

WHEN THE CURTAIN WAS LIFTED

These committees carry on their colorless routine and also their real work—promoting thievish legislation, preventing decent legislation, devising ways and means of making rottenest dishonesty look like honesty and patriotism—these committees carry on their work in secrecy. *Public* business in profound privacy! Once Vest, angered by some misrepresentation made by Aldrich, had part of the minutes of a meeting of the finance committee read in open Senate—a gross breach of "senatorial courtesy"! Before the rudely lifted curtain was dropped, the country had a rare, illuminatory view of Aldrich. Here is this official minute:

"At a meeting of the Committee on Finance on March 17, 1894, on motion of Mr. Aldrich, the committee proceeded to a

consideration of the provisions (of the Wilson bill) in regard to
an income tax. Mr. Aldrich moved that the whole provision be
stricken out of the bill."

He and Allison, that lifelong professional friend of the
"plain people," had both voted aye. A pitiful sight he and
Allison were, flustering and red, as this damning fact was read
in open Senate, with the galleries full and all the reporters in
their places! It is the only time the people have ever had a
look at Aldrich in his shirt sleeves and hard at his repulsive but
remunerative trade. But the people do not need to see the
processes. They see, they feel, they suffer from the finished
result—the bad law enacted, the good law killed.

When Bacon, in 1903, moved to call on the Department of
Commerce and Labor for full facts about the selling of American goods at prices from one-fourth to a full hundred per cent.
cheaper abroad than at home, Aldrich at once moved to refer
the resolution to his committee, and his motion was carried. A
year later, Bacon reminded the Senate of his former resolution
and of how it was sleeping in Aldrich's committee, and rein-
troduced it. He backed it up with masses of facts—how "our"
sewing machines sell abroad for fifteen dollars and here for
twenty-five dollars; how "our" borax, a Rockefeller product,
costs seven and a half cents a pound here and only two and a
half cents abroad; how "our" nails, a Rockefeller-Morgan product, sell here for four dollars and fifty cents a keg and
abroad for three dollars and ten cents; how the foreigner gets
for one dollar as much of "our" window glass as we get for
two dollars; how Schwab, in a letter to Frick on May 15, 1899,
had said that, while steel rails sold here at twenty-eight dollars
a ton, he could deliver them in England for sixteen dollars a
ton and make four dollars a ton profit; how the beef trust sold
meat from twenty-five to fifty per cent. dearer in Buffalo than
just across the Canadian line; how the harvester trust sold its
reapers cheaper on the continent of Europe than to an Illinois
farmer coming to its main factory at Chicago; how on every
article in common use among the American people of city,

town and country, "the interests" were boldly robbing the people.

And Mr. Aldrich said, "Absurd!" And the Senate refused even to call upon the Department of Labor for the facts.

An illustration of another form of Aldrich's methods: When House and Senate disagree on a bill, each appoints a conference committee; and the two committees meet and try to find common ground. At one of these conferences—on the war-tax bill—Aldrich appeared, as usual in all matters which concern "the interests," at the head of the Senate conferees. He pressed more than a score of amendments to a single paragraph in the House measure. The House committee resisted him, and he slowly retreated, yielding point after point until finally he had yielded all but one. He said: "Well, gentlemen of the House, we of the Senate have yielded practically everything to your body. We dare not go back absolutely empty-handed." And the House conferees gave him the one remaining point—the "mere trifle." It afterwards appeared that this was probably the only one of his more than a score of amendments that he really wanted; the others were mere blinds. For, that "mere trifle" subtly gave the tobacco "interests" (Rockefeller-Ryan) a license to use the war-revenue tax on tobacco to exort an additional four or five cents a pound from the consumer! There are half a dozen clauses, at least, in the present so-called Dingley tariff that protect the many-sided Standard Oil trust alone. But it takes an expert to find them, and doubtless many have escaped detection.

THE MAN WHO LAUGHS

Such is Aldrich, the senator. At the second session of the last Congress his main achievements, so far as the surface shows, were smothering all inquiry into the tariff and the freight-rate robberies, helping Elkins and the group of traitors in the service of the thieves who control the railway corporations to emasculate railway legislation, helping Allison and

Bailey to smother the bill against the food poisoners for dividends. During the past winter he has been concentrating on the "defense of the railways"—which means not the railways nor yet the railway corporations, but simply the Rockefeller-Morgan looting of the people by means of their control of the corporations that own the railways.

Has Aldrich intellect? Perhaps. But he does not show it. He has never in his twenty-five years of service in the Senate introduced or advocated a measure that shows any conception of life above what might be expected in a Hungry Joe. No, intellect is not the characteristic of Aldrich—or of any of these traitors, or of the men they serve. A scurvy lot they are, are they not, with their smirking and cringing and voluble palaver about God and patriotism and their eager offerings of endowments for hospitals and colleges whenever the American people so much as looks hard in their direction!

Aldrich is rich and powerful. Treachery has brought him wealth and rank, if not honor, of a certain sort. He must laugh at us, grown-up fools, permitting a handful to bind the might of our eighty millions and to set us all to work for them.

EDITOR'S NOTE.—*In the March instalment of Mr. Phillips's articles on "The Treason of the Senate," the statement was made that a candidate for a federal district attorneyship, recommended by Senator Platt, "had been caught stealing trust funds," and that on this account his candidacy was rejected by the President. Mr. Phillips has since ascertained that this statement was untrue, and that the reason for the failure of his candidacy was not his character, which is above reproach, but was his zealous espousal of the Platt side of the New York factional warfare.*

It is requested that any other publication which may have reprinted such statement will publish this correction, as the COSMOPOLITAN *and Mr. Phillips wish to be fair and just and accurate throughout this series.*

III

LEFT ARM OF THE MONSTER

WE have now seen,

First: That there has been in the past quarter of a century an amazing and unnatural uppiling of wealth in the hands of a few; that there has been an equally amazing and equally unnatural descent of the masses, despite skill and industry and the boundless resources of the country, toward the dependence of wages and salaries; that the massing of wealth and the diffusion of dependence are both swiftly increasing.

Second: That these abnormal conditions have come with, and out of, the development of a small group of controllers of railways and, through them, of finance and manufactures; that this little group controls and freely levies upon and trims the twenty thousand millions of our annual internal commerce, three-fourths of which is interstate and therefore subject to the supervision of Congress only.

Third: That this little group owes its power and its wealth, in part to legislation favoring it, but in the main to the failure of Congress to safeguard the people in the possession of the fruits of their labor by enacting the laws in regulation of interstate commerce which the public welfare has clearly demanded and which the Constitution clearly authorizes.

Fourth: That the responsibility both for legislation in favor of "the interests" and for failure to legislate in restraint upon their depredations rests wholly and directly upon the United States Senate.

Fifth: That, as the Senate's legislation for "the interests" and its failure to legislate against them have not been frank and open, but tricky, stealthy and underhanded, the Senate cannot plead in its own defense either ignorance or honest motives; that its conduct has been and is deliberate, has been and is an intentional serving of "the interests" and an intentional betrayal of the people, has been and is treason.

Sixth: That the right arm of this treason has been and is Senator Aldrich.

But the monster has a left arm, also. And that left arm, almost as powerful and quite as useful as the right, is Arthur P. Gorman, of Maryland.

The common enemy, "the interests," dominate the political as well as the industrial machinery of the nation. In the political machinery of both parties they have at the important points faithful, well-paid agents, shrewd at fooling the people or at selecting those who can fool the people. Their control of state legislatures is such that they determine nearly three-fourths of the senators. Whoever may be, "for appearance's sake," in charge of the Republican machine, Aldrich is really in charge. Whoever may be nominally at the head of the Democratic machine, Gorman is really there. For only to men approved by them or their lieutenants will "the interests" supply the "oil" indispensable to a machine. Popular movements and heroes and spasms of reform rage and pass; but the machine abides, and after the storm it resumes; indeed, it works exceeding well even through the roughest cyclones. To our national political machine, with its label that reads "Republican" on the one side and "Democratic" on the other, Aldrich and Gorman are as the thumb and the forefinger to a skillful hand.

GORMAN, FROM PAGE TO "PATRIOT"

Gorman was born in Maryland sixty-seven years ago. After a few years at public school, he, at the age of thirteen, entered politics; his father, a contractor and lobbyist in a small way, got him a place as page in the United States Senate. This was in 1852, when the slave oligarchy, then in the heyday of its haughtiness, was using the same methods of sophistries about alleged "constitutional law" and alleged jealously for the "grand old Constitution" that the industrial oligarchy is using in this heyday of its haughtiness. The slave oligarchy, to maintain and strengthen itself, was strenuous for the state as paramount over the nation; to-day, we have the doctrine resurrected by alleged Republicans from its grave under the battlefields of the Civil War, rehabilitated and restated to make the nation impotent before enemies far worse than the slave oligarchy. And under the renovated banner of "states' rights," "the blue" and "the gray," the "bloody shirt" Forakers and Spooners and the Confederate Baileys and Stones march shoulder to shoulder in protecting "the interests" in their lootings.

Gorman, the brightest of bright boys, absorbed and assimilated all the mysteries of the Senate—all its crafty, treacherous ways of smothering, of emasculating, of perverting legislation; how to thwart the people and shift the responsibility; when to kill a just bill in committee and when to kill it in open Senate in the midst of a wild scrimmage among "honest patriots contending only for the right but conscientiously differing in views." For the Senate, not elected by the people, not responsible to them, and containing a controlling nucleus of men who have their seats as securely and for as long a period as the members of any hereditary legislative body in the world— the Senate has almost from the beginning been the bulwark of whatever form of privilege happened to be struggling to maintain itself against the people.

Gorman continued his invaluable education in the Senate throughout the stormy, corrupt days of the Civil War. In 1866 he received from a Republican President the internal-revenue collectorship for the Fifth Maryland District. It has been charged that he was in those days a Republican, and that this appointment is proof of it. But the charge is foolish. He was no more a Republican then than he is a Democrat now. Such men have no politics of principle; and no one will think they have if he will take the trouble to glance from the badge to the man and his deeds. In the spring of 1869, Gorman ceased to be a Republican officeholder; in the fall he was elected to the lower house of the Maryland legislature by the Democratic party. There, at the age of thirty, he entered upon his real career.

Aldrich's simple home problem has been to rule Rhode Island by means of an aristocratic old constitution which puts all the power in the hands of the ignorant and cheaply purchaseable voters of a few sparsely populated rural townships. Gorman's has been less easy, yet far from difficult. Maryland, being a border state, has a great many white Republicans; and there is a negro vote large enough to hold the balance of power. It has been Gorman's cue to keep "negro domination" ever before the eyes of the Maryland voter, to make the whites feel that, rotten though his machine is, it is yet the only alternative to "rule by and for the black." When the Republican machine, usually his docile dependent, would in some brief spasm of reform cease to play his game, he has sometimes lost; not always, because the uncertain conditions in Baltimore compelled the machine to maintain at all times an army of thugs, repeaters, ballot-box stuffers and the like, and several times the lost day has been saved to him by a carnival of ballot-box debauchery and bloody rioting.

In a speech in Baltimore, on October 15, 1895, Theodore Roosevelt said,

"I caught Mr. Gorman in an *ugly falsehood*, one that might be termed better in the plain Anglo-Saxon *word of three letters*."

Mr. Bonaparte, the present secretary of the navy said on March 31, 1904:

"A good many years ago Mr. Gorman was described on good Democratic authority as a 'generalissimo of the lobby.' Senator Gorman calls me a professional reformer. Whether it is more commendable to be a professional reformer or a professional lobbyist I must leave each to judge for himself. But I must own that Senator Gorman's 'profession' has had one advantage over mine—it has been vastly *more profitable.* Although the senator seems to think *honesty* is of minor importance in determining a man's qualifications for high public office, it is certainly true that *a conspicuous absence of this qualification* has not proved fatal to at least *one man holding a high office* and aspiring to a higher." (Gorman was then a seeker of the nomination for President.)

On October 22, 1888, Henry E. Wooten, a distinguished Marylander living at Ellicott City, issued an open letter to Gorman in which he challenged him to sue for libel on the following statements:

"That you, with your own hands, assisted by others, distributed three thousand dollars among the ruffians that thronged the city in 1875.

"That you were an active participant in the fraud of 1879. You had Higgins at your headquarters in Baltimore, and he was in this county at least upon two occasions closeted with you and other conspirators against the rights and liberties of the people, perfecting the details of the conspiracy, conferring as to what names should be dropped and what names misspelled, and by which route the negro repeaters should be sent out.

That you are *steeped in corruption and saturated with official perjury.*"

Gorman did not sue Mr. Wooten for calling him a briber and perjurer. Nor did he sue Mr. Roosevelt for calling him a liar, nor Mr. Bonaparte for calling him a notoriously dishonest professional lobbyist. Nor did he sue Bernard Carter, the eminent lawyer and Democrat, who denounced him as "generalissimo of the lobby" when he was handing over the streets of Baltimore to the Baltimore and Ohio Railroad, which was the section of "the interests" he chiefly represented in those days.

BASIS OF GORMAN'S POWER

The original basis of Gorman's power in Maryland was the state-built and state-owned Chesapeake and Ohio Canal, connecting the coal regions with tide water. This canal had two values for a boss: it offered an indefinitely large number of "soft snaps"—good for heelers of all grades—and it enabled corrupt and highly profitable negotiations with the railways, which would be prevented from looting the people through extortionate freight rates if it were honestly administered. Gorman appreciated both of these values to the uttermost. In 1872, at the very outset of his career, he had himself made president of the canal company, and that soon enabled him to make himself boss of the party and of the state, at first a levier upon the corrupt controllers of big corporations, then a partner and promoter of those controllers in "milking" both the corporations and the people. In 1880, a suit was brought by Daniel K. Stewart to enjoin Gorman and his gang in control of the canal from entering into contracts to give the railroad companies rebates. The testimony revealed Gorman as a grafter, great and small. There was the big side to the scandal—the huge loot in rebates, and in packing the service with idle heelers. Then there was the minor stealing revealed in expense accounts, of which this is only one typical specimen from a mass offered in evidence:

> Dec. 13, 1874.
> Gorman—
>
> | | |
> |---|---:|
> | Board and rooms | $13.50 |
> | Boy, 25 cts.; fire, $1.50; cash, 50 cts. | 2.25 |
> | Fires in two rooms | 1.50 |
> | Two carriages, $4; telegram, 30 cts. | 4.30 |
> | Champagne, $2; hack, $1 | 3.00 |
> | Cash to waiters | 10.00 |
> | | $34.55 |

Despite scandal and outcry Gorman, giving Maryland

choice between thug domination and "nigger" domination, was able to hold on to the canal until it had been "milked dry," had been rendered worthless and had been turned over by Gorman's legislature to the Baltimore and Ohio and the Western Maryland Railways. And with it went the people of Maryland's protection against railway-rate extortion through the necessities of life.

It was by stupendous open frauds that the gang elected the legislature which put Gorman into the United States Senate in 1881. Several of the heelers afterwards confessed. Harrig, for instance, told how "Gorman and Higgins called the body of men (repeaters) together to meet them at a certain hotel in this city (Baltimore). He (Gorman) wanted a certain man in Howard County defeated for the legislature." Charlie Goodman, who had twenty-eight entries in the criminal docket against him, told how "Higgins paid me five dollars apiece for my forty men." He told about various Baltimore elections—the gangs of roughs sent by the political machines of New York, Philadelphia, etc., in exchange for similar services from the Gorman gang. "Those repeaters," said he, "have been put in my hands forty strong. I was ordered not to put in less than five thousand votes; but I usually put in fifty-eight hundred."

So diligently did Gorman reward the assiduity of his humble allies who lifted him to the Senate by these methods that the Independent Democrats of Maryland, in a public address in 1887, said, "Of twenty-three state and federal employees in one ward (of Baltimore) we have found nineteen whose names appear on the criminal records." There were money rewards also; these, of course, came chiefly from the Baltimore and Ohio Railroad, which financed the Gorman machine and which had the first call upon Gorman himself until the Pennsylvania Railroad bought control of the Baltimore and Ohio. Then, naturally, Gorman passed to the service of that powerful section of "the interests" called the "Pennsylvania."

We may not linger upon Gorman's home record—upon the treachery to the people of Maryland, equal proportionately to

Depew's and Platt's in New York, to Aldrich's in Rhode Island
—the hundreds of millions of loot, the great licenses to loot in
perpetuity handed over, with no public compensation, to railway companies, gas companies, traction companies, or, rather,
to the greedy few who "milk" those companies and, through the
companies, the people. The distinction between the corporation and the thief who seizes and robs it and uses it as a tool for
robbing others should not be lost sight of. It is precisely that
abysmal but too often overlooked distinction which makes the
men in control of our industrial machinery, not leaders and developers of the national resources, but looters and national
enemies, parasites upon prosperity, and upon the producers of
prosperity.

"WHERE A MAN'S TREASURE IS"

Gorman entered the Senate as a senator twenty-five years
ago this spring. He already knew the mysteries of the Senate.
He had been studying and practicing the black art of politics
for nearly thirty years. Inevitably he was soon a leader, the
trusted counselor of those of his party who wished to be led
skillfully in the subtle ways of doing the will of "the interests"
without inflaming the people against them. He, of course, entered the Senate primarily as an agent of the eminently respectable among his pals and sponsors, the interstate looters through
the railway corporations of his state. Every traitor senator,
whatever else he represents in the way of an enemy to the
people, always represents some thief or group of thieves through
railways. For the railway, reaching everywhere, as intimate a
part of our life now as the air we breathe, is the easy and perfect instrument of the wholesale looter of investors and of the
public, and is also the natural nucleus and subsidizer of a
political machine. And, as the railways have merged—even
Aldrich now publicly concedes that competition has been almost abolished—the senators have "merged" also. And peace
reigns in the Senate Chamber under a "community of interest"

in treason corresponding to the "community of interest" in spoliation.

But it is with the "merging" of the Republican and Democratic political machines that we are now concerned. And let no one be distracted by the roaring eloquence and the sham battles of the Senate or by the "eminent respectability" of the senators into losing sight of the central fact that the machines, drawing their revenues from the one power, ruled by the twin agents of that power, are the property of that power—never more so than when the politicians, wearing and disgracing official robes, beat the air and "jam the wind" to make the people confuse party and party principle with party machine. To appreciate the Senate look, not at its professions, not at the surface pretenses of the measures it permits to become laws, but at the effect of those laws—how plutocracy and plunder thrive under them. And to understand why the laws always somehow fail to serve the people, always somehow relicense the people's enemies, look at Aldrich and Gorman and their band— how they got, how they keep their seats; whom they associate with; their private fortunes; how their fortunes are invested. "Where a man's treasure is, there will his heart be also."

Rarely does the Senate hold a session without there cropping out some indication of the existence of this secret "merger" of the two party machines under which they work together in harmony wherever "the interests" are interested—befogging the responsibility for acts hostile to the public interest, lining up senators from both parties for a debate or a vote, and releasing to perfunctory, though always perfervid opposition, senators who have "insuperable conscientious objections" in the particular matter or dare not offend the people of their state in that particular crisis. For, while many of the "merged" senators can all but leave out of account the feelings of "my people," there are more who have to be "conscientious" and careful and crafty, except during the first two or three years after they have been elected, and when they have three or four years before they come up for election again. Occasionally the evidences of the existence and smooth working of the "merger" are so plain that only the very stupid or the stone-blind partisan would fail to see.

AN HISTORIC ACT OF TREACHERY

But these almost daily indications of the "merger" and of the real inwardness of most of the senators on both sides are rarely clear enough for any but the well versed in the mysteries and undercurrents of practical politics. For a clear proof, let us recall the historic act of treachery which revealed Gorman publicly and branded his ownership in national affairs as indelibly and conspicuously upon him as it had long been branded upon him in Maryland state affairs.

Whenever there is a revenue or a railway-rate bill up before the Senate, there is obviously a crisis of the first magnitude between "the interests" and the people. The Senate is extremely slippery at manipulation in public. Besides, it has its committees for doing in secret the traitorous acts that could not be done publicly; and, in times of crisis, the "merger" uses all the cunning of its double-headed leader, Aldrich-Gorman, and his adroit staff, in arranging the public side of the act of treachery so that appearances will be deceptive or at least will deceive a people always heretofore disposed too generously to give their public men the benefit of every conceivable doubt. But in 1894 the "merger" was not working as smoothly as it is now; "the interests" had not yet either driven honest senators from public life, or coerced some of them, cowed others and flattered the rest into silence or into no speech stronger than futile, general, and impersonal protest couched in terms redolent of "senatorial courtesy." So the great act of treason of 1894 was done with much and terrible public scandal.

The revenue or tariff bill—the Wilson bill—had come up from the House, with much loot in it for "the interests," for Mr. Wilson and the honest among the Democratic representatives in the House were no match for the sly "Democratic" and "Republican" "tariff experts" of "the interests." But it did contain free sugar, free coal, free iron and free barbed wire; and, as the majority of the senators then posed as Democrats pledged to tariff reform, the bill bade fair to pass—so the country thought—in some form that would give partial relief from the exactions of "the interests," in so far as those exactions arose through abuse of the tariff system. We get some faint idea of how vast that plundering is when we note that the United States Steel Corporation, worth actually about $350,000,000, makes in *net* profits upward of $120,000,000 a year; and, as in all large corporations, there is, in addition to the profits for the stockholders, an usually larger "rake off" for "the inside ring" that is hidden by bookkeeping and other devices of "high finance."

As usual, Aldrich and Gorman retired to their finance committee with the tariff bill—as the Senate was "Democratic," Gorman had taken the chairmanship of the committee and the leadership of the Senate that goes with it, and Aldrich had become nominal second in command. All the mischief, all the treachery that was put into that bill in the secrecy of that committee by those slippery twins, will never be known; it is impossible for anyone not in the secret to grasp the effect of the sly amendments slipped in here and there. But there could be no concealment of the treachery in giving the looters of the people renewed and enlarged licenses to rob in such necessities as iron and coal. Gorman's public pretext was that the tariffs on those articles were needed for purposes of revenue! This, when we are exporters, not importers, of iron and coal; and the duties on those articles therefore serve only to enable the iron and coal monopolists to charge us what they please without fear of foreign competition. The "merger" lined up for the treason by Gorman, was composed of all Aldrich's men and the five from Gorman's band necessary to piece out a majority of the Senate: Gorman, Brice of Ohio, Murphy of New York,

Smith and McPherson of New Jersey. With this secure majority
Gorman and Aldrich faced the infuriated House. So aroused
was the whole country that the House would not have yielded
to the traitor Senate had not Gorman given a solemn pledge
that, if the Gorman-Aldrichized Wilson bill were passed, he
would see to it that the Senate would afterwards pass and
send to the House for passage four separate bills placing sugar,
iron, coal and barbed wire on the free list. The House took his
word and yielded; the Gorman-Aldrich bill, denounced by President Cleveland as "party perfidy and party dishonor," became
a law.

And what of Gorman's solemn pledge? He prepared and
offered the four promised bills. Then the Senate referred them
—to the Aldrich-Gorman finance committee! And they died a
midnight death there. Their consignment to that chief senatorial
slaughter-pen of "the interests" was made by a "merger" vote—
the Aldrich men plus eight supplied by Gorman.

THE SUGAR SCANDAL

The public scandal centered about sugar. Havemeyer had
been too blatant, the trust had distributed and tendered bribes
almost openly, and senators and representatives had gambled in
sugar stock. When the whole country was ablaze, Senator Peffer
of Kansas offered a resolution to investigate. Senator Quay,
among the "Republicans" then second only to Aldrich in ardent
and efficient service of "the interests," promptly moved to lay
the resolution on the table, that is, to kill it. He was seconded
by Gorman, himself at that very moment in the public pillory
as a traitor to party and country. Here are a few characteristic
sentences from Gorman's speech:

"I denounce the outrageous misrepresentations of senators
which have been made. I trust that this case will bring the Senate
of the United States back to its old-time method of action. Let
senators on both sides of the chamber, without regard to party,

vindicate this body by resenting the attempt to bring in here such a matter as is included in the resolution of the senator from Kansas. If he or any other senator on the floor believes that his vindication is necessary, let him ask for an investigation. But to take up these sweeping charges as to senators against whom there has heretofore not been a breath of scandal, who have done nothing but discharge a public duty, as they understand it, is, in my judgment, an outrage!"

This will vividly and amusingly remind the reader of some of the utterances of distinguished senators and conspicuous newspaper servants of "the interests" since the present series on the "Treason of the Senate" was announced.

However, the "merger" lined up its motley band, and the Peffer resolution was "tabled." But the scandal grew and grew and grew until, when Lodge, still in the "reformer" stage of his career, offered another and similar resolution, it was passed. Senatorial investigations of the Senate form about the most derisive and disgusting of the many varieties of senatorial solemn farce. This particular one was no exception. But despite the rotten insincerity and connivance at suppression, so frightful was the corruption and so inadequate to the situation was the then newly formed and awkwardly working "merger," that a few facts were brought out. The majority or "merger" report gave everybody a nice, clean character. The minority report, got up by reformer Lodge, who had not yet learned the Senate's gospel that the Almighty created the American people for the benefit of "the interests," was less careful of the "dignity of the Senate." It contained some facts as to Gorman's secret work. It showed that the sugar trust magnates, Havemeyer, Searles, Henry R. Reed and Cord Meyer, were in Washington more or less constantly and that "they addressed their arguments principally" to Gorman and the other "Democratic" members of the "merger." Said the Lodge report:

"It appears, by the testimony of Senator Vest, that Senator Brice of Ohio, Senator Gorman of Maryland, Senator Smith of New Jersey, Senator Hill of New York, and Senators White and

McCafferty of Louisiana, after said conference (a Democratic caucus) came to the rooms of the finance committee in regard to the sugar schedule. *Senator Vest testified that Senator Gorman urged a duty of forty per cent. ad valorem, and one-fourth of a cent a pound differential in favor of refined sugars as the proper schedule."*

That is, Gorman was not satisfied with presenting over twenty million dollars a year from the pockets of the people to the sugar trust—the gift which the "merger" had previously arranged to grant. In his enthusiasm he tried to make the gift forty millions a year! The two Louisiana Democratic senators balked at this and prevented it.

The Lodge report continued:

"The sugar trust, by the evidence of its president and treasurer, has contributed freely to the state and city campaigns of both parties, and these contributions have been made in years when national elections were held. This is a thoroughly corrupt form of campaign contributions, for such contributions, being given to two opposing parties, are not for the purpose of promoting certain political principles, but to establish an obligation to the giver on the part of whichever party comes into power."

But nothing was done, except to improve and extend the "merger." It works better nowadays. Aldrich and Gorman are more skillful, and the orators of treason are more adroit. Aldrich had no such smooth sophist as Spooner then, nor had Gorman a Bailey; the "new" or loot-licensing "constitutional interpretation" was in its blundering infancy; the Senate was just beginning to discover that the Constitution is unfortunately so worded that it contains nothing to protect the people from their enemies, but only provisions for protecting their enemies from them.

EJECTED FROM HIS SEAT BUT BACK AGAIN

Gorman was ejected from his seat in the Senate in 1896. But he retained his old reliable Maryland machine, which, being financed by the Maryland branch of "the interests," was proof against the brief inconstant winds of popular clamor however cyclonic. And now he is back in the Senate again, and on duty for those who sent him there, for those with whom his treasure is. He is more stealthy than before—he has learned to be more cautious. But his modest shrinking does not interfere with his usefulness. A senator's best work is done in the "conference," in the "caucus" and in the committee—all secret.

It must not be supposed, because the "Democratic" representation in the Senate is in a hopeless minority before the "Republican," that Democratic senators are useless to the "merger" or that Gorman is not valuable. True, Aldrich has more than enough votes on his own side of the Senate to perpetrate almost any act of treason "the interests" may demand. But, remember, there are many senators who must be let off from voting for this or that measure, must even be allowed to speak in opposition that they may make themselves "solid" with their constituents. For, while the "interests"-owned legislatures can elect as senator almost anybody "the interests" advocate, still there is a limit—the man must not be a stench in the nostrils of the people, unless the state is a rotten borough like Rhode Island or Montana or West Virginia, or has peculiar political conditions like New York, Pennsylvania or Maryland. Sometimes the "merger" has to draw heavily upon the band shepherded by Gorman. Again, it is wise for both parties to the "merger" to assail in vigorous, honest, nonpartisan fashion some measure hostile to "the interests" and helpful to the people which millionaire yeoman Joe Cannon has had to send up from his House. In many ways, and at every session, Gorman is useful—as useful as Aldrich.

For a small but classically perfect instance: On April 11, 1904, a resolution to investigate post-office conditions, including the huge railway graft upon the Post-Office Department, came before the Senate. Gorman moved to eliminate the paragraph providing funds for the investigation. Aldrich rose and pointed out that another paragraph, overlooked by Gorman, might be construed as ordering the appropriation. Gorman at once modified his motion. The resolution, freed of its hasty and ill-considered features by the Gorman-Aldrich amendments, was passed by a "merger" vote, and there could be no investigation of railway postal loot for lack of funds!

GREAT WEALTH OF GORMAN

The Senate is a great stickler for form. Places on committee are assigned by rigid rule of seniority. Thus, all the important committees are composed of a secure majority of seasoned veterans in treason, men who know how to serve "the interests" with celerity, skill and noiseless stealth. A new senator gets nothing, is nothing; and if he should revolt, should develop the courage to rise up and in open Senate denounce the band of smooth, rich, socially prominent, always affable, traitors, he would simply make himself a senatorial pariah, and would be laughed at by the press of "the interests" as an overheated crank. Thus far, none among the few honest senators has developed that really heroic courage. Gorman, by his defeat in 1896, lost his place in the Senate's line of promotion, and was on his return, in 1903, a new senator. Yet, we find him immediately back on the all-powerful finance committee! And whenever a measure marked for death by "the interests" enters that secret chamber, there he is, ready to drive with expert hand a knife into its heart, while Aldrich closes expert fingers on its throat to prevent outcry.

Gorman is very rich, almost, if not quite, as rich as Aldrich. He is a multi-millionaire, a partner in sundry railways and mines. He and his cousin, Senator Elkins, chairman of the

Senate interstate-commerce committee and therefore chief executioner of all measures aimed at railway looters, are in many enterprises together. But Gorman, though rich, lives modestly and does nothing to cause the people to speak of him as a plutocrat, or to wonder "where he got it," nothing to cause his poorer henchmen to turn upon him and demand a "square deal."

Such is the "Democratic" leader of the Senate—a matched mate to the "Republican" leader, Aldrich. And this being the character of the leadership, what is the necessary conclusion as to the led?

IV

CHIEF SPOKESMAN
OF "THE MERGER"

WE have now seen the Aldrich-Gorman "merger" of the two party machines, and what sort of men Aldrich and Gorman are, and how they got their power. We have seen how, now by legislation and now by preventing or emasculating legislation, this "merger" diverts to its master, "the interests," more and more of the earnings and savings of the American people. We have seen that the "merger," with the Senate as its citadel, does the most, and most important, of this traitorous work in secrecy through a cunningly contrived system of committees, operated by chairmen who are stanch and skillful servants of "the interests." We have seen that, whenever it becomes necessary to complete the work in the open, the "merger" arrays a secure majority, usually made up of senators from both parties, to vote down the "hasty and ill-considered" measure of the people or to pass the "safe and sane" measure of "the interests."

The open part of the treason is, of course, preceded by a debate to fool the people. The "merger" senators who are to vote for it must explain, with specious and learned eloquence, how public-spirited they are and how patriotic is their action; the "merger" senators who are assigned or let off to join the opposing minority must help their fellow-conspirators of the majority by extolling their honor and purity of motive, while deploring that prejudice should so blind them. And the galleries are thrilled; and the honest senators sit glumly silent, trying to keep down the gorge and longing for the courage to transgress "senatorial courtesy" and defy "the interests" by plain, honest speech.

For its dexterous and delicate senatorial floor-work the "merger" has many eloquent and adroit orators and debaters, all of them men whom the powerful press of "the interests" has built into distinguished and admired public figures. The head spokesman of the "merger" is John C. Spooner of Wisconsin.

Many of our foremost newspapers, Republican, Democratic, and independent, have been assuring us for the past few years that Spooner is a great statesman, an honor to his state, his country, and his era. But they have cited no acts of signal or even of modest public service in the one direction in which a statesman could serve the people—in correcting conditions that have built up a plutocracy in a single generation, that have reduced the average American family's income to a scant six hundred dollars a year, and have driven our little children by the hundreds of thousands to hard labor in mines and factories. Now if you take all the acts of the life of the very worst man that ever lived, you find that most of them were either innocuous or positively good. To get the character and the influence of the man, you must take his *crucial* acts. If you take all the acts of the Senate at any one session, you find that most of them, almost all of them, were harmless enough; to get at the reality of the Senate, you must take its crucial acts—what it does in the great crises between the people and their enemy, plunderer and oppressor, "the interests." Spooner is all right when busy about purely foreign affairs. But the Spooner that concerns the American people, the Spooner that interests us here, is the Spooner of the crisis.

He is now sixty-three years old. After a brief nominal war service, he entered public life at the age of twenty-two, as secretary to Governor Fairchild of Wisconsin. He has therefore been a public man forty-one years. We cannot, need not, rehearse the whole record here. Typical acts at crucial times will be enough.

EARLY CONNECTION WITH "THE INTERESTS"

To begin with his first appearance in public life: Wisconsin was then dominated by two bands of thieves engaged in robbing the people of vast areas of valuable agricultural, timber, and mineral public lands. One of these bands was in control of what afterwards became the "Omaha" railway system, the other of the Chicago, Milwaukee & St. Paul. The United States had conditionally given to Wisconsin certain large tracts, larger than several states, to be granted to companies that would agree to build *and would build* railways. The St. Croix and Lake Superior Company, a possession of the Omaha gang, had conditionally got one of these conditional grants; but it had never built a foot of railway. The Omaha problem was how to keep this land without doing anything to earn it. "Cush" Davis, afterwards a senator from Minnesota, and our Spooner, then a poor young lawyer working for the West Wisconsin Railroad, later a branch of the Omaha, got from the United States Circuit Court a ruling that—

"Such lands do not, *ipso facto*, revert to the United States by mere failure to build the road within the time specified by Congress; to effect the forfeiture, some act on the part of the general government evincing an intention to take advantage of such failure is necessary."

The Supreme Court sustained this apparently fair but really dishonest Spooner proposition, so useful to land thieves throughout the West. The courts did not take judicial cognizance of the fact that the land thieves controlled the Senate and the federal land office, and so could prevent federal interference while their legislatures were giving them the people's land.

The ruling was got in 1872—and in 1872 Spooner entered

the legislature under the auspices of the Omaha gang. And in 1872 the legislature made the thieves, organized as the Wisconsin Railway Farm Mortgage Company, a present of the first large slice of the people's property. So, intending settlers, instead of getting the land for a nominal sum from the government, as was their right under the homestead act, had to pay the thieves a good, stiff price, the thieves of course having first exploited the timber and the minerals. Note the "patriotism" and "constructive statesmanship" of that ruling got from the compliant lower court and the unconscious higher court, and of the present of millions on millions of the people's property to a gang of thieves and bribers and debauchers of public life.

These two gangs, typical of the gangs working throughout the West at "developing the resources of the country," as it is called in "high-finance" circles, finally so stirred the wrath of the people that, partisan though they were in those days just after the war, they elected a "granger" legislature. Our budding statesman "side stepped" into the job of solicitor for the Omaha. The popular fury against, not the railways nor honest railway investors, but against railway thieves, was not easily allayed. It wasn't until 1881 that the gangs could again elect a "safe and sane" legislature, and resume and complete the steal. When the steal was being completed, in the corrupt and corrupted legislature, our Spooner was not only *general solicitor* of the Omaha, and therefore in charge of all its legal business; he was also a *stockholder* and a *director* in the system!

Philetus Sawyer, Spooner's friend and employer in the railway system, was a powerful man in Wisconsin politics. Sawyer had had himself elected senator in 1881 by his "safe and sane" legislature. But he was coarse, rough, a buyer of men, not a diplomat or speaker. He was now in a big interstate railway combine, and he needed for his more delicate work at the national capital some glib fellow, a first-class lawyer and a plausible "wind-jammer" as well. One of his local partners in those days was Isaac Stephenson. Spooner, in 1884, was put forward for the Senate, with Sawyer and the Omaha back of him: the

gang of railway rogues in control of the Chicago, Milwaukee &
St. Paul, the Omaha's rival, put up Gen. Lucius Fairchild,
Spooner's first introducer to "practical" politics. The Omaha
crowd was the stronger, and Spooner joined Sawyer in the
Senate.

Two years ago, Stephenson, at outs with his former pals,
publicly charged that the legislature was bought for Spooner,
that he (Stephenson) had put up twenty-two thousand dollars
and Sawyer thirty thousand dollars to "do the trick." Spooner
hysterically denied this. Cried he,

"Does anyone suppose that if I had been elected to office by
corrupt means it would have taken twenty-one long years to find
it out?"

This is not Spooner at his best; usually he is plausible.
Obviously corruption of that kind cannot be uncovered until a
principal "peaches"; and it was twenty-one years before Stephenson got in the mood to give the game away. Spooner's plea
that there is a statute of limitations against truth tends to
confirm Stephenson's confession. On the face of the facts, is it
likely that the people of Wisconsin would select as senator the
chief lawyer of their chief despoilers?

TREACHERY TO THE PEOPLE

We need give here only a characteristic instance or two
of Spooner's treachery to his new client, the people—quite
enough to reveal the "patriot" and "constructive statesman." In
those days, as now, the Senate was busy with the "vast problems
of constructive statesmanship in connection with railways"—
said problems consisting in devising ways and means of preventing interference with "the interests" industriously exploiting the railways and their stockholders and, through the railways, the people. Spooner began his senatorial career in December, 1885. Three months later there came before the
Senate a bill to restore to the public domain all public lands
which a railway had forfeited by not complying with the con-

ditions of the grant. Spooner moved an ingeniously worded amendment, one worthy of the "great constitutional authority" and "constructive statesman." Its effect was to exclude from the operations of the bill a large part of two huge Iowa counties claimed by the Omaha system. Senator Plumb, chairman of the committee on public lands, exposed the scheme. Said he:

"There never has been a more *flagrant violation of public right*, a more *complete contempt for the public*, than is exhibited by the claim of this railroad company. For more than ten years after they completed their railway they never set up a single claim to these lands. It was not until the fact that the lands were lying idle became the subject of inquiry among people who would like to be settlers that the railroad came on and set up any claim to them, and they then sought to do it by indirection."

But on March 12, 1886, the Spooner amendment was adopted by a Senate dominated then, as now, by "interests" of various kinds. On March 16th, four days later, Spooner, the senator, the retained and paid lawyer of the people, the sworn guardian of the people's rights, *stepped over to the Supreme Court of the United States and appeared in precisely the same matter as the lawyer of the Omaha.*

This classic specimen of senatorial treason brought to a climax the scandal of congressmen, especially senators, *openly* acting in the courts as lawyers for the enemies of the people. On June 1st, Senator Beck of Kentucky introduced a bill making it unlawful for any senator or representative to act as the attorney or agent for any railroad which had received a land grant from Congress. The penalty for transgression was five hundred dollars fine or a year in prison or both. Said Beck in the debate on his measure on June 22d,

"Will any gentleman insist that any man who is the attorney of any railroad, any man who is retained in any way by any of these roads, when these great questions involving perhaps fifty or a hundred millions to the tax-burdened peoples of this country come up for consideration, shall *advocate the interests of the road whose money in the shape of retainers or fees he has in his pocket,*

*keeping the fact concealed, professing all the time that he is acting
and arguing in the interests of the United States?"*

Spooner, Allison, Cullom and Frye, all doughty defenders
of "the interests" then, as now, opposed the bill. An attempt was
made to refer it to the judiciary committee where it could be
quietly done to death. But Beck was in earnest and forced a
vote, and the Senate dared not refuse to pass it.

But—one day, when the public scandal had died· down, a
motion to reconsider was suddenly sprung; and though Beck
fought gallantly the motion passed, to be followed by a motion
to refer the bill to the judiciary committee, which also passed.
The bill was never heard of again. But "the interests" profited
by the warning of the scandal. Their senators do only senatorial duty nowadays—in public.

SPOONER LOSES HIS SEAT

In 1890 the people of Wisconsin revolted against the
shameless corruption and robbery by and under the auspices of
the Republican branch of the merged political machine; they
flung it out and put in the Democratic branch. It was one of
those frequent amusing farces which the American people have
been enacting in national, state, and local politics for a quarter
of a century. Spooner was ejected from the Senate, and William F. Vilas, wearing a Democratic label, took his place and
assumed his "duties." And "the interests" in whose service Vilas
was an old and efficient employee, had no cause to complain.

Spooner, however, was as busy as ever. He still had his
"private" duties as a lawyer in the pay of "the interests." There
was also the work of going about among the people, extolling
"the party," seeking to show, with the adroit eloquence of
which he is a master, that the Republican branch of the merged
machine should be restored to its former place as chief exploiter
of the people, and that the Democratic branch should be rele-
gated again to the minor and supplementary place in the service

of the master of machines, "the interests." It is hardly necessary to quote any of those speeches. Like all the speeches of
these secret traitors to country and people, of these men who
are so directly responsible for the uppiling of huge, ill-gotten
fortunes and for the increase of poverty and child labor and of
the vast armies of unschooled children, Spooner's speeches
abounded in virtue, piety, and patriotism. Let us pass to typical
instances of Spooner's "constructive and constitutional statesmanship" for right, people and country as a distinguished private citizen and party leader.

Henry Villard's wrecking of the Northern Pacific was exposed by the stockholders' committee in its scathing report of
February 18, 1893. On August 15th of that year three receivers
were appointed, the chief of them Henry B. Payne, Spooner's
"next friend" in politics after the death of Sawyer, and a corrupt boss and boodler whom death recently rescued from final
and crowning exposure and disgrace. As Payne was boss of
the Wisconsin merged machine, "next friend" Spooner of
course became chief lawyer for the receivers. They began to
cut wages on the plea that the road was in bad financial condi-
tion. After a second huge cut which reduced wages all along
the line from fifteen to thirty per cent. below the market rate,
the employees of the road asked for a conference with the
receivers. The receivers assented. On the eve of it, Spooner
and his associate, Miller, got Judge Jenkins—one of our "interests"-selected, Senate-recommended, and Senate-confirmed,
federal judges—to issue an injunction which prohibited the
men "from combining or conspiring to quit, with or *without*
notice"—that is, an injunction forbidding twelve thousand
American fellow-citizens of statesman and patriot Spooner
under any circumstances to quit work! Jenkins followed this
up with a supplementary injunction forbidding these American
citizens from "ordering, recommending, *approving* or *advising*
others to quit the service of the receivers!"

This outrage upon freedom, with few parallels, if any, in

all modern civilization, caused the House of Representatives to investigate through its judiciary committee. At a session of the committee at Milwaukee on April 10, 1894, Spooner denied part in the supplementary injunction, but was forced to admit his joint authorship with Miller of the "constructive statesmanship" and "constitutional interpretation" involved in the principle that an American citizen can be forbidden and restrained,

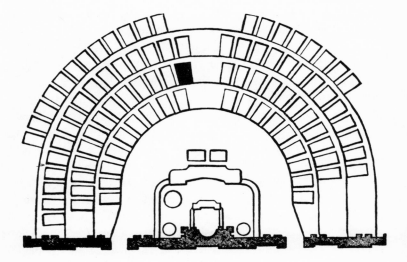

DIAGRAM OF SEATS IN SENATE CHAMBER, SHOWING SPOONER'S COIGNE OF VANTAGE AS THE MOUTHPIECE OF SPECIAL PRIVILEGE. (Black rectangle indicates position of Senator Spooner's desk.)

under jail penalty, from quitting work, even though he give due notice! The House judiciary committee, in its report (H.R. No. 1049—53 Congress, 2 Session, June 8, 1894) denounced Spooner's statecraft and constitutional law as "in violation of a constitutional provision, an abuse of judicial power and without authority of law." It denounced Jenkins's proceedings as "an oppressive exercise of the powers of his court" and "an invasion of the rights of American Citizens." But what did Spooner and his pals care for this? The injunction had been obeyed by the men.

And what were Payne and his pals doing with the money they took by such high-handed tyrannies from the pockets of workingmen? The year after the injunction, on August 7, 1895, Brayton Ives petitioned the federal court at Seattle to remove the receivers on the ground of gross misconduct in office. Two days later, Spooner and a long train of lawyers began to fight for Payne and his pals. When all their ingenuity was exhausted—which was not long, as this was a family quarrel between two branches of "the interests" and the anti-Payne branch had the stronger "pull"—the receivers resigned to escape appearing in court and showing their books. Ives challenged them to show their books; the challenge was not taken up. But the resignation of Spooner's friend and his pals was confession, and the refusal to show the accounts was confirmation.

It is said that Spooner's fee in this one case was eighty thousand dollars. Certain it is that he has been well paid, as the pay of "the interests" for mere brains goes. Spooner has been at times a very rich man; again, not so rich—this according to his luck in the "street." It must have been in one of his lean periods when, on his reëntry into the Senate in 1897, he said in an interview, "The newspapers are accustomed to say I am a millionaire; but it is not true." The highest sum with which Spooner has been credited in Wisconsin gossip is two millions. The figure usually given is "about a million."

RETURNS TO THE SENATE

The occasion of Spooner's 1897 outpouring about his wealth, was a charge as to the manner of his getting back to the Senate. It was known that the people of Wisconsin did not want him; they had shown their opinion of him by beating him for governor in 1892. It was known that the legislature which elected him to the Senate did not represent the people, that it was for the most part a rotten aggregation of Republican and Democratic hacks swept in by the Payne-Spooner gang on the tide against free silver. It was not unnaturally suspected that Spooner's friends had had to "give down" for his election. But Spooner denied this with angry virtue.

"I have nothing to say about the way in which I got to the Senate, except that it was the clean way. No improper influence of any kind was employed in my behalf."

He did not explain how he could possibly know this, and know it so positively. Nor did he explain how anything clean could be got from a Payne legislature which soon showed itself to be so shamelessly in the control of "the interests" that the Republicans turned to La Follette and wrecked the Payne machine.

In the Senate again, Spooner was immediately busy. We need here note only a few typical activities. An anti-trust bill came up from the House in 1900. There was in it a provision that, when a trust was declared criminal by the Supreme Court, it should be barred from the mails and from domestic or foreign commerce, just like a common, ordinary criminal who gave nothing to campaign funds and owned no senators or congressmen. The House passed the bill; the Senate referred the "hasty and ill-considered" measure to Spooner's judiciary committee, and there it slept until February 5, 1901. Then a free senator, Pettigrew of South Dakota, moved that the bill be brought before the Senate. Spooner's debating on this, on February 21, 1901, was in his best vein. He fairly yearned to smash the wicked trusts, but—always that Spooner "but"—as to this bill, he had grave doubts about its constitutionality. Always the Constitution! It never interferes with "the interests"; it always solemnly stops the people—at least, that is the effect of having it interpreted in Congress always by agents of "the interests."

Next, a motion was made in the judiciary committee to

report the bill without recommendation. The motion was voted down, Spooner of course supplying the Aldrich members of the committee with the pretext for doing it. Finally, a motion to take the bill from the committee was forced in open Senate. The Aldrich gang "lined up," led by Aldrich himself, by Spooner, Foraker, and Fairbanks. The motion was defeated; the bill died in Spooner's committee—a peaceful death, for Spooner is not a harsh man.

Another instance: In many speeches, notably on October 13, 1902, at Milwaukee, he came out strongly against the corrupt and law-defying trusts. It would have made a patriot's blood leap to hear him cry out, "The American people will have no masters, either in business or in politics!" He was especially fierce about the coal trust. But that was Spooner on the stump; let us look at Spooner in the Senate, that is, on duty. On January 5, 1903, less than three months after Spooner's stump speech, Senator Jones of Arkansas moved that the attorney-general be called on for what evidence he might have that the coal roads and the coal operators were conspiring to monopolize coal. Up sprang Spooner. To second the motion? To call for immediate inquiry into that cruel conspiracy to rob the people through an absolute necessity, and to cause the poor to suffer and their children to die? No; Spooner asked that the resolution be referred to his committee, his particular slaughter-pen for "the interests," almost the equal, in treasonable work, of Aldrich's finance committee and of Elkins's interstate commerce committee. As the "merger" was working smoothly, there was no rude attempt to transgress "senatorial courtesy." Spooner got the resolution, bore it away to its doom; it is one of the many, many corpses of measures for the public good buried under the floor of that committee room.

Again, on March 3d, of last year, it was Spooner who dealt the final blow to the pure-food bill for that session and so issued the seventeenth annual senatorial renewal of license to the poison trust. But we will not here take up the matter of pure-food legislation. In like manner Spooner's part in the pending railway-rate legislation, interesting, typical, and repellent though it is, will not be described until we have before us the completed law, with all the mischief and emasculation of the Aldrich-Gorman "merger" ineffaceably a part of the record.

In these debates, in all the debates wherewith the "merged" senators led by Spooner, amuse and excuse themselves, the method is tediously the same. It consists in discussing judicial decisions and precedents as to constitutionality. The innocent lay spectator or reader is impressed; but an intelligent lawyer or judge would be disgusted that grown men should so waste time, and the man who loves his country is exasperated that there should be such heartless trifling with the vital interests of the people, with matters that mean food, clothing and shelter or lack of it to millions of Americans. As any competent lawyer will say, when an honest judge is interpreting a law he looks first at what is just and sensible in the particular circumstances which the law purports to meet; then, having found what is the best way to interpret the law in the interests of the people, he goes to the law books and selects from among the masses of conflicting and contradictory decisions and precedents those that will sustain the position honesty and common sense command him to take. In the light of this, how contemptible, how vicious, how cynical become those vaunted debates of the Spooners and Baileys, the Knoxes and Forakers! Those sham battles in the Senate tourney—and the people being plundered the while, and begging in vain for the relief that is their right!

LA FOLLETTE FORCED TO ACCEPT HIM

How did Spooner get reëlected to the Senate in 1903? La Follette, the splendid fighter of the corruption in control of his party in Wisconsin, had triumphed. His associates in that battle to destroy all that Spooner stood for in Wisconsin politics, were a majority of the legislature. Spooner, for obvious reasons, announced an "unalterable purpose not to be a can-

didate for reëlection." He having thus secured himself against
any public humiliation from possible defeat, the press of "the
interests" and all the newspapers that do not look beneath sur-
faces or remember history, cried out that it was a shame "to
deprive the country of a great constructive and constitutional
statesman like Spooner." But this clamor—which was truly
"hasty and ill considered"—was not what decided La Follette
and his friends; they knew Spooner too well—what he was in
Wisconsin, what he was at the capital, the real Spooner under
that fluent and learned plausibility and sweet geniality. What
decided them was that the broken Spooner-Payne machine
effected a combination with the Democratic machine—under
the "merger" system—and announced that, if Spooner was not
sent back to Washington for "the interests," all the reform
measures for which La Follette and the people had been
striving, would be defeated. To avert this, they let Spooner
return. It was a hard dilemma that was there forced upon La
Follette; whether he chose wisely it is not easy to judge. To
realize what it might have meant to the people to have another
La Follette in the Senate from Wisconsin, it is only necessary
to recall that La Follette, in his third month in the Senate, exposed a Rock Island railroad grab of lands worth, not millions
but *billions* of dollars, that was smoothly on its way through
the Senate. And so complete was his work that the "merger"
hastily secured a postponement of the measure until next year
—when doubtless another and slyer attempt to consummate the
grab will be made.

A VAIN SEARCH

Ever since Spooner attained manhood's age and influence,
the great, vital, all-dominating, all-dwarfing issue, has been
justice in the distribution of wealth—the product of a man's
labor to the man himself. The politicians, serving the plunderers
and diverters of the people's property and prosperity, have

been trying, often successfully, to obscure or to pervert this issue. But it has always reappeared, stronger, clearer, more insistent. In preparing this article about the foremost senator in talent and in reputation for respectability, his record has been searched diligently with the desire in fairness to present, if possible, some act of his that would show at least an occasional impulse toward the side of right and justice on the one great issue. The search has been in vain. Spooner has been in deeds steadfastly and constantly where he was when his Omaha patrons and pals were stealing the vast tracts of the people's lands, where he was when he devised an injunction making the workingman the slave of his employer. So much for domestic affairs. In foreign affairs the only matter wherein senatorial action was greatly important to the American people in a quarter of a century was the reciprocity treaties. These the traitor Senate killed at the bidding of "the interests"; and Spooner's record there is the record of all the "merged" senators.

Wisconsin—Spooner's "home folks"—has long known him, through and through. His oratory has been admired, listened to and applauded—and that is all. His presence in the Senate, despite the home opinion of him and feeling about him, is characteristic of our senatorships, so unrepresentative of the people except in a few more or less accidental instances. Further, everybody at Washington has long known Spooner as thoroughly as Wisconsin and his friends in the Wall Street district know him. Yet the country at large has looked on him as an almost ideal senator. He has been put forward by the leaders of his party, by the leaders of the other party, by his fellow-senators, by the entire "merger," as an ideal senator and as typical of the Senate. "Yes, there *are* a few queer fish in the Senate. But most of the senators are like John Spooner."

Well, so they are. Are they not willingly led by Aldrich and Gorman, whose characters and conduct have been heretofore exposed? Are they not willingly spoken for by Spooner, whose character we have just outlined? And Aldrich, Gorman, and Spooner are in their essence of a piece and pattern with the representatives of the foremost state in the Union, with Platt and Depew.

SPOONER SAYS "NO TREASON"

It was said at the outset of this series that treason was a strong word, but not too strong in the circumstances. We have only begun to penetrate into the real Senate. Yet, is not that statement already justified? Spooner, defending the Senate at a banquet in Washington on March 27th, said:

"There is no treason in the Senate! The one man I despise most is he who takes upon his lips in blasphemy the good character of a woman; next to that is the man who will tear down the character of the man in public life. Above all things, my brothers, believe in your republic and in the general fidelity of your public servants."

In view of Spooner's record, is it difficult to understand why he is so eager for us to shut our eyes and silence our consciences as lovers of our country and give ourselves up to blind belief in the "general fidelity" of our Spooners? Spooner is right about the infamy of "the man who will tear down the character of the man in public life." But, the only man who can do that is the man who makes the record of the man in public life, the faithless, treacherous public servant himself. And Spooner's only successful assailant is Spooner himself, the maker of Spooner's record. It is not victim nor prosecutor nor judge that brings the criminal to justice, but the criminal himself.

V

BAILEY, THE "PATRIOT"

WE have now read the records of the three chief men of the Senate—Aldrich, the master of the Republican machine; Gorman, the late leader of the Democratic machine; Spooner, Aldrich's chief lieutenant, the chief spokesman, chief legal adviser, and chief floor-manager of the great senatorial "merger" to license and protect "the interests" in levying greedily upon American labor and capital, especially upon America's annual twenty billions of interstate commerce. There is a fourth leader, younger than these three and newer to the Senate; but, because of his aggressive abilities and because of the death of Gorman, he is rapidly pushing to the front. If this young man, Joseph Weldon Bailey, is reëlected by the Texas legislature next winter, and if the present so-called Republican but really Aldrich majority is replaced before 1913 by the Gorman kind of Democratic majority, he will be the leader of the Senate. We have found the Senate to be the citadel of the present unfair distribution of our national prosperity, the chief cause of the elevation of luxurious chicanery and of the depression of honest industry; therefore, it behooves us to scan Bailey's record carefully.

Of course, in the House, in the Senate, and on the stump,

Bailey has spoken as strenuously for people and country as any other politician. He is not surpassed in that respect by any of the rest of the band of expert raisers of dust over the Senate arena as a cover for the acts of treason. But words are not significant of the real man. If words meant character, Judas himself with his "Hail, Master!" would rank as a very Jonathan of fidelity. Let us disregard Bailey the talker. Let us ask only, What has Bailey *done?*

He came to Washington, to the House, fourteen years ago last December, when but twenty-eight. His obstreperously unconventional dress and his frank physical, as well as mental, vanity made him something of a butt at first. But soon through his fast-peeling surface there appeared a strong and developing personality. So rapidly did he disclose power and shrewdness that his becoming House minority leader at thirty-four, and after only three terms, would not have seemed mysterious had he not been highly unpopular with his party colleagues, especially with those least in sympathy with "the interests" that were financing and dominating both party machines. Soon the feeling against him became open, led to frequent and fierce rows between him and his colleagues. Those were the days when the "merger" of the two party machines was not so apparent, nor indeed so complete, as now; the House had only just submitted to the yoke of its committee on rules, controlled by "the interests." If speech were conclusive, there would be no room for doubt of Bailey; for he discharged his picturesque vocabulary of vituperation upon his enemies in a philippic on April 15, 1897, in which he equaled Joe Cannon or Gorman or Spooner or Lodge at their best in proclaiming their own patriotism.

HOW STANDARD OIL GOT INTO TEXAS

Was the distrust of Bailey just or unjust? For answer, let us in fairness go to his home state, where he was in the van of the leadership of the responsible party.

Texas is overwhelmingly one-sided, politically, like overwhelmingly Republican Pennsylvania; so "the interests" have had no more difficulty in building a rotten machine there than in Pennsylvania. Occasionally there are popular revolts; but by one subterfuge and another the people are soon fooled or wearied back into submission. To get office in Texas, one had to have, and one must now have, "the interests" with him or at least not against him. In one of the popular spasms of revolt, the machine of which Bailey was then, and is now, the star statesman and spellbinder, was forced to put upon the statute-books a model antimonopoly statute. The whole country has heard of this statute and of vague wonders wrought under it. The fact is that it has never permanently nor for long excluded any monopoly from the state. Thanks to the power of "the interests" over the dominant machine—labeled Democratic just as the Pennsylvania machine is labeled Republican—the grand total of achievement has been several futile prosecutions, fourteen hundred dollars in fines and about five hundred dollars for refiling forfeited charters and revoked permits—and the monopolies are steadily gaining ground. The insolent extortions of the Standard Oil Company, disguised for its Southwestern activities as the Waters-Pierce Oil Company of Missouri, were the chief cause of this typical "sop to the mob"; and, naturally, the first effect of the law was the ejection of the Waters-Pierce Company from the state. The monopoly fought from court to court, up to the Supreme Court of the United States, and lost. Then——

Let us give Bailey's and his friends' own version of the story. Bailey said, in newspaper interviews, before the Democratic state convention at Waco in the summer of 1900, and before the Texas legislative investigating committee in January, 1901, that his friend, Dave Francis, ex-governor of Missouri and a rich advocate of the "safe and sane," introduced him in St. Louis in the spring of 1900 to H. Clay Pierce, president of the Waters-Pierce Oil Company, and vouched for Pierce's character. Bailey explained that Pierce told him how repentant the company was, how it was not part of the Standard Oil Company, how it would reform, anyhow, and behave itself. Bailey's friends say that for no compensation, not even for a "fee" (Bailey is a lawyer and could therefore call it "fee" or "retainer"), he went back to Texas to see what could be done for the friend of his friend. This, though the "friend" had been expelled for crimes, thus described and *proved* before state and federal courts:

> That the (Waters-Pierce) oil company has abused its franchises and privileges; has monopolized the oil trade of the state; has carried on a system of threats and intimidation and bribery to prevent parties from buying or selling competing oil, to the great injury of the people of the state."

When D. H. Hardy, then secretary of state of Texas, an associate of Bailey's in the machine and one of his adherents, was asked for the facts last March, he said that Bailey came to see him at his office in Austin about the readmission of the Waters-Pierce Company. But said Hardy, "Bailey's talk to me was as exalted and patriotic as any talk, speech, or statement ever made by any Texas man in behalf of the welfare of Texas." The company might be readmitted only if it would obey the laws, and he (Bailey) "believed that their solemn obligation was genuine and sincere," and he thought "it would be for the benefit of Texas, because Texas needed all the honest money and honest industries that could be brought into the state."

WHAT BAILEY MIGHT HAVE DONE

Hardy related how he talked with Attorney-General Smith about Bailey's corporate friend and how they decided that under the law the oil company must reorganize before it could enter the state again. Presently, according to Hardy, Pierce reappeared at Austin. Says Hardy:

> "What was I to do? The law required that all the secretary of state had to do was to make the head of a foreign corporation

applying for a permit swear to an affidavit that his company was not a monopoly and was not connected with a monopoly. *This affidavit was signed and sworn to by H. Clay Pierce, president of the Waters-Pierce Oil Company. I issued the permit on May 31, 1900."*

Hardy—and Bailey—might have done several things before readmitting the Standard Oil Company to prey upon the people of Texas. For instance, they might have inquired of Missouri whether the Waters-Pierce Company had really reorganized. Had they done so, Henry Troll, clerk of the circuit court of the city of St. Louis, would no doubt have sent them, as he sent another inquirer, an *official* statement that *"no corporation known as the Waters-Pierce Oil Company has ever made application for dissolution,"* and that *"no judgment of dissolution of any corporation by the name of the Waters-Pierce Oil Company has ever been rendered."* Obviously, if the company did not dissolve, it could not reorganize under the same name. Further, Hardy and Bailey might have insisted on a public hearing, and so have anticipated Attorney-General Hadley of Missouri, who, at hearings in St. Louis last March, got official admissions from Standard Oil witnesses that *"all of the shares of the Waters-Pierce Oil Company standing on its books in the name of M. M. Van Buren"* (son-in-law of Vice-President Archbold of the Standard Oil Company) *"are held for the Standard Oil Company."* There were 2747 of these shares, 746 more than a majority of the whole capital stock. Further, they might have got proof, as did Hadley, that the Waters-Pierce Company had, from its beginning, been owned and controlled by the Standard. Further, when the Standard or Waters-Pierce duplicity was legally established last March, Bailey might have demanded that it be straightway ejected from Texas, where it reigns supreme over oil. But Bailey has not uttered so much as a murmur.

Bailey says he believed Pierce, the friend of friend Francis. Yet Pierce, as Bailey knew, was president of the Waters-Pierce Company, which had been, as Bailey knew, tried, condemned, and ejected for criminal acts against the people of Texas whose interests were supposed to be Bailey's chief concern. Did Bailey believe? Then how explain Bailey's silence and inaction since last March?

DISTRUST OF THE TEXANS

Bailey got the Standard back into Texas on May 31, 1900— the date of Hardy's permit. On June 25th of the same year, Bailey bought the splendid "Grapevine Ranch" of six thousand acres near Dallas. Said Gibbs, owner of the ranch, in an innocently indiscreet newspaper interview at the time:

"The deal represents a land trade of two hundred and fifty thousand dollars. I sold to Bailey at fifty thousand dollars less than the property is worth."

This "land trade of two hundred and fifty thousand dollars," less than a month after the Standard resumed sway over Texan oil, aroused public interest of a kind which Bailey could not ignore. His hundred-thousand-dollar share in the trade astounded those Texans who had been assuming that the struggling young lawyer and politician's congressional salary was his chief income. It was charged that Joe Sibley, an ex-congressman from Pennsylvania, an oil magnate, enormously rich, and a great friend of Bailey's, was behind him. Bailey replied in a newspaper interview:

"Mr. Sibley offered to stand behind me financially to any amount I might need or desire. But affairs shaped themselves so that I did not need the proffered assistance. Ex-Gov. D. R. Francis of Missouri is alone in the trade with me. I can unload on him if I wish or can keep the property and have forty years' time, if I desire, to settle with him."

Bailey further said that he gave for the ranch eighty thousand dollars in cash, and land in the Pecos valley worth twenty thousand dollars. He explained to the Texas legislature's investigating committee that he had borrowed the eighty thousand dollars of banks and others by giving "notes secured by a deed of trust and mortgage." He said the land belonged to friend Francis, who was to get from him five per cent. interest on its value until the debt was settled. And still envy of Bailey's luck in being able to assemble eighty thousand dollars and in having such rich and ready friends, has not been shamed into silence! When the legislature met, six months after the "land trade," with Bailey as the machine candidate for United States senator, Representative D. A. McFall of Travis County, a public man of high character and repute, offered, on January 11, 1901, a resolution to investigate the readmission of the Waters-Pierce Oil Company and candidate Bailey's connection therewith. Speaker Prince, of the machine, appointed the committee—and in violation of fundamental parliamentary procedure *left McFall off it*.

The committee met, and in a large, general way called upon any member or any citizen to appear and prosecute the charges. Of course, no one appeared. The machine in Texas is so powerful and so aggressive that, for fear of financial ruin and even of physical violence, Texans of independent mind hesitate to speak out, except in those futile generalities such as honest but timid senators now and then vent against the Aldrich-Gorman "merger."

THE MCFALL AFFIDAVIT

McFall, however, on January 17th, submitted an affidavit to the committee. He rehearsed the facts of the Waters-Pierce ejectment from the state and charged:

"That by reason of Bailey's influence and personal and political popularity and prestige, they (the Waters-Pierce Company) were enabled by a mere sham of dissolution and reincorporation to continue in business in Texas.

"That the said Joseph W. Bailey did, on or about May 2, 1900, accompany H. C. Pierce, president of the Waters-Pierce Oil Company, to Waco for the purpose of holding a consultation with the county attorney of McLennan County, with a view of compromising said suits (the suits were for one hundred and five thousand dollars in fines); that the proposition of compromise by said Pierce was ten thousand dollars to the state in full of her claims and the payment of three thousand five hundred dollars to the county attorney as an extra fee for advising the compromise; and that the said Bailey endorsed said proposition and urged its acceptance."

Bailey was present when this affidavit was read to the committee. He arose and denied that he had made any proposition to give the county attorney of McLennan County (Cullen F. Thomas) anything in addition to his legal fee. We have already given the Bailey version of the other charges.

Cullen F. Thomas, a machine and a Bailey man, testified that Bailey had come to Waco in May, 1900, and had said to him that he, Bailey, wanted to talk to him regarding the Waters-Pierce Oil Company; that he, Bailey, had promised his friend, Dave Francis, to see if something could not be done to settle the matter; that Bailey said he had become interested in the case at the instance of his friend Francis, for whom he could vouch and who said he (Francis) could vouch for Mr. Pierce. The civil cases, Thomas testified, *were later dismissed.* Thomas said he knew nothing to lead him to believe in Bailey's dishonesty.

On the same day, January 17th, the committee fully exonerated Bailey and the state officials!

On January 21st there was a heated debate in the Texas House over the committee's report. Several speakers declared that Bailey had packed the committee; that every witness before it was a friend of Bailey's; that the proceeding was a farce, conducted strictly in Bailey's interest by Bailey and his friends. But Bailey's adherents indignantly denounced these attacks and lauded his patriotism and statesmanship; and the report was adopted by a vote of seventy to forty-one.

Bailey was elected United States senator on the same day.

In view of the facts, and making every allowance which justice commands or charity begs, had the people or "the interests" gained a senator?

In September, 1902, Bailey bought stock in the Kentucky

Horse Breeders' Association. In August, 1902, he had twenty trotters in training at Lexington, Kentucky. It was reported in May, 1904, that he had disposed of his interests in the association and removed his trotters to Texas. Bailey was quoted as saying that "the newspaper reports made the pleasure of breeding horses a burden." He disposed of the Grapevine Ranch, and so far as is known he has not complained of loss. He is established at Washington in a style befitting his wealth and rank; he entertains generously, patronizes a private school, and no longer distresses fashionable society with unconventional evening dress. And of the many warm friends who welcome him when he visits Wall Street, none is warmer than Thomas F. Ryan, insurance, gas, trolley, tobacco, and railway financier and chief backer of the "safe and sane."

In the course of the inquiry into the sources of Bailey's affluence, application was made at the office of that stanch friend of Bailey's, the "Houston Post." "See Kirby," was the answer. "Bailey is Kirby's attorney, and Kirby will tell you that he got it in legitimate fees."

BIG FEES FOR BAILEY

Who is Kirby? John H. Kirby is one of the "big men" in Texas, a dominant factor in finance and in politics. A resident of Houston, he controls lumber, crude-oil and other companies. He built a railroad in Texas and sold it to the Santa Fé branch of the railway department of "the interests." One of the county attorneys of Texas brought suit against him in 1904, charging him with organizing a lumber trust; but the machine attorney-general refused to join. When asked about Bailey, and whether he had contributed to enriching him, Mr. Kirby replied, with the direct frankness characteristic of his type of "the business man in politics":

"Yes, I paid Bailey more than two hundred thousand dollars in fees, first and last. I employed him in the fall of 1902. I controlled more than a million acres of timber land in East Texas.

That land was supposed to be underlaid with oil. Two companies were organized, the Kirby Lumber Company and the Houston Oil Company."

Mr. Kirby described at length intricate deals with New York and other Eastern financiers. He was then, October, 1902, in New York. He telegraphed Senator Bailey to come on. Senator Bailey came. Continued Kirby:

"Bailey took hold as my attorney and also as attorney for the Kirby Lumber Company. After several months of effort he recovered for me more than a million dollars in securities and aided me otherwise. During this period he also assisted in raising money for the Kirby Lumber Company, of which it stood in great need. From whom did he raise it? Well, he sold for the account of the company $1,600,000 of the company's preferred stock to the 'Frisco railroad system. Thus he saved us from bankruptcy. He procured loans to the company aggregating more than $1,500,000 in additional cash from the Rock Island Railroad, from Kountze Bros., Brown Bros., Third National Bank of St. Louis, American Loan and Trust Co. of Boston, the Riggs National Bank of Washington, Ladenburg, Thalman & Co., North American Trust Company of New York, H. B. Hollins & Company, and other concerns. In addition, he sold treasury stock for about $1,000,000 and Houston Oil preferred stock for $733,000. For all this service the Kirby Lumber Company paid Senator Bailey $200,000. I paid him for services to me individually an additional sum of $25,000 and still owe him something."

The readmission of the Standard Oil Company into Texas in May, 1900; the purchase of the Grapevine Ranch in June, 1900; the election by the machine legislature to the Senate in January, 1901; the entry into the breeding of trotters in 1902; the large and lucrative employment by boss Kirby beginning, as Kirby himself says, with 1902; the negotiations with such notorious exploiters of prosperity and politics as the controllers of the 'Frisco and Rock Island systems; the hawking of securities and notes among the high financiers of Wall Street and their Western and Southern dependencies—all these things together compose an arresting picture of sudden, dazzling prosperity, and delicate, intimate commerce with interests not suspected either of warm friendship for the people or of warm interest in pure politics and honest, equal progress. Does this composite picture, of Bailey's own painting, suggest in any of its lineaments the "tribune of the people," the fit leader of opposition to the traitor "merger," encitadeled in the traitor Senate?

The destined successor of Gorman in the actual, if not in the nominal, leadership of the Democratic branch of the "merger" hails from Gainesville, within forty miles of the border of Indian Territory. He has lived in that part of Texas, has been in politics there, since 1885. "The interests" have been for twenty years industriously absorbing the vast natural resources of Indian Territory, preparing for that time, not far distant now, when its coal, iron, oil, lumber, and agricultural products will be the necessities of twenty or more million Americans. And these preparations have been in defiance or evasion of law and public policy, a menace to the future of the entire Southwest. Bailey, from just over the border, is one of the men whose direct duty it was and is to oppose and expose the Indian Territory monopolizings and exploitations by "the interests." Yet, never has he opened his lips in protest; never has he introduced a measure looking to stopping or checking or curbing the rascality.

THE INDIAN TERRITORY GRAB

Last April, when a huge Indian Territory coal, timber, and oil grab was on its stealthy way through the traitor Senate, under the auspices of the "merger," and under cover of fake railway-rate-bill excitement, it was La Follette, a new senator from far-away Wisconsin, who exposed it. Mr. La Follette offered several amendments to the Indian appropriation bill, to protect the people's remaining rights there. He urged, on April 27th, in behalf of one amendment, that it was recommended by Mr. Hitchcock, secretary of the interior, who is an honest and efficient official. Up rose Bailey, for the "merger," to say, "When the senator understands more fully the situation in Indian Territory, he will pay less attention to what the secretary of the interior says." And the amendment, which made it possible for home-seekers to buy Indian lands, but impossible for corrupt corporations to grab them, was killed on a point of order—raised by Spooner!

Bailey's chief concern last spring was the railway-rate bill. If that bill had been an honest measure, still Bailey's "popular" activities would not be significant. He is seeking a reëlection next winter; also, the "merger" has voices and votes to spare at present. But Republican Senator La Follette and Democratic Senator Rayner of Maryland, both experts in railway matters and both "unmerged," have revealed to the public the fundamental futility of that bill; have revealed it as a companion fraud to the deliberately futile Cullom interstate-commerce act of 1887; so all intelligent Americans know that the entire railway-rate debate was simply another Senate sham battle, another fake to fool the people with a stone painted to look like a loaf of bread. Bailey was playing the game of "the interests" by posing in railway-rate debate as a "learned constitutionalist" —this, when constitutional questions are decided, not in the Senate, but in the Supreme Court, and there by votes of five to four, with no man able to forecast on which side will be the five, and on which the four.

On the other hand, the "Congressional Record," so full of surprises for the careful reader, reveals that Bailey has been, in his fourteen years at Washington, one of the chief introducers of Indian Territory railway and land bills—bills granting rights of way to railways, bills renewing, extending, and broadening charters. He introduced Gainesville, McAlester & St. Louis bills, the Gainesville, Oklahoma & Gulf bill, the Denison, Bonham & Gulf bill, part of the Choctaw, Oklahoma & Gulf legislation. And in 1904 he, become a senator, introduced a bill which permitted the Kiowa, Chickasaw & Fort Smith to sell out to the Eastern Oklahoma Company, and permitted this company to sell to the Santa Fé system. His interest in and information about these matters are suggested by a colloquy in the House on February 26, 1900, over a Choctaw, Oklahoma & Gulf bill, which Sherman of New York, high in the so-called Republican branch of the "merger," was pushing. Representative Sulzer asked a question; up popped Bailey to help Sherman out. Said he:

"Mr. Speaker, if the gentleman will permit me, I never heard of this bill until it was read, but I know the circumstances of the corporation."

And he proceeded to explain how innocent the measure was; he and Sherman together quieted Sulzer's doubts. In a speech on March 28th last, Senator La Follette brought out that this corporation, whose "circumstances" Bailey professed full knowledge of, has been notoriously and from its start a corrupt exploiter of Indian Territory.

All the measures introduced by Bailey looked well enough; no doubt many of them were harmless enough in and of themselves; no doubt many of them might have been most beneficent, if properly investigated and freed of all sly looting schemes. But in his Indian Territory work he has shown the uninquisitive and credulous nature so conspicuous in the Standard Oil transaction. And when we consider the cumulative effect of all the Indian Territory legislation by the "merged" Senate and House, the handing over of the resources of the people's great and rich domain to "the interests"; and when we consider that Bailey has been either mentally or morally paralyzed as to the people's rights there, how is it possible to be reassured by eulogies of his "constructive statesmanship" and "constitutional learning" from Spooner and other spokesmen of the "merger," and from the powerful press and the controlled news-services of "the interests"?

WHERE BAILEY STOOD ON THE PURE-FOOD BILL

Bailey's speech against the pure-food bill gives concisely the plausible line of his leadership for the "merger" and "the interests." The orators of "the interests" are all sticklers for the

Constitution. The Aldrich gang take the ground that, while the Constitution should be interpreted broadly, still, alack and alas! there is no way of interpreting it so as to protect the people from the depredations of "the interests." You can "constitutionally" pass any kind of legislation to "provide for the common defense" and to "promote the general welfare"—provided always such legislation helps, or does not hinder, "the interests" plundering the American laborer and independent capitalist. But, if any legislation threatens the "high finance" bandits who supply funds to both political parties and control nearly three-fourths of the senators and possess the machinery of the House and, through the Senate, have dominant influence in selecting federal judges and district attorneys—why, there stands the Constitution like a rock to prevent it. The Bailey, or the so-called Democratic, gang reaches the same end of protecting the plutocracy by the way so long used by and for the ante-bellum slavocracy: The Constitution must be *strictly* interpreted; the rights of the states must not be violated! Here is Bailey, denouncing, last March, the bill purporting to check the poison trust:

"I believe that the man who would sell to the women and children of this country articles of food calculated to impair their health is a public enemy, and ought to be sent to prison. No senator here is more earnestly in favor of legislation against adulterated food and drink than I am."

Fully as impassioned as Bailey's protest that he would "fight to the last ditch" against admitting to Texas a monopoly to prey upon his beloved constituents! But— Hear the "tribune of the people" further:

"But I insist that such legislation belongs to the states and not to the general government. When something happens not exactly in accord with public sentiment, the people rush to Congress until it will happen after a while that Congress will have so much to do that it will do nothing well."

No suggestion that Congress might find ample time for doing the people's work in the time it now devotes to smothering or emasculating legislation against "the interests" and to preparing and plausibly covering and enacting legislation for "the interests"! No suggestion that time, and other advantages, might be gained if leaders of Senate and House dabbled less in stocks or had less business for their private clients with the politico-financial powers of Wall Street. No suggestion that it would be fully as sensible and patriotic to propose, in time of foreign invasion, that the task of repelling the foe be left to the states severally, as to propose that Congress leave to the states the repelling of the raids of "the interests" operating on commerce which is but partially, where at all, subject to state laws! Could "the interests" ask anything better than this sly grant of immunity on the ground that to attack the national foe by national measures violates the national law?

Bailey is rich with wealth acquired in the service of corporations and men whose doings and alliances have not always been, to say the least, for the public good. Bailey is a political leader whose record reveals no act of effective friendship for the people in the struggle between them and "the interests" that prey upon labor, honest capital, and honest investors. Bailey is a leader of the body that is covertly but literally the final arbiter of the distribution of our prosperity, is covertly but literally the final fixer of wages, salaries, incomes, and prices. And his leadership consists in befogging issues by contributing to what he himself calls "the endless and confusing wrangles of the lawyers" about a Constitution which the Supreme Court, when the legislative and the executive departments have given it a chance, has rarely failed to interpret broadly for the people and in amusing disregard of the "learned constitutionalists" in Congress for "the interests."

Aldrich is and Gorman was the master of the Republican and Democratic machines, the deciders what "the party" shall do and what it shall merely pretend to do. Spooner and Bailey are their chief spokesmen, the men who strike the "keynotes." With such leaders, what must be the leading? Is it strange that "the interests" grow and the people diminish?

VI

CONFUSING THE PEOPLE

THESE articles have been attacked, but their facts—the facts of the treason of the Senate, taken from the records—have not been attacked. Abuse is not refutation; it is confession. New to this democratic republic, and more than suspicious, is the doctrine that the people must not be shown the public records of their public servants; that the people may not learn how the "merged" senators, with Joe Cannon's "merged" House concurring, license and protect the "high financiers" in piling up vast fortunes for the few and in multiplying for the many the difficulties of getting a livelihood and a competence; that the people must not be told how the Senate has never moved to use its ample Constitutional powers to protect the people until public anger compelled; how it has then merely passed some deliberately ineffective measure, like the Cullom interstate commerce act of 1887; and how, by killing reciprocity treaties and by injecting robber schedules into tariff laws, it has penned the people in from even such slight relief as might have come from abroad.

A great deal is said by apologists for treason about there being nothing "constructive" in exposing public corruption. If trying to bring it about that only men of character can get public honors, if trying to make it impossible for tricksters and traitors to live in our public life—if these objects are not "constructive," then what does the word mean? Are only lying speech and perfidious act "constructive"? The exposed cry out that these exposures endanger the Republic. What a ludicrous inversion—the burglar shouting that the house is falling because he is being ejected from it! The Republic is not in danger; it is its enemies that are in danger. The treason of the Senate is a disease to be cured; but it is a disease of the skin, not of the bones.

We have noted the "merger" of the two national political machines, and have watched it in operation, its Republicans and its Democrats playing into one another's hands. We have examined the records of its leaders. We have seen that they, the avowed chief men of the two political parties, the chosen arrangers of campaigns and legislative programmes, are of, by, and for "the interests." We have seen, beneath the dust of senatorial debates, measures in the popular interest maimed or assassinated, so-called Democrats coöperating with so-called Republicans, each crowd of the sham battlers wearing an angry front toward the other—to fool and confuse the people.

The fact that these leaders are obeyed, are followed, is in itself proof of the character of the followers. But there are those who would say: "True, such men as Aldrich, Spooner, and Bailey ought not to be in command. But their followers are honest, are honestly deceived." But to say that men of enough ability to get anywhere at all are so foolish that they do not understand the politico-financial game, though playing it daily for years, is to draw too heavily upon credulity; and to excuse them is to stretch the mantle of charity diaphanously thin. However, let us go on until the deplorable but necessary truth about the overwhelming majority of the senators is established beyond even groundless and shadowy objection.

Spooner and Bailey are, as we have seen, the first lieutenants of the "merger." There is a group of senatorial leaders who may be fittingly called second lieutenants—big figures in the public eye, influential in the Senate, that is, in the "merger," dangerous to the people because they are adroit, specious, reputed "eminently respectable." From this group let us select two for the present article—Elkins and Knox.

ELKINS AND WHAT HE STANDS FOR

First—Stephen B. Elkins of West Virginia.

We have seen that the "merger" does the main part of the work for "the interests" and against the people in the secure secrecy of Senate committees. Aldrich has Elkins on several important committees—rules, commerce, appropriations, etc. He has intrusted to him the chairmanship of the interstate commerce committee. Thus Elkins, under the Senate rules and "senatorial courtesy," is practically master of the committee which, with the exception of Aldrich's own finance committee, is the most important to the gang that finances both party machines and promotes the fortunes of senators and other high politicians in exchange for license and protection. For to this committee—to Elkins—are referred all proposals to enable the people to regulate their twenty thousand millions of annual interstate commerce, to secure a just distribution of prosperity. And only such measures as Chairman Elkins approves, or as Aldrich and he decide can or must be "taken care of" in the open Senate, ever see again the light of day.

Who and what is the man Aldrich has intrusted with this vital command?

Every man, woman, and child who makes or spends a dollar anywhere in this country is more interested in this question than in the immediate source of his or her own income. You can change your employer; but not so easily can you change this man who by his power over interstate commerce legislation has more to say about your material welfare than has your employer, more to say than have you yourself, no matter how well you may be using your energy and intelligence. Also, the answer to "Who and what is Elkins?" will broaden our light upon the Senate, where he has honor and authority by the votes of the majority of the senators. In reading his public record, let us not forget that its facts are well known to his colleagues, and that they can no more plead ignorance of him than they could of Aldrich or Spooner or Bailey—or of themselves.

Elkins, having graduated from the University of Missouri in 1860 and been admitted to the bar in 1863, went to the territory of New Mexico, and, by interesting himself in politics, got the federal office of district attorney. The Mexican system of peonage, slavery for debt, was in full operation then, and Elkins laid the foundations of his fortune by wholesale prosecutions, each of which netted him a tidy sum whether there was conviction or compromise. With the capital thus gained lawfully, the young lawyer and politician went into the business of grabbing public land—keeping firm grip, of course, on his political power, and getting successively the, to a land-grabber, invaluable offices of attorney-general of the territory and territorial representative in Congress. As a citizen of New Mexico, a "captain of industry," and a "developer of resources," he was compactly described by the distinguished George W. Julian, one-time surveyor-general of New Mexico and a careful, honest man, in a speech at Indianapolis on September 14, 1892. Said Julian:

"Elkins's dealings were mainly in Spanish grants, which he bought for a very small price. Elkins became a member of the land-ring of the territory; and largely through his influence the *survey of these grants was made to contain hundreds of thousands of acres that did not belong to them.* He thus became a great landholder, for *through the manipulation of committees in Congress grants thus illegally surveyed were confirmed with their fictitious boundaries.*

"He made himself particularly conspicuous as the hero of the famous Maxwell grant which, as Secretary Cox decided in 1869, contained only about ninety-six thousand acres, but which, *under the manipulation of Elkins, was surveyed and patented for 1,714,-764 acres, or nearly 2,680 square miles.* Congress, through the action of its committees, was beguiled into the confirmation of the grant, and thus the Supreme Court was compelled to recognize this *astounding robbery* as valid. By such methods as these *more than 10,000,000 acres of the public domain in New Mexico* became the spoil of the land-grabbers; and *the ringleader* in this game of spoliation was *Stephen B. Elkins,* the confederate of Stephen W. Dorsey, and the master spirit of the movement. I do not speak at random, but from official documents and ascertained facts with which I became familiar during my public service of four years in that territory."

Let us not linger upon the scores of instances of successful and unsuccessful jobbery in those days—how, for instance, he tried, but failed, to grab a group of rich copper mines by having a grant, which lay in one direction, surveyed as if it lay in exactly the opposite direction; how he took up and tried to force a claim against the Brazilian government for fifty million dollars, which claim Secretary of State Thomas F. Bayard characterized as "an outrage upon any nation with which the United States has a desire to have friendly relations." Let us pass with him to West Virginia, where his father-in-law, Henry Gassaway Davis, was one of the overlords—a Democrat as Elkins was a Republican, and finally, in the last national campaign, the Democratic "merger" candidate for vice president. Davis and Elkins were soon in a sort of general partnership for exploiting West Virginia by means of political finance and financial politics.

HOW HE "DEVELOPS" HIS STATE

Elkins has been "assisting in the development of the resources" of West Virginia since 1875. He came there rich; he has grown enormously rich in coal lands, railways, and public facilities of all kinds—the Morgantown & Ringwood Railroad, the Security Trust Company of Wheeling, the Wheeling Traction Company, the West Virginia Bridge & Construction Company, etc., etc., etc. His interests have destroyed independent towns that were thriving, and have built up in their place other towns that are dependent upon him. One illustration of his methods, being typical, will serve us as well as a hundred. The Fulmers owned coal mines which Elkins wanted. He owned the railway upon one of whose spurs the Fulmers depended to get their coal to market. The Fulmers found they could get no cars; then the spur somehow fell into such disrepair that it was unsafe to run cars over it, if the Fulmers should get a court order compelling Elkins to furnish cars; finally, he began to tear up the tracks of the spur. A succession of utterly lawless acts; a miniature of the man's career! Bold where boldness was necessary, sly where slyness would best serve, always energetic, implacably greedy, unscrupulous—such is Elkins, the citizen. And he has got together more than thirty million dollars; he "represents" the debauched state of West Virginia in the Senate; and there he is the man who passes upon all measures relating to our interstate commerce—the bulk of the labor of the American people, the bulk of their prosperity, for just or unjust distribution, as Elkins, under Aldrich and "the interests," may decide!

What has Elkins done in the Senate? Except only the recently compelled rate bill, which as we shall see in due time is a fraud, no measure even pretending to be for the people or against the looters has been reported from his committee. That fact alone is enough to stamp the man, just as the fact of vast robbery rampant and big thieves unmolested and unafraid throughout the nation would be enough of itself, and without the crowding confirmatory evidence, to convict the Senate of treason. But let us recall, as a specific instance of Elkins's treason, his most conspicuous act of perfidious commission.

In the winter of 1902-1903 he reported, and the "merged" Senate passed, an amendment repealing that provision of the law which made punishable by imprisonment the infamous crime of rebating—infamous is a fit word to characterize the crime that is almost on a par with murder as an assault upon vital rights. To jail with the man who steals an overcoat or a loaf of bread; but only a fine for stealing by "high finance" sneak-thievery the property, the business, the prosperity of tens of thousands! This is Elkins's climax of senatorial achievement, thus far. It is significant of the power of the "merger" over the House that the Elkins act passed it by two hundred and forty-one to six, so eager are the Washington politicians to serve the "merger" and "the interests" if they can get plausible reasons for doing so. The fact that President Roosevelt signed it shows how unconscious he then was of the perfidy he had to deal with at the other end of Pennsylvania Avenue. The reason advanced by Elkins for his bill, and accepted by many who should have known better in the excitement of the tremendous applause from the agents and newspapers of "the interests," was that railway officials would let themselves be convicted if the penalty were a fine only, whereas they would not permit it if they had to go to jail. The common sense of the matter was expressed with more than judicial moderation by Federal Judge Bethea at Chicago last April, when, in imposing a fine upon some rebaters, he said he doubted if any fine would prevent the criminals from "repeating this offense or cause others to hesitate to follow their example," and that "if there were a provision of imprisonment, much more might be accomplished."

EXPOSED BY LA FOLLETTE

The real reason for the Elkins act was exposed by Senator La Follette in a speech in the Senate on April 27th, last. He told how the Wisconsin legislature in 1903 ordered an expert investigation of the books of the railways. Said he:

"That was *just about the time of the passage of the Elkins act.* It was disclosed that the railroads had made more than seven million dollars of deductions for rebates."

Obviously, if Elkins and the Senate had not hastened to the rescue, the high officials of the railways radiating to the North and Northwest from Chicago would have had to go to jail; for the proof was complete.

To befog the railway situation in the public mind, the

railways, about two years ago, appointed as a committee for a "campaign of popular education" President Spencer of the Southern, President Underwood of the Erie, and President Wilcox of the Delaware & Hudson. Spencer, with his offices at Washington and with his direct opportunities socially and otherwise to influence public men, was the chief director of this education. Part of the scheme, and a very important part, was a series of public hearings on the railway question by Elkins's Senate committee a year ago last spring. For six weeks railway men poured in testimony to the fairness and impartiality and honesty of the management of the big railways. About the only discord was introduced by Governor Cummins of Iowa, a Republican who is fighting to destroy the grip of the "merger" upon his party in that state. In a speech at Storm Lake, Iowa, on February 16th, last, he described his treatment by Elkins. Said he:

"For four hours and a half not one single question was put to me except with the intent to overwhelm me. I was the only man in that large room crowded to the doors who had not gone there on the invitation of the railroads and on a free pass. While the chairman was probing me there sat by his side the general attorney for all the railroads of the United States. And when I saw that attorney passing to the chairman question after question to embarrass me, and when I observed the tender relationship existing between them, the hot blood of indignation ran through me. That chairman was Stephen B. Elkins. *The people of West Virginia did not put him in the Senate. The railroads placed him there. He is there to do what the railroads command him to do.*"

The attorney to whom this stanchly Republican governor referred was ex-Senator Faulkner of West Virginia, a so-called Democrat, one-time chairman of the Democratic Congressional campaign committee. Elkins issued a long denial in May last; but Governor Cummins has ample corroboration for his main points.

The Republican Governor Dawson of West Virginia was last spring forced by the desperate anger of the people of West

Virginia publicly to describe and protest against the conditions resulting from Elkins-Davis "merged" politics. Wrote he:

"West Virginia to-day is in the grasp of a railroad trust which practically says what part of the state shall be developed and what part shall not be developed, how much coal shall be shipped out of this state, to what points or parts it shall be shipped, and when it shall be shipped. Of course it makes its own rates and our people are helpless. I have been trying since 1881 to get a railroad commission in West Virginia, but the railroad lobby would never let us have it."

This Republican governor sent this protest and appeal, not to Republican Senators Elkins and Scott of West Virginia, but to Senator Tillman, a Democrat from South Carolina. And when the Bituminous Coal Trades League of West Virginia made its similar protest and appeal, it addressed itself, not to the "merged" senators or to the cowed representatives from its own state, but to Representative Gillespie from far-away Texas.

When Elkins and Aldrich found that the railway-rate bill could not be suppressed they had it reported from their committee in charge of Senator Tillman. The newspapers called this a bit of spite work against the President. As if old, experienced, cool-blooded experts in the politics of chicane like Aldrich and Elkins acted from spite in crucial matters! The real reason was that the enmity between Mr. Roosevelt and Mr. Tillman would necessitate go-betweens in the negotiations to get as strong a bill as possible through the Senate. The whole country now knows how shrewd that Elkins-Aldrich move was, and how easily they and their agents entangled the bill in a snarl of personal hatreds and distrusts, and took out of it what little strength it originally had.

Is there doubt in anyone's mind whether Elkins is with "the interests" or with the people? Is it possible to conceive Elkins doing anything for the people? Yet he is a power in the Senate, one of the men who can do things, while honest senators like Republican La Follette and Democrat Tillman can only talk.

ANOTHER CREATURE OF ALMIGHTY ALDRICH

But some one is saying: "There is Knox. He is a power. Yet he is of the highest respectability, a man of character and of impartiality, a representative of the people." Let us see. Let us neither trust nor distrust "appearances"; let us look beneath them at actualities.

Philander C. Knox, a graduate of Mount Union College, Ohio, in the class of 1872, became a lawyer and, in 1875, United States district attorney at Pittsburg. "The interests" are always alert to annex the bright young men who enter public service and who show capacity for mischief—and for usefulness. Knox graduated from the office of people's prosecutor into the service of those whom the people most wish and most need to have prosecuted; he has been in that service without a break ever since. His most profitable client for many years was the scandalously corrupt Carnegie Steel Company, as to whose vast rebating crimes President Cassatt of the Pennsylvania has lately "peached." He had the Pittsburg, Bessemer & Lake Erie, the Pittsburg, Fort Wayne & Chicago, the Pittsburg and Birmingham Traction, and other powerful corporate clients, several of them always in need of the skill of an adroit lawyer, because, like the Carnegie Company, they were engaged in wholesale law-breaking and law-dodging. Knox performed many signal and well-rewarded services for his law-cheating clients, who were just as much thieves as is the tramp who steals a nickel to get at a free-lunch counter; but to recite them all would be to repeat the familiar story of the successful lawyer for big, rascal-controlled corporations. One most notable instance will suffice:

The Carnegie Company was manufacturing armor-plate at a cost of less than two hundred dollars a ton, was selling it to the Russian government for two hundred and forty-nine dollars a ton, and to the United States government at from five hundred and twenty dollars to seven hundred dollars a ton.

These are all official figures. The difference in price was not in value but in "patriotism"—our Carnegies with their "blow-hole" plate for the navy and our Armours with their "embalmed beef" for the army are nothing if not "patriots"; to criticise them or their agents in public life is "anarchy," is "pessimistic," is "muck-raking." A Congressional committee, after examining thoroughly into the Carnegie Company's methods of manufacturing for American warships, reported (House Report No. 1468, 53d Congress, 2d session):

"The company was hired to make the best possible armor-plate and was paid an enormous price. Resting under these obligations the company or its servants have perpetrated manifold frauds, the natural tendency of which was to palm off upon the government an *inferior armor whose inferiority might perchance appear only in the shock of battle and with incalculable damage to the country.*

"The efforts of the company, and of its superintendents Cline, Corey, and Schwab, have been to satisfy your committee that the armor is up to the requirements of the contract, notwithstanding the false reports to inspectors, doctoring of specimens, plugging of plates, fraudulent re-treating of test-plates and 'jockeying' of the testing-machine. The *unblushing character of the frauds to which these men have been parties and the disregard for truth and honesty* which they have shown in testifying before your committee render them unworthy of credence."

The committee made charts showing the exact location of many bad plates upon thirteen American warships and specifying the defects so far as they could be ascertained. Did Knox throw up his retainer of fifty thousand dollars a year from this company, thus convicted? No! Did he refuse to defend it? No! Did he demand the dismissal of the men who had been detected and branded as untruthful and dishonest, parties to crimes against their and his country? Not he; not Patriot Knox. On the contrary, he continued as chief lawyer for them, continued intimately to associate with them, continued to grow rich out of fees and dividends earned from and by them. And when the Carnegie Company entered the United States Steel

Corporation, with first Schwab and then Corey as president, Knox was made one of the legal sponsors of that gigantic tax upon industries and fraud upon investors. And to that same crowd he owes a large part of the money which makes him a millionaire. As we shall see, he also owes it his seat in the Senate.

March 22, 1901, J. Pierpont Morgan, the big man of the steel corporation, called, in the evening, upon President McKinley, at the White House. The next morning Mr. McKinley announced that the attorney-general, the head of the national Department of Justice, the legal guardian of the people against the common enemy, "the interests," would be—Philander Knox! And Mr. Roosevelt, charmed by his engaging personality and manifest abilities, impulsively retained him. The Anti-Trust League, petitioning the Senate judiciary committee —in vain—not to confirm the appointment, put the matter thus pertinently:

"Is it proper for a lawyer to appear against his former clients? Can a lawyer willing to appear against his former clients be trusted to prosecute them if guilty? The charges we have filed refer not only to his dereliction of duty in the cases we have filed with him, but also bear upon his admitted intimate relations and *his collusion with the criminal practices of the armor-plate trust* which, we are informed, robbed the government of millions of dollars during the time Mr. Knox was their associate and adviser."

KNOX BETRAYS ROOSEVELT

During Knox's custody of the national Department of Justice the expected happened. Nothing was done to reëstablish justice, to drive off or even seriously to hamper the insolent thieves of "high finance." Mr. Roosevelt ordered Knox to proceed against the notorious Northern Securities Company which Morgan, Jim Hill, Harriman, the Rothschilds, and the Rockefellers had had cooked up by their lawyer lackeys. And what did Knox do? Let the answer come from the United

States Supreme Court, from the opinion delivered by Mr. Justice Holmes on March 14, 1904:

"It is vain to insist that this is not a criminal proceeding. The words cannot be read one way in a suit which is to end in fine and imprisonment, and another in one which seeks an injunction. I am no friend of *artificial interpretations. . . .* So I say we must read the words before us as if the question were whether two small exporting grocers should go to jail."

That is, Mr. Justice Holmes, in judicial language, exposed and rebuked Knox's sly betrayal of the President and the people in bringing a *civil* action against men who, as the justice said, were guilty of crime, if guilty at all. The court held that they were guilty; but the faithful Knox had seen to it that there could be no "running amuck," no jailing of rich law-breakers as if they were poor devils with no education and with their poverty in extenuation of their crimes.

Such was Knox as the efficient attorney-general for "the interests" and against the people. When Matt Quay died there arose the question, who could best represent what he had so long and so efficiently represented. The two great powers in Pennsylvania are the steel trust and the Pennsylvania Railroad —the steel trust that earns annually one hundred and forty millions *net,* on an actual investment of hardly twice that sum, by extortionate prices for a prime necessity of civilized life; and the Pennsylvania Railroad, the criminal betrayal of whose stockholders and of the people by its controllers was exposed before the Interstate Commerce Commission last May. It was published by newspapers of all parties, as a matter of routine news, that Frick, one of Knox's old employers in the Carnegie Company and a controller of the steel trust, and A. J. Cassatt, the presiding genius at the Pennsylvania's carnival of swindling, favoritism, and rebating, got together, agreed that Knox was the man for the job and "recommended" his appointment. The "recommendation" was, of course, heeded by Governor Penny-packer and ratified by the legislature.

What has Knox done in the Senate? Nothing that suggests that the people have rights or even existence—except as material for his friends and patrons to exploit. The most conspicuous of his typical and natural activities has been his effort to amend the railway-rate bill. Like all the "merged" senators, he was greatly agitated lest it should be "unconstitutional"; and, in the "merged" Senate and in the "merged" House, "unconstitutional" always means dangerous to the big leeches that are sucking away with greedy lips at the prosperity of the American people. His amendment provided for the point which Aldrich afterwards secured—every effort to curb the railways subjected to a court review which would enable the railways' lawyers to nullify the law by endless technicalities and delays. It contained a further provision that the orders of the Interstate Commerce Commission could be reviewed "in the Circuit Court of the United States *for the district in which any portion of the line of the carrier or carriers may be located.*"

That is, the railways could drag the wronged shipper to a part of the country remote from his business, could make it all but impossible for him to press his case. Attorney-General Moody pointed this out to Mr. Roosevelt, who cooled toward Knox. Throughout the railway debate, Knox was second only to Spooner in eagerness to serve corrupt controllers of railways, was second only to Bailey in confusing the issues and, so, aiding Aldrich to secure the complete triumph of the "merger" over President Roosevelt and Senators Tillman and La Follette representing the people.

MUCK-RAKING AND TREASON

Knox is fifty-three years old; he has been in public life thirty years—and that in a state in which there is clamorous opportunity for a man with conscience and patriotism, and with talents such as his. Yet we search his record as vainly as we searched Aldrich's, Spooner's, Bailey's, Platt's, and Depew's.

To him, as to the other leaders of the Senate, America has meant, not the American people, but the men who exploit the labor and the capital of the American people of all classes, even of their own small class of the colossally rich; to him, as to the rest of the band, patriotism has meant serving those exploiters. Looking at this suave, complacent man, made a millionaire by fees from armor-plate and rebate rascals, or in listening to his smooth eloquence in behalf of robbers by methods worthy of footpad or assassin, who would imagine that he was supposed to represent the people of a state where there are such conditions as are described in the following extract from the official report of the Child-Labor Commission?

"If Pennsylvania's *working-children* were to stand shoulder to shoulder, the line would reach more than *twenty-two miles.* If one of them were to pass your door *each minute, day and night,* it would take *three months* for the entire number to go."

There is a real problem for real "constructive statesmanship"! And a Senate of and for the people would consider it to the exclusion of all other problems until it was solved. But in a Senate of Knoxes and Elkinses, of Aldriches, Depews, Baileys, Burtons, Spooners, and Platts, the only problems that concern the "statesmen" are how to keep the people docile under saddle and curb, and how to maintain the plutocracy in the saddle, hand on the curb-rein.

Admit that it is "muck-raking" to write and publish the records of the Senate, the biographies of the senators as made by themselves. Still, how does the epithet "muck-raker" change the fact of senatorial treason to the people, incessant, flagrant, deliberate? How does it change the fact that the Senate is licensing and protecting the sneak-thieves that pilfer daily, hourly, from your wages, your savings, your till, your larder, your coal bin?

VII

THE RISE OF FORAKER

IN the Republican-Democratic "merger" for protecting and aiding the big exploiters of the American people, there is, physically and oratorically, no more attractive figure than Senator Foraker of Ohio. In intellect he is not the equal of Knox, hardly the equal of Spooner or Bailey; he lacks the cold audacity which has got Aldrich and Elkins their enormous riches, though he has made the service to which he has devoted the last twenty-five years pay well enough to net him a large fortune and to keep him in the millionaire class, despite his extravagance. His chief usefulness to "the interests" and to his private fortunes has been his oratory. He is about the best stump speaker at the command of the backers of the merged political machines.

Foraker's beginnings were away back in the late seventies, when the domestic enemies of the people, enriched by the spoils of Civil-War contracts and bond jobbings, were covering their huge grabs of franchises and privileges in the nation and in the states by having their political agents wave the "bloody shirt" and call on the people to "vote as they shot." Nowadays, Foraker, like Aldrich, Bailey, Cannon, Williams, Spooner, and all the "merged," is an ardent advocate of states' rights, flares fiercely at any suggestion of repelling the national foes by national enactments, demands in the name of God and Constitution that the states be left to deal with "the interests"— it being, of course, impossible for the states singly to do so. But in the days when the "bloody-shirt racket" was as good for fooling the people as "the interests" think "Beware of socialism!" is now, Foraker was a wild and winning waver of the "bloody shirt."

Thus Foraker became the *protégé* of the respectable traders of campaign contributions for licenses to loot, became the pet of his own Cincinnati's notorious George Cox gang. They made him a judge; they and their pals throughout the state ran him for governor, finally elected him, reëlected him—and gay and rich was the carnival he presided over. But when, in 1889, he ran for another term, he was beaten. The people had had enough of him and his gang; stump oratory as a cover for public plundering ceased to charm. The people revolted against the rule of the "boys" calling themselves Republicans, and turned to the so-called Democratic "boys"—who were equally "boyish," and hungrier and clumsier about stuffing themselves. The Republican "boys" soon got back, but not "Fire Alarm" Foraker; his public career, in office for which the people vote, was at an end. While waiting for a senatorship to be vacant so that the "boys" could reënter him in the "service of the people" without their consent and all but beyond their reach, he became a lobbyist and the chief negotiator between the "boys" in control of the state legislature and "the interests" feeding upon Ohio's rich resources and industrious population. We find him in 1892 installed, not in a Columbus hotel like a common lobbyist, but in the state Capitol itself, using its library and committee-rooms as his offices. The legislature was called "the Foraker legislature"; the supreme court of the state was known as "the Foraker court."

AN IMMENSELY PROFITABLE JOB

To relate his doings in detail would serve no useful purpose. There was the law permitting parallel railways to consolidate and so create monopoly and install extortion; there was the Cincinnati waterworks law, a six-million-dollar job for Foraker's overlord, Cox, and the Cincinnati "boys" both Republican and Democratic—for, in Ohio, the two machines work in joyous harmony, with no quarrel except about which shall be harvester and which gleaner, just as they do in New York and Pennsylvania, in New Jersey and Illinois and Massachusetts, and so on through practically the entire list of states where there are two parties. But let us pass over the enactments of "the Foraker legislature" for financiers seeking to rob the people by means of railways and telephones and insurance, etc., etc.; let us content ourselves with citing in some detail only Foraker's immensely profitable street-railway job.

He first tried to give the street railways of the state a free gift of a ninety-nine years franchise with freedom from taxation. This was too much even for patient Ohio; the "popular clamor" against this overstiff dose of the "safe and sane" frightened the politicians, especially as the "free-silver peril" was beginning to loom. But, just after his legislature elected him to the Senate—that is, in April, 1896—he did push through a bill authorizing the "boys" in control of Mark Hanna's Cleveland and George Cox's Cincinnati to grant a fifty years' franchise to consolidating street railways—fifty years' license freely to pick the pockets of workingmen and workingwomen by an extortionate five-cent fare! And, in spite of public uproar and adverse decisions of lower courts, the "law" held for Foraker's home city, Cincinnati, thanks to supplementary acts of the legislature and to the decision of "Foraker's court." He appeared before his court as lawyer for the robbers to give it the plausible legal pretext for this assault upon the wages of the poor. Cincinnati traction stock boomed to 130; the "law" netted the

inside traction ring upward of ten million dollars. Foraker's
son is now vice president of the company and his brother is its
counsel. It was charged that in addition to his stock profits he
got a fee of one hundred thousand dollars. In denying this
charge, the worthy senator said he got only a "present of five
thousand" from an officer of the company! Such was our fiery
patriot and statesman's first public act on his promotion to
the field of national service, as a member of the body that is
the final arbiter of the distribution of prosperity for us all. A
most propitious inaugural!

In 1896, Senator Foraker, paid attorney for the Southern
(Morgan-Ryan) Railway Company, advised and urged the
people of Cincinnati to sell their Cincinnati Southern ("Queen
and Crescent") Railway for a paltry sum, compared to its
value. His eloquence was in vain; the fact is, though his great
personal vanity may still hide it from him, Ohio people know
him for what he is. They like to hear him "wind-jam," just as
Wisconsin people like to hear Spooner "orate"; but they would
no more elect him to an office than Wisconsin people would
Spooner, or than Texas people will Bailey when they get a little
better acquainted with him. In 1905, the Southern Railway
gang, having failed to get Cincinnati's road outright, leased it
for *between three and four hundred thousand dollars a year
more than the interest on the Foraker purchase price would
have been*—and at the end of sixty years *Cincinnati will still
own the road.*

What is Foraker's record in the body that is, as we have
seen, officered and used by and for treason against the people
in their struggle with our common enemy, the exploiters of industry, the trimmers of wages and savings?

Of course, like all the "merged" senators, he has voted
with the "party, that is, with Aldrich, for all the great tariff and
commerce measures for "the interests"; has voted against every
notable measure in the people's interest; like his fellow-conspirators, he has made occasional farcical, but with the unthinking highly effective, shows of "independence" when his vote or

voice was not needed by the "merger." Aldrich has him as aid
to Steve Elkins on the committee on interstate commerce,
whose sins of omission and sins of commission are, as we noted
last month, in large measure responsible for the fact that wages
have remained about stationary for thirty years while rents and
prices have greatly increased and the profits of the parasites
upon capital and labor have become the wonder and the scandal of the world.

LOOT SIDE OF RAILWAY BUSINESS

There is probably no senator who knows the loot side of
the railway business so thoroughly as does Foraker—not even
Spooner, not even Bailey, not even the presiding officer of
the Senate, Vice-President Fairbanks, to whose railway-got
millions we shall advert. Yet not a word has Foraker ever
spoken against the colossal stealing, except the usual "hot
air" generalities to be expected of a rhetorical politician; and
not a measure has he introduced or advocated even looking
toward lessening the enormous burden upon American industry
through the monopolizing of the highways and the exaction of
unequal and exorbitant tolls. He concocted and urged a bill to
permit the railways to "pool," that is, to abolish even the pretense of competition. And last spring his "great Constitutional
speech" against the railway-rate bill was devoted to proving
that under the Constitution *the people have no right to regulate
railway rates!*

To show how minute is his attention to the "problems of
statesmanship" he is in the Senate to wrestle with: on December 17, 1902, Patterson of Colorado, one of the "unmerged"
senators, asked unanimous consent to a resolution directing the
Interstate Commerce Commission to send the Senate a report
on the unsanitary sanitary appliances of sundry great railways;
Kean of New Jersey, for the "merger," objected to this effort
to look after the health of the vast traveling public, and the
resolution went over; when it came up again on January 5, 1903,

Foraker, for the "merger," had it referred to the committee on interstate commerce. We have learned what that means. We can imagine what chance a measure for the people and against "the interests," would have of escaping alive from a committee presided over by railway owner Steve Elkins, and containing railway owners Aldrich, Kean, and Foraker.

JOSEPH BENSON FORAKER OF OHIO, A LEADER OF THE SENATE, WHOSE RECORD SHOWS NO ACT OF FRIENDSHIP OR EVEN NEUTRALITY TOWARD THE PEOPLE IN THEIR STRUGGLE WITH "THE INTERESTS."

Once more we search in vain the record of an avowed and admired leader of the Senate for a single act of friendship or even of neutrality toward the people in their struggle against the great, the real enemy. Foraker in the Senate has always been against the people, always for his franchise-grabbing, stock-and-bond-watering, pocketpicking clients who have given him the retainers that make him rich. But, after all, what reason—except such trifles as honor and self-respect—has a Foraker for keeping his oath and serving the people? They didn't send him to the Senate; they don't keep him there; they didn't pay him the sums which enable him to swagger in "society." Indeed, if they got a good, square chance they would probably "give it" to him where he has for so many years been "giving it" to them—in the region between the head and the shoulders.

LODGE AND THE "BOY" METHODS

Foraker naturally suggests Lodge. There are many surface differences between the senior senator from Ohio and the senior senator from Massachusetts. Foraker rose from poverty; Lodge was born rich, inheriting one of those "rum and nigger" fortunes that form the basis of the amusing aristocratic pretenses of so many of the New England "old families." Foraker pretends to be democratic in his ideas; Lodge is frankly contemptuous of "the mob" and morbid on the subject of his haughty lineage. Foraker is as magnetic as Spooner or Knox, or as Depew used to be; Lodge is so vain and self-centered that he is almost friendless. Foraker is eloquent and has originality of thought and expression; Lodge is as dry and commonplace as an old-style college professor. These surface differences obscure from the casual glance the essential likeness of the two men—the fact that they are the product of precisely the same conditions, owe their office to them and are maintained in office by them. They are of about the same age—Foraker, sixty; Lodge, fifty-six—and they entered public life at about the same time.

Lodge, like Spooner and Knox, makes a specialty of prim "respectability," and does it with better countenance because he does not take "fees." Also, he deceives because his manner is forbidding instead of apologetic, and because he has been careful rarely to speak for the "merger" but only to vote with it and play its game by standing for "strict party discipline," and has made foreign affairs seem to be his specialty. Like

Foraker, he is a product of the petty grafters, not of the big grafters. In the days when the two were not thoroughly united, when the big respectable thieves in the two parties looked disdainfully down upon the Coxes and Crokers and "Bathhouse Johns," Lodge, like Foraker, took sides with the "boys." The last open battle in the Republican party between the "boys" and the "big fellows" was over the nomination of Jim Blaine. Jim was the idol of the "boys," was abhorred by the "big fellows," and also, of course, by the high-minded men still influential in the party in those days. The "boys" won and nominated Blaine in 1884. Foraker was heart and soul with them; Lodge, striving in vain to establish himself in politics in Massachusetts, then wholly under the domination of the big tariff and railway corruptionists, hesitated at the Blaine dose. He almost bolted with the moral element and with those big financial backers of the party who thought Blaine a demagogue and likely to do almost anything, even possibly to attack them, in his pursuit of his passion for popularity. The temptation to get political power triumphed over the desire to be thought moral and the natural hankering of a conventional man like Lodge to herd with his "social equals." Lodge swallowed Blaine.

It has often been charged that Lodge is responsible for the low plane of Massachusetts politics, that he introduced the "boy" methods. This, however, is unjust to Lodge. He simply conformed, stooped to use and to be used by the forces that have created and made powerful the chain of bosses and boodlers of which Aldrich and "the interests" are the lock-links.

THE "SCHOLAR" IN POLITICS

The Massachusetts Republican machine, deserted for the time by the big grafters, needed money; Lodge had money, and spent it freely. The machine needed "respectability"; in Massachusetts, to be a Lodge and a Cabot, a relative of the Quincys and the Adamses, is to be "respectable." Lodge won the gratitude of the "boys" throughout his state, became boss of the machine at Nahant, to which he had removed in the early eighties after his failure to get into politics in his native Ninth Ward of Boston. He was beaten twice for Congress, in 1882 and again in 1884; but by 1886 his good work among the "boys" began to tell; he was elected, and held his place through three more elections until he intrigued himself into the senatorship. It must not be imagined that he abandoned for an instant his game of respectability. He spoke with heavy and therefore convincing solemnity for civil-service reform, got himself dubbed a "practical reformer," a "successful type of the scholar in politics." The solemn farce goes far everywhere, nowhere farther than in New England. While Lodge was preaching civil-service reform like a dedicated missionary, he was filling the public service with his henchmen, was one of the most assiduous and successful securers of places for janitors, elevator men, messengers, etc., etc. One example out of scores, literally scores, which might be cited: In October, 1889, he drafted and put into the Republican state platform a strenuous civil-service plank; yet at the very time he was using his influence with the newly installed Republican national administration to fill the Charlestown navy yard with his heelers. In the first seven months of that administration, when the "Blaine gang" was still powerful with Harrison, there were *eighteen* removals at the Charlestown yard above the grade of laborer, two "extra" men were appointed, and *no less than forty Democratic laborers* were removed. All these places were filled with Lodge "boys."

We have seen enough to identify beneath the robe of the "gentleman scholar" the familiar coarse type of machine politician. But Lodge is not merely that; he is far more dangerous. He, the disguised "boy," got the senatorship by a deal with the "big fellows" who had returned to the party which could be most useful to them in Massachusetts, just as they "stand by" the Democratic party in Texas. To realize the nature of this Lodge deal with the "big fellows" through the eminently respectable Drapers, General W. F. and Eben, rich manufacturers and tariff-troughers of Hopetown, let us recall the once famous outburst of indignation from State Senator W. D. Butler on January 4, 1893, when, by the "snap" action of a caucus, Lodge was foisted on the party as its senatorial nominee:

"Away back—perhaps two years ago in some instances—one of the candidates who has been suggested with reference to this great and honorable office, began his efforts to obtain it. He employed methods never before heard of in this commonwealth with reference to this office. Prior to the election on November 8th this state was gone over with a fine-tooth comb, not in the interest of the Republican party, but of the man who is a candidate for this place. . . . There has been such a use and abuse of the machine in his campaign that the precedent may be established in this state that no man can go to the United States Senate in the future except by resorting to similar means."

At that time "Harper's Weekly" was universally recognized as an organ of intelligent, honest public opinion. In its issue of January 21, 1893, it summed up the authentic facts thus:

"He (Lodge) pressed upon the legislature a 'gerrymandering' scheme from the shamelessness of which even his followers recoiled; he laid the wires for the election of members (of the legislature) favorable to himself; he brought about the holding of a 'snap' caucus, outdoing our own Hills and Murphys. Had he devoted the ability and time and labor he squandered on this miserable business . . . to the earnest study and treatment of public questions and to the establishment of a solid reputation as a statesman, the senatorship would have come to him as a free offering by a state proud of him, *instead of his running after it like a man who would steal it if he could not get it honestly.*"

And who elected Lodge to the Senate? From whom did he get this office "like a man who would steal it if he could not get it honestly"? From a legislature that in its betrayal of the people, in its subservience to public plunderers great and small, was the worst Massachusetts had known up to that time. It is manifestly impossible in the limits of these articles to go into the record of the Massachusetts legislature since the rise of the machine of which Lodge is the chief manager and chief political beneficiary—he leaves the financial spoils to others. The legislature has been bought again and again, every session, several times, by gas, railway, traction, and insurance interests; it has killed child-labor legislation, legislation seeking to prevent the extortion of monopoly; it is openly attended by an expensive and active lobby. At this writing it has once more been forced to make pretense of investigating itself because it is being really investigated by District Attorney Moran and a grand jury at Boston—this time because it killed a bill to stop that bare-faced form of plain stealing, the bucketshop. Representative Frank Gethro, who was expelled last June for attempting to bribe fellow-members, became so enraged by the action of the "mob of hypocrites who have taken ten bribes to my one" that on June 23d he gave inside facts as to a typical session:

"Scarcely a measure came before the House but came with it money offers for my vote from representatives, senators, and lobbyists. . . . I found what prices were being paid to leaders, both senators and representatives, and to the rank and file, and determined to get for myself the contract to buy a large block of votes. I agreed to buy Republican votes, got the contract and bought the votes. The Republican leaders told me if I would not divulge the names, they would stand by me. I depended entirely upon them for my escape in the investigation, and this was my fatal error."

And this is notoriously typical of the body which has three times elected Lodge. A stream can rise no higher than its source—that is not an axiom of physics only.

If Lodge were a patriot, would he not have been using his talents and energies in striving to make decent the political conditions in his state? *Yet never, not once, has he opened his lips against corruption there.*

We have seen that the "boys" were with Lodge, and who the Massachusetts "boys" are. Since the healing of the factional quarrel between the "boys" and "big fellows," he has had these latter with him also. Their stronghold is the Arkwright Club— and that is Lodge's stronghold now. The idea of patriotism, of the glory that is American, which those gentlemen entertain, was well illustrated in the report of the committee they sent down South to see why it was compelling them to cut their huge dividends. Said the committee (December, 1897):

"The working day in North Carolina is twelve hours, and the price paid per day for common labor in the mills is from fifty to seventy-five cents. So far as we could learn there is no disposition to organize labor unions. . . . *It seems a duty to apply at once to the legislatures of the New England states to put us back on a footing with the manufacturers in other parts of the country.* It is particularly incumbent on us to urge the legislature of Massachusetts to *repeal the legislation reducing the hours of labor to fifty-eight.*"

HOW LODGE WORKS THE PEOPLE

Not to be content with fair returns on their actual capital. Not to urge Lodge, their especial friend, to press legislation forbidding anybody anywhere to degrade and enserf an American man, woman, or child. But to try to get *ten*-hour laws and *child-labor laws* repealed! To "put us back"—what a significant phrase! And in 1905 the legislature that reëlected Lodge for the third time killed in its upper house a bill prohibiting the employment of women and children in factories before six o'clock in the morning and after six at night. We are in a position now to understand why Lodge the senator has never done or tried to do anything effective for the people, why he has pretended to concern himself with foreign affairs, talking not against corporate oppressions or child-labor or the corruption of politics in the nation and in his own state, but about war with Germany, whose only difficulties with us have been when she refused to receive without inspection the rotten products of the beef trust and again when she refused to let the big insurance companies ravage the German people as the American people have since learned they were ravaging them. In all ages and countries "foreign affairs" has been the specialty of the politician who wished to distract attention from the operations of a devouring privileged class within his country's borders. Lodge knows well that no country on earth would contemplate the insanity of making war on us with our boundless resources and our absolute ungetatableness. But inasmuch as his pose of Spartan purity will not permit of his openly aiding "the interests" that finance his machine and rule his party, he "saves his face" by manufacturing war clouds and

SENATOR HENRY CABOT LODGE OF MASSACHUSETTS, WHO IS THE FAMILIAR COARSE TYPE OF MACHINE POLITICIAN, DISGUISED BY THE ROBE OF THE "GENTLEMAN SCHOLAR."

puffing them away; thus, he can affect ignorance of the real war, the struggle between the people and their Senate-guarded and Senate-licensed plunderers, and can deceive the unthinking into believing that he does not know what he is doing when he "stands pat" on Aldrich's tariff law for robbery chiefly, or votes and even occasionally speaks in favor of some "safe and sane" measure for the perpetuation of privilege.

We need give space to only a few illustrations of Lodge

in senatorial action—not the Lodge who talks and occasionally proposes some petty futility of "popular" legislation, but the real and efficient Lodge. On December 17, 1895, Senator Call of Florida moved that a special committee of five senators investigate the efforts of "the interests" to control federal elections and to influence legislation. Here was a chance for Lodge, the reformer, the denouncer of corruption. Did he speak for the resolution? No; he sat silent. Did he vote for it? On the contrary, when Hale of Maine, for the "merger," moved its reference to the committee on privileges and elections, where it could be secretly strangled and buried, Lodge lined up in the "merger," with Republicans like Elkins and Democrats like Brice of Ohio, to protect the corrupt sources of the "merger's" revenues for financing the two party machines.

As we have seen, the two obvious and conclusive tests of the treason of the Senate, and the obvious and conclusive proofs that the "merger" of the machines of the two parties on all vital questions, all questions affecting food, clothing, shelter, wages, prices, plunder, and privilege, is in force and effect, are found in the Senate's attitude toward the high financiers who misuse the railways for wholesale robbery of the people and misuse the protective tariff system for binding the people and making them helpless under robbery.

A PERSISTENT "STANDPATTER"

What is Lodge's record on the tariff? In 1894 he spoke against the income tax and voted with the "merger" to inject more than four hundred robber amendments into the so-called Wilson, but really "merger," bill to use the tariff for robbery. In 1897, Lodge lined up with the rest of Aldrich's band to stuff the Dingley bill with "good things" for "the interests," to make it over completely into a "merger" measure, to make it the traitorous thing which that stalwart Republican, Governor Cummins of Iowa, thus concisely described last spring,

"All the robberies and thefts committed by all the insurance officers since the life insurance business was originated do not amount to the extortion due to the Dingley law in one year."

Lodge is a "standpatter." And what is his record on the railway test of senatorial treason? Let us not linger on his part —that of the railway lawyer—in the debates and votes on the railway-rate bill. Like all the "merger" senators, he voted against the "unmerged" Republican La Follette's amendments that would have made it a reality of justice instead of a sham and a fraud. Let us not waste space in explaining his futile little "popular" amendments with which he sought to confuse the public mind as to his real self. Let us recall a real achievement, his specific proclamation of himself. It has been proved again and again that the people pay the railways for mail service *no less than ten times what the express companies pay for exactly the same service,* that by clearly extortionate charges the railways have got *in loot* about a billion dollars since 1873. Not since 1878 has there been a reduction of the rate. Again and again honest senators have tried to end this robbery, but the "merger" has always prevented. The last very vigorous attempt was made in 1895 by Senator Blackburn of Kentucky, who, by the way, is being retired by the Louisville and Nashville Railway, which is almost as powerful a factor in Kentucky politics as are the New York Central and the Boston and Maine in New England politics. When Blackburn moved an amendment to the post-office bill giving the postmaster-general discretionary authority as to railway-mail rates, up jumped Lodge to defend "the interests." The debates on this and kindred motions in January and February, 1895, spread in the "Congressional Record," make exceedingly interesting reading. Lodge is not an adroit debater; his shifts and squirms at that time were very amusing. Allison and other "merger" senators had to help him out, though they evidently enjoyed his unhappiness—he is unpopular in the Senate because of his obstreperous egotism and lack of tact. It was a sad plight for Lodge the poseur to have to face such shots as, for instance, Peffer's in saying:

"I asked Postmaster-General Wanamaker why he did not propose legislation, or why Congress did not act. His reply was that the *railway companies see to it that the representatives in Congress in both branches take care of the interests of the railway people,* and that it is practically impossible to procure legislation in the way of reducing expenses." (Debate of February 11, 1895.)

When the debate ended, the "merger"—the Senate then had a small "Democratic" majority—voted down the attempt to reduce the railway steal.

One more instance: On May 12th of this year Senator La Follette proposed as the penalty for rebate thievery a heavy fine *and* imprisonment for from two to five years at hard labor; that is, Mr. La Follette proposed that the law be no respecter of persons among thieves. Up rose Lodge to move that the imprisonment be for *not more than* two years and *without hard labor*. Need it be said which amendment the Senate accepted?

But enough of Lodge. Clearly, he is like the other leaders of the Senate whose records we have examined; is of the "merger," is against the people, is for "the interests." To expect him to originate or to endorse any measure of democratic justice would be like looking for potatoes among the roots of a dock-weed. Let us pass on to his new-elected colleague, Crane.

ACTS OF PATRIOT CRANE

Crane is a paper, woollen goods, and shoe manufacturer, grown hugely rich by some of the most inexcusably predatory schedules in our tariff. Quiet, seemingly retiring, of great tact and adaptability, charitable, with aspirations to be a part of our aristocracy of wealth, "birth," and "breeding"—such is Crane as a private man. But all that is of no interest or importance to the people. A man may be good to his family and friends, may pay his debts and give alms and attend both church and Sunday-school, and still may be a Rockefeller. A man may profess, indeed may have, the best motives in the world, and still be an enemy of his country. Benedict Arnold said, and probably believed, that it was for the best interests of the American people to have England take care of them. And the Cranes may honestly believe that the American people would go to the "demnition bow-wows" if "high finance" didn't take away from them the surplus money they earn and might

SENATOR WINTHROP MURRAY CRANE OF MASSACHUSETTS, A FAVORITE OF SENATOR ALDRICH, AND CONSCIENTIOUSLY DEVOTED TO PLUTOCRATIC RULE.

waste. They will "stand for" the very worst plundering scheme of "the interests" as "better than mob rule."

Murray Crane was appointed to the Senate in October, 1904, by Governor Bates of Massachusetts, who had just ruined himself politically for anything but a senatorship or federal judgeship or other non-elective office by vetoing a bill forbidding the employment of women and children more than twelve hours a day. In 1905 Crane was elected to the Senate by a legislature whose upper house killed the same bill, rein-troduced. But we have seen what kind of legislatures "the interests" elect in Massachusetts. Crane had hardly taken his seat in the Senate when the "merger" *chose him for a place on the powerful committee on interstate commerce.* This, in itself, without the facts of the origin of his senatorial honors, would be enough to arouse strong suspicion of Crane; for new sen-ators never get such places as that unless they come with home records which make Watchman Aldrich sure they are "safe and sane."

What was Crane's home record which satisfied Aldrich?

His crucial acts as governor were two—the Boston and Albany and the Fitchburg transactions.

The Boston and Albany Railroad was built by a combina-tion of public and private capital, the city of Albany supplying one million dollars first and last, the people of Massachusetts $4,300,000 and the most valuable part of the franchise, and private capital supplying only eight hundred thousand. By a series of the familiar juggles of "the interests," the share of Massachusetts had been reduced and "the interests" were in control and were using the road to loot the people and to cor-rupt politics. Governor Crane had been a large stockholder; but on his election, he virtuously got rid of his holdings—to his brother and partner, Zenas Crane! With mind thus completely freed from the faintest shadow of personal interest, he was ready to consider strictly on its merits the proposition which was made by "the interests," with whom he was allied by personal friendships and by very large holdings in the infamous Bell Telephone monopoly and other similar enterprises for corrupting politics and levying upon the industry of the people. The legislature, amid a storm of protests from the people and the independent press, accepted the terms of "the interests."

HOW HE SOLD OUT THE PEOPLE

What were those terms which Crane recommended and ratified and, so, made legal? Under the terms of the original charter, the state could have acquired the entire road for about thirty millions; and so rich a property was it, *the state could have reduced freight charges twenty per cent. and still easily have made annually enough entirely to have abolished state taxation.* Also, state ownership of the road meant freedom from monopoly. Under the Vanderbilt-Crane perpetual lease, the state gets only two million dollars a year and "the interests" are absolutely free to loot and to monopolize. No wonder Crane refused even to recommend that the question be referred to the people for a vote. No wonder the legislature killed a bill to compel a popular vote before final action. No wonder Representative Dean of Wakefield was able to charge, during the debate, that it was "common rumor in the state house that members were receiving three hundred dollars apiece for their votes."

But this was not Crane's worst. That worst is the Fitchburg transaction. The people of the state had built at great expense the Hoosac tunnel, the key to New England for direct traffic with the rest of the country. The Boston and Maine, a harmonious part of the so-called Vanderbilt but really Rockefeller-Morgan branch of "the interests," got various governors and legislatures of Massachusetts to loosen the state's hold upon the tunnel and its traversing Fitchburg railway, until at last, with Crane in the governor's chair and a good "safe and sane" legislature of Lodge's "boys" in the Capitol, the time was ripe for the grand stroke. The state's hold upon the system had been reduced to fifty thousand shares of the common stock, but these shares were necessary to "the interests" for complete control. By the familiar manipulations the common stock had been rendered completely worthless. The state commissioners in their report filed in January, 1900, gave the full facts of that corrupt performance. Did Crane proceed

against his offending "high finance" friends? Not Crane! When
the Boston and Maine with an air of magnanimity offered thirty
dollars a share for these fifty thousand shares which, if the
laws had been enforced, would have been worth at least ten
times that much, not to speak of their greatest value—the
guarantee of railway freedom for the people of New England
—Governor Crane announced, not that they could not have
them at any price, not even that they could have them at their
real value, but that they could have them at par, that is, for
five millions instead of one and a half millions. This offer was
eagerly accepted by "the interests" on January 29, 1900. The
people had been trained to regard the stock as all but worthless, their treacherous servants having let the Boston and
Maine crowd depreciate it for so many years. So, the controlled
press's acclaim of Crane's shrewdness and patriotism as a bar-
gainer was echoed by the people until they began to realize
that by the two transactions together they had been delivered
over, bound hand and foot, to a transportation monopoly, and
had got in return a sum that was paltry as a bare purchase
price for the Fitchburg stock alone. If Crane had shown this
kind of sagacity at bargaining in his private business, he would
not be the vastly rich man he is to-day. He cannot divide the
responsibility for the Fitchburg sell-out of the people who en-
trusted him with the governorship. He personally made up the
deal with Ledyard of the American Express Company and
President Lucius Tuttle of the Boston and Maine—the famous
Tuttle who dominates all New England politics and consults
with the New England senators whenever the railways want
anything at Washington. The whole transaction, by the way,
was in direct violation of the state law which declares that the
Fitchburg line must be maintained "permanently as an independent line from Boston to points in New York state."

AN ALDRICH FAVORITE

Is it strange that Crane, on his arrival in the Senate, should step at once into high favor with Aldrich? Is it not natural that he should at once get into Steve Elkins' committee, which determines the present scandalously unjust distribution of the annual twenty thousand millions of interstate commerce, the bulk of the year's product of the brains and brawn and capital of the whole American people?

Foraker, Lodge, Crane—three more leaders of the Senate to be added to the galaxy whose records we have examined; three more seated in the body that is the final arbiter of wages and prices, and seated there in the interest of the only dangerous enemies of their country. As in the cases of Aldrich and Spooner and Bailey and Elkins and Knox, it is impossible to imagine these three originating or favoring or not fighting any measure that would disturb the greedily sucking lips of the class to which they belong, the class they associate with and serve. They are as harmonious with the present Senate as La Follette and Tillman are discordant. And of the three, Crane, the quiet, the good mixer, the sincerely and conscientiously devoted to plutocratic rule, is far the most dangerous. When Aldrich passes, Crane will succeed him—unless Massachusetts learns that good character and good motives are of no more importance than plausible speech, if the man's *acts* be not for the public good. It would be more sensible to call in an English duke to decide a controversy between us and England, than it is to let such men as the Aldriches, Elkinses, Baileys, Lodges, and Cranes arbitrate between us and their friends, associates, and political sponsors, our enemies.

VIII

THRIFTY PATRIOT ALLISON

IN Allison of Iowa the Republican-Democratic "merger" for betraying the people to "the interests" has about its craftiest senatorial agent. If he were a man of courage and decision, and if he "represented" a Rhode Island whose senators could flout its public opinion, not Aldrich but Allison would be the leader of the "merger." His skill at duplicity needs no other tribute than the fact that, despite an unbroken record of forty-three years of betrayal of the people to "the interests," especially the people of his own state, he has been a senator continuously for thirty-three years. How politically careless have we been, how short-memoried, how credulous of words and neglectful of deeds, how easily tricked by cunning appeals to prejudice! We have been struggling with the great thieves operating through railways and tariffs, and have not seen that it was the Senate that determined our national laws, superintended the distribution of our prosperity, and selected our national judges. We have been defeated because we have not realized that it was our Allisons and Aldriches and Lodges and Baileys in far-away Washington, in the Senate, who were making our struggles futile—were making, and *are.*

Allison's public beginnings were in 1863, when he, a poor

Dubuque lawyer of thirty-four, was sent to the House because about all the best young men of that then sparsely populated state were at the war. He found Congress, which the people thought absorbed in patriotic labor, really possessed by and busy for the great graft-seekers through war contracts and Union Pacific and other Western enterprises in vast land and franchise looting. Like him who journeyed from Dan to Beersheba, young Allison had fallen among thieves. But they did not despoil and despitefully use him; they made friends with him. Like latter-day Joe Bailey, he was poor; but, unlike Joe, he did not have to wait until he was a senator before he suddenly struck "pay-dirt" in quantity. To go into that part of his career in detail would be to retell the stupendous graft story of the Union Pacific Credit Mobilier, etc.; Allison was more or less active in and for all of those huge "loans" and land grabs which cost the people and netted "the interests" thousands of millions, besides licenses in perpetuity to extort rents and exorbitant freight rates. He was hand in glove with the chief "developers of the resources of the country"—with John I. Blair, Morris K. Jesup, Jim Fisk, L. B. Crocker, Oakes Ames, and the rest.

One typical instance: It came out in 1873 that our poor young patriot had been for some time owner of at least sixty thousand dollars of Dubuque and Sioux City stock; that he got it soon after his début at Washington, along about 1867, when with his aid the road got the valuable favor of a Congressional act saving it from the just forfeiture of its charter (act of March 2, 1867). Before the Congressional (Wilson) investigation committee, compelled by the public scandal over the many vast and open robberies with Congressional aid, they asked Allison on February 1, 1873, what his interest was, and when and how he acquired it. Here is his reply:

"I cannot state when I acquired it, nor can I state precisely what it was. My impression is that it was fifty or sixty thousand dollars originally that I subscribed to the construction company. I think it was sixty thousand dollars."

And with this answer, so candid, so obviously truthful, the kindly committee let him off. But John I. Blair, the chief of the gang, testifying on February 7, 1873, shed a little light on where our poor young patriot and public servant got the trifle of "fifty or sixty thousand dollars" which made such a vague impression on his memory:

"Q. Do you know who furnished the money for Mr. Allison? "A. No, sir, I do not. I am under the impression it was a gentleman from New York or Boston. I think it was a banker in New York."

THE SIOUX CITY AND PACIFIC GRAB

How strangely these habitually cautious financiers become hypnotized into prodigality to our poor but virtuous young statesmen, our Allisons and Baileys! But let us hasten over his long record to pause for a moment upon his connection with the Sioux City and Pacific grab. Allison, Jesup, Blair, and Crocker were among the incorporators; Allison was a *member of the House,* and most active when, on July 2, 1864, the road got life, franchise, an eventual loan of $4,200,000, and huge grants of fine public lands. It picked up many millions more in lands and terminal sites as gifts from Iowa and Nebraska counties and cities. Expert testimony before the Pacific Railroads Commission gave the total cost of construction as not more than $2,600,000, the cost of honest construction as about $1,000,-000. Yet the Allison-Jessup company reported the cost as $49,865 a mile or just over $5,000,000! A nice "profit," and this exclusive of land and other loot—and the road only one hundred and one miles long! No wonder our patriot Allisons and our philanthropist Jesups became multimillionaires. Allison is now credited with being the richest man in Iowa.

The final chapter of this typical Allison instance, typical also of the origin of our statesmen and plutocrats, was written in 1900—only six years ago—when, on June 2d, Allison, "merger" senator, pressed a "local bill" the effect of which was to let the Sioux City and Pacific looters off with a payment of less than one-tenth of the people's cash loan of $4,200,000 with thirty-odd years' interest. Senator Harris of Kansas exposed the grab, recited the many scandals concerning that one small road, and demonstrated that the road was not poor but rich. But

SENATOR WILLIAM B. ALLISON OF IOWA, ONE OF THE CRAFTIEST AGENTS OF THE "MERGED" SENATE IN BETRAYING THE PEOPLE TO "THE INTERESTS."

the "merger" lined up—Aldrich, Allison, Cullom, Foraker, Elkins, Frye, Lodge, and the rest, to the necessary number—and passed Allison's "local bill."

Another instance of his patriotism, taken at random from a multitude: Nine years ago Congress authorized the creation of forest reservations. It is not often, as we have seen, that any measure for the public good, aside from the absolutely necessary routine measures, gets a chance in the Congress of Aldrich and Joe Cannon. Invariably, such a measure is passed because the anger of the people forbids longer denial or because it has been charged with "jokers" which mean graft for "the interests"—and usually the measure compelled by public sentiment is not passed until it is juggled into harmlessness and stuffed with steals. The main graft "joker"—in "practical politics" this kind of treason goes by the name of "joker"—the main graft "joker" in the forest-reservations bill was put into it in conference committee by Allison and Cannon, leading respectively the Senate and the House conferees. The original bill provided in simple justice that a homesteader whose lands were taken for forest reserve could change them for equally good land elsewhere in the public domain. Patriots Allison and Cannon slipped in, after "homesteader," these four innocent-looking words *"or any other claimant."* Not until 1900, not until the robber railway barons had exchanged millions of acres of desert and of denuded timber lands, of snowy peaks and rocky slopes, for millions of acres of the best remaining homestead lands in the public domain, did it come out — through the "unmerged" and therefore soon retired Senator Pettigrew's vigilance—what Allison and Cannon had done for their friends, "the interests," and against their country. Mr. Pettigrew, on May 31, 1900, called attention to the steal; the Senate virtuously passed his amendment. The amendment went to conference in charge of Allison and Hale; it emerged so altered that the stealing could go on. Pettigrew saw what had been done. Here is an extract from the record:

"PETTIGREW: I should like to ask the chairman of the committee on appropriations (Allison) if the secretary of the interior did not think the law should be entirely repealed?

"ALLISON: The secretary did.

"PETTIGREW: Did he not think there were great frauds being practiced under it?

"ALLISON: I have no doubt that is all true, but *that is a subject we cannot deal with now.*"

Obviously not. How could a "merged" Senate find time to interfere in behalf of the people and the country, when interference would cut off rich plunder from "the interests"? Not until last year, when "the interests" had grabbed all possible loot, did Congress find time to repeal the loot clause. Such traitorous doings as this, taken with senatorial license to the controllers of railways to rob through extortionate and unequal rates, explain why the farm mortgages of the West increase, why we year by year lose more and more of our best farming population to Canada.

BACKED BY THE BIG LOOTERS

The Senate seat which Allison has held for thirty-three years was got for him by the big looters of and through railroads. They sought, in 1872, to elect Allison; by the use of money, by corruption so flagrant that it is still remembered, they succeeded. Allison has since maintained himself, not indeed with the people but with the legislature, by federal patronage, by attaching to himself all Iowans active in politics; and "the interests," by the use of passes and advertising contracts, have seen to it that even the opposition press dealt gently with their handy man. Said Republican Editor F. W. Faulkes of the stanchly Republican "Cedar Rapids Gazette," in an interview in the "Kansas City Star," on January 18, 1890:

"Mr. Allison does not now represent and never has represented the interests of Iowa or of the West; he has stood as the special champion of . . . the elements and measures that have permitted, induced, and aided the inauguration and upbuilding of the trusts, combines, and commercial conspiracies which have been plundering the producers of the country. . . . I was secretary of the Republican state committee in 1883 when Allison was a candidate. He had rooms near the committee rooms, and he had agents to give out money to be used in helping to elect Republican candidates for the legislature. Some of those, if not all, so helped, voted for Allison. The same thing will be done again this winter."

But fully as valuable to him as his railroad backing and the direct use of money as described above have been his skill and power as a place and "pork" securer. No man, not Lodge even, has proportionately so many heelers and henchmen upon the federal pay-roll. And, as chairman of the Senate committee on appropriations, he is the custodian of the federal "pork barrel." This "pork barrel" is the "merger's" great instrument for keeping senators and representatives docile to "the party," which we have learned means "the interests" behind the Aldrich-Bailey "merger." Those who offend the "merger" by voting or speaking against its measures without permission, get upon Aldich's black list and get no "pork"—and "pork" means to the politician power in the machine. The business of the Senate appropriations committee is to see to it that the federal appropriations—now nearly a billion a year—are distributed as far as possible for the benefit of friends and agents of "the interests," are distributed among those loyal to "the party" and withheld from the "disloyal." Using the people's money to punish their friends and to reward traitors and those acquiescent in treason! While appropriation bills originate in the House, they take final shape in the Senate. Thus Allison, under Aldrich and the "merger," has all but absolute control over the popularity or unpopularity of senators and representatives with their constituents and with the heelers and backers of the local machines throughout the country. Making an appropriation bill "safe and sane" is, therefore, a delicate, difficult task; no other senator works so hard as does Allison.

This is the power that chiefly enables "Uncle Joe" Cannon and Lieutenant Williams to keep the House "in order." Halfway through his brief two years' term, a congressman must stand for renomination and reëlection. He has no chance to build himself up in a manly way; he can't even speak without Uncle Joe's permission. And if he has antagonized the "merger" his failure as a place and "pork" getter usually ends him. If he by chance is renominated, where is he to find campaign funds, when the "merger," which has those funds, will have none of him? Is it strange that Uncle Joe rules the Republican majority and Lieutenant John Sharp Williams the Democratic minority with such ease? Superb "'party discipline"! And Aldrich's chief disciplinarian is Chairman Alli-son. We begin to understand now how it has come about that the machinery of our two political parties has passed under the control of two harmonious, intimate agents of "the inter-ests"—Aldrich and Bailey's friend, Ryan.

Allison's typical "merger"-senator record, in all its thirty-three industrious years—years that have seen his private

SENATOR SHELBY M. CULLOM OF ILLINOIS, WHOSE GREAT ACHIEVE-MENT, THE CULLOM ACT, WAS DELIBERATELY WRITTEN TO MAKE THE INTERSTATE COM-MERCE COMMISSION POWERLESS.

pocket fill with stealthy millions—contains, so far as diligent search has disclosed, not an instance of service of the people, except, of course, lip-service. To recite here any large part of his acts for "the interests" and against the people and the nation would be impossible and useless. We already have cut enough samples from the cloth to show that its pattern is uniform. Let us stop with one more illustration—this from his record as a loot-securer for "the interests'" by abuse of tariff legislation. When the Dingley tariff bill of 1897 came up to the Senate for "perfecting," it fixed the duty on white-pine lumber at the old McKinley bill rate of one dollar the thousand feet. In conference, Aldrich, Allison, and Jones of Arkansas being the Senate conferees, the duty was raised to two dollars the thousand feet. When this was reported from committee on July 20th, Senators Vest and Teller pointed out that the duty of one dollar had absolutely barred foreign lumber; that therefore the extra dollar was a frank present to the lumber barons, the great thieves who had stolen public lands and were stripping them of trees. Senator Pettigrew quoted from the "Northwestern Lumberman" of February 27, 1897, an account of a meeting of lumber barons in the Senate committee room of that mighty Michigan lumber baron Blodgett's protégé, Senator Burrows of Michigan. One had an envelope and a lead pencil. Said the "Northwestern Lumberman":

"He walked around the room and ciphered out a little bit, and he said, 'Mr. Burrows, do you know what one dollar a thousand feet would mean to this little crowd of men here? $6,125,000 on last year's product.'"

But the "merger" voted the steal—and more than four hundred other steals, in the same bill, of equal and of greater magnitude and of like treachery to the people. Were not Aldrich and Allison in charge for "the interests"? Of what avail the few unmerged senators, Democrats and Republicans, against the "merger" in control of the machines of both parties and of the campaign funds and the patronage—the "oil" and the "pork" which enable those machines to live?

Allison, we find, is like the rest of the leaders of the Senate—like Aldrich and Bailey, like Lodge and Spooner and Foraker, like Elkins and Knox and Crane— against the people, for "the interests." His misdeeds are not of the long ago or the result of ignorance of public questions and moral responsibilities, but are the deliberate habit of a lifetime, as are the misdeeds of all those senators with whom "the interests" have filled the Senate. Let us pass to the minor leaders, and then to the rank and file of the Senate—the men who follow Aldrich and Cannon, Bailey and Williams, and by vote make valid the decisions of "the interests" as to party policy, as to legislation, as to suppresing legislation. A crucial fact or so about each will be sufficient. Of course they, all the senators, all our politicians, have been patriotic in speech, have voted with their country on questions of foreign affairs and on such insignificant home questions as did not affect "the interests." The "merger" men use these questions to gain false repute as patriots. But in this article, as in all the preceding articles, we deal only with acts really important to the people, really significant of the character of the public man.

HOW CULLOM SERVES THE PEOPLE

Cullom of Illinois has been in public life since 1856. As a state legislator, as governor of Illinois, as representative, and as senator, he has now had just *half a century* of opportuity to serve the people. If he has ever served them except in nonessentials, his record fails to show it. That record shows throughout that, except in demagogic "wind-jamming," he has either held aloof or has actively aided "the interests," usually in "shaping legislation" in the secrecy of a committee, rarely by open speech, but always with his vote. He was Elkins's predecessor in charge, for Aldrich and "the interests," of the Senate interstate commerce committee. His great achievement was the interstate commerce act of 1887, which goes by his name. That "Cullom act" was the result of the first great exposure of the rascalities of high finance and of the public demand that Congress cease to license and aid the rascals. The Cullom act, passed with blare of virtuous triumph, was, as "unmerged" senators pointed out, deliberately so written that the Supreme Court could not but declare its main creation, the Interstate Commerce Commission, powerless. The favorite trick of the "merger," where it has to "pander to public sentiment," is to pass laws which the Supreme Court cannot but declare invalid. On January 14, 1887, when the Cullom act was on its way to final passage, Cullom in his most patriotically heartfelt manner said:

> "It has been said over and over again that the railroad companies would build up one man and crush another; that their policy has been to destroy one locality or city and build up another. Here (in the Cullom bill) we have undertaken so to regulate them as to prevent them from doing these things, so far as we could do so."

There was nothing to prevent him and his fellow "mergered" in control of the Senate from entirely doing away with the crimes of "the interests" through railways—nothing to prevent it but "the interests" themselves. The worthlessness of the Cullom act and its treachery to the people were demonstrated within a year. Interstate Commerce Commissioner Prouty, a Vermont Republican, well described it when he said:

> "If the Interstate Commerce Commission were worth buying, the railroads would try to buy it. The only reason they have not is that the body is *valueless* in its ability to correct railroad abuses."

Yet for fifteen years this so-called law, this act of treason to the people, protected and licensed "the interests" and was used by the traitor Senate as a pretext for not interfering with wholesale rebating and the charging of exorbitant rates.

Cullom prides himself upon his physical resemblance to —Abraham Lincoln!

KEAN, STONE, AND NELSON

Kean of New Jersey is a hugely rich man, rich by inheritance, richer through his manipulations of his heritage. There was the Perth Amboy Water Company, of which he was chief bondholder. The company had a contract from the city to supply "pure and wholesome water" for ten years. It supplied water from an unsanitary pool known as the "duck pond." And when it became a public scandal Kean strove in the courts and lobbied in the legislature to compel the city to buy him out. Then there was the Elizabeth Gas-light Company, of which he was president and controlling owner. It

SENATOR WILLIAM J. STONE OF MISSOURI, ONE OF THE DEMO-CRATS OF THE "MERGER," WHO DECEIVES THE PUBLIC BY MAK-ING CHEAP POLITICAL CAPITAL WHENEVER IT CAN BE DONE WITHOUT EXPOSING "THE INTER-ESTS" TO SPECIFIC CRITICISM.

supplied poor gas at $2.50 the thousand feet. A competitor entered the field; Kean fought it in the legislature and in the courts, wrecked it by reducing gas to seventy-five cents the thousand feet, bought it in, and then put the price of gas back at the old extortionate figure. These are typical of his many vastly profitable and onerous petty monopolies. He went to the Senate because, to quote Congressman Thomas Dunn English, "behind Kean at the present day you find all

the coal-carrying railways, because he is a heavy stockholder
in all of them, and as such is a beneficiary of the rise of
coal." His alliances, offensive to the people, beat him for
governor in 1892; but those same alliances, so popular always
with legislatures, elected him senator in 1899 and again last
year. In the Senate he is openly with "the interests"; he said
frankly in last winter's struggle between the people and their
railway despoilers, "Like Senator Foraker, I am opposed to
all government rate-making." He is chairman of the committee on audit and control of the contingent expenses of the
Senate; that is, he arranges the disbursements of the Senate's
annual graft for mileage, perfume, razors, chatelaine bags, etc.,
etc. It was he who let the convicted criminal, Burton, draw
many thousands of unearned dollars of the people's money by
making "constructive appearances" at the glass cloak-room
doors of the Senate. As the senators love their petty graft,
some of the richest being among the greediest, Kean's position
carries with it a surprising amount of power for the "merger"—
as Aldrich well knew when he gave it to a "safe and sane"
man.

   Stone of Missouri is one of the Democratic or Bailey
"bunch" in the "merger." An ancient and experienced lobbyist,
familiarly known as "Gum-shoe Bill," he was made nationally
famous when his fellow-lobbyist, Bill Phelps, said, "We both
suck eggs, but Stone he hides the shells." In 1899 he opposed
the assessment of the St. Louis street-railway companies at
seven million dollars as "overvaluation"; they now pay on
twenty million dollars, thanks to the great Folk reform wave.
It was that wave which, soon after Stone's election to the
Senate in 1903, caused the exposure of his lobbying in 1901
for the baking-powder trust, and how he disguised himself as
the "Missouri Pure-Food Society"—said society consisting of
himself and two other men. Yet he said to the legislative committee, "I appear before you at the request of the Health
Society of Missouri, composed of good people, both men and
women, living in different parts of the state."

In the Senate Stone has done nothing beyond making a few famous buncombe speeches. Like his fellow-Democrats of the "merger," now that their votes are not needed by "the interests," he is helping to make cheap, showy "political capital" wherever it can be done without exposing "the interests" to specific criticism. Thus, when the people grow weary of the so-called Republican wing of the "merger," the leaders of the so-called Democratic wing can cry: "Put us in! We are real patriots! We voted against the steals! We will serve you!" The result, or, rather, lack of result, from substituting one set of agents of "the interests" for another set equally devoted was shown in 1892-1896 when Bailey's predecessor, Gorman, was Aldrich's lieutenant in charge of the so-called Democratic Senate.

Nelson of Minnesota. A most impressive figure personally; and in patriotic speech as eloquent for people and country as Bailey or Spooner, and as effective in his way on the stump as was Foraker until he was found out. He is the foremost of the "Jim Hill bunch" of senators, the Jim Hill contribution to "the interests'" secure majority of the Senate. He got his seat from Hill (through Hill's legislature) in 1895, after a long public career during which the people of Minnesota had loaded him with honors and he had rewarded them by aiding their chief enemies, "the interests." As "the interests" ask chiefly the preventing of legislation that would interfere with them, the Nelsons have small difficulty in deceiving the people. All they have to do is "stand pat" and oppose any proposed legislation as "unconstitutional" or "unsafe" or "a cure worse than the disease," etc., etc. Nelson, a master of the "standpatter's" art, has as his greatest individual service of treachery to the people since he became senator a trick that was exposed recently in the "Northfield (Minn.) News." It will be remembered that Mr. Roosevelt has uttered two sharp rebukes of Judge Humphrey for giving an "immunity bath" to the beef-trust rebaters, and, by implication, to the Standard Oil, United States Steel, and other rebate assassins. If Mr.

Roosevelt had been less impetuous, if he had reflected on the text of Judge Humphrey's decision and on the law before speaking, he would have seen that under the law the judge had no option. He would have denounced the treason of the Senate, instead of the treason of the judiciary. The bill creating the Department of Commerce and Labor emerged from

SENATOR JOHN KEAN OF NEW JERSEY, WHO HAS THE COAL-CARRYING ROADS BEHIND HIM, AND WHO IS OPPOSED TO ALL GOVERNMENT RATE-MAKING.

conference committee on February 9, 1903, with an amendment by Nelson, the crucial clause of which was a provision that "all the requirements, obligations, liabilities, *and immunities* imposed by" the just-passed Elkins amendment to the interstate commerce act "shall also apply to *all* persons who may be *subpoenaed* to testify as witnesses or to produce documentary evidence" before the commissioner of corporations. That is, the devoted Nelson had slipped in a clause changing the law to ferret out crime into a law to grant immunity to criminals. Through Elkins, the "merger" gave a "bath" to the railway robbers; through Nelson to the rest of the corporate criminals. Nor can Nelson and the "merger" agents who voted the Nelson amendment onto the statute-books claim that he and they were innocent. In the House debates on the amended bill, before its final passage, the "Nelson amendment" was specifically exposed by Representative Richardson on February 10, 1903; it was denounced by Representative Adamson on the same day as "a delusion and a snare, a hollow mockery, the meanest sham, the most contemptible fraud and false pretense." That is, it was a typical "merger" measure— seeming to give the people what they demanded, while really giving them nothing and giving "the interests" a larger license. We shall have to return to Nelson when we examine the fraudulent railway-rate bill passed last winter.

NEW WORKER FOR THE "MERGER"

To know where stands Senator Clapp, Nelson's new colleague from Minnesota and a Jim Hill lawyer, it is only necessary to read in the "Congressional Record" how he concocted, with the approval of the "merger" Senate, an amendment to the above-mentioned Elkins bill of January, 1903, to grant immunity baths to criminal railway extortionists and to safeguard them against jail. The Elkins bath was,

"The claim that any such testimony (before the Interstate Commerce Commission) is evidence tending to criminate the person giving such evidence shall not excuse such witness from testifying; *but such evidence or testimony shall not be used against such person on the trial of any criminal proceeding.*"

That is, officers of corporations could get immunity, but it was not absolutely clear that corporations themselves could. So forward came Clapp for "the interests" and the "merger," and (Congressional Record, February 3, 1903) said, "We find that the immunity is not broad enough." Then he proposed that

> "No person or corporation shall be prosecuted or *subjected to any penalty or forfeiture* for or on account of any transaction, matter, or thing concerning which he or it may testify or *produce* evidence, documentary or otherwise, in such proceeding."

The Senate promptly passed the full and free extra bath for its masters; but the House did not dare go so frankly to such lengths, and the Elkins immunity bath, equally good for all practical purposes, became a law. A law! And these men *law*makers!

Last winter Congress, with a campaign record to make, and with Mr. Roosevelt and the people clamoring, passed a bill introduced by Knox to make possible official inquiries into crime without necessarily granting the Elkins-Nelson immunity bath. But the object of the Elkins-Nelson "joker" had been in the main accomplished. Also, who knows but that a "joker" is hid in the Knox law or in some other law which may have been slipped through and whose purpose will not appear until after this fall's elections are over?

Very important are those elections to the "merger"; for, to note only the chief point, the legislatures then elected will choose the successors of Bailey, Elkins, Nelson, Crane, and Cullom—five highly important men to the "merger." It will be interesting to see just how far the people are awake to the real cause of the futility of their struggles against the arch-enemy, to the real reason why prosperity is trimmed and clipped and adversity made more burdensome. For the Senate, the "merger," controls the pockets of the people—controls *your* pocket!

IX

FAIRBANKS, HALE, AND FRYE

FAIRBANKS, the presiding genius of the Aldrich-Bailey Senate, is, technically, not a member of it. But no account of the leadership in the citadel of "the interests" would be adequate if it neglected him. The story of his rise from a young Indianapolis lawyer with rich, influential relatives, in 1874, to senatorial multimillionaire, vice-president, and Harriman candidate for the Republican presidential nomination, is a typical Senate biography. Soon after he began to practice law, his uncle, General-Superintendent Smith of the Chesapeake and Ohio Railway, got him the job of attorney to the receiver of the Indiana, Bloomington & Western Railroad. For fourteen years thereafter he devoted his talents to the service of railway wreckers and reorganizers and stock and bond waterers. He laid the broad foundation of his great fortune early. The I. B. & W. was popularly regarded as much poorer than it really was. A pool was formed by the inside ring and the heavily discounted wage-checks of the road's badly paid employees were brought up; the checks were paid in full—and the young lawyer became a financier, a bulwark of conservatism and probity!

It was his clever railway work that got him Morgan's

favor and the coveted position of Morgan's Middle-Western lieutenant. To indicate the man as a public factor we need not linger on the jobbery of Indianapolis, Bloomington & Western, the Cincinnati, Hamilton & Dayton, the Cleveland, Cincinnati, Chicago & Indianapolis, the Père Marquette, etc. Fairbanks grew richer and richer, bought Indiana Republican heelers, financed Indiana Republican and independent newspapers, including the chief Republican papers of the state, the "Indianapolis Journal" and the "Indianapolis News"; he made addresses to religious bodies, backed the machine with his money bags, became a statesman, a senator in 1897, and vice-president through the popularity of Roosevelt in 1905. While he was "representing" the people of Indiana as a senator in 1901, he and his protector, Morgan, quarreled over the famous, or rather infamous, Joss railway bill drawn by Morgan's chief lawyer, Stetson. Fairbanks promised Morgan that Governor Durbin would sign the bill. Durbin either would not or dared not. Though the Fairbanks machine punished Durbin's "treachery" by retiring him from public life, Morgan remained "sore." This and some C. H. & D. matters caused Fairbanks to find it expedient to transfer himself to the service of Harriman. It is with the Harriman branch of "the interests" that he is now identified, and under its auspices delegates— chiefly colored delegates from the South—are in the way of purchase as Fairbanks's support for the Republican presidential nomination.

As senator, Fairbanks was always quick to rally with the faithful round Aldrich, against the people. As presiding officer of the Senate, his opportunities for direct service are necessarily limited. He is still a Wall Street speculator, for his political expenses are a heavy drain. His most ardent senatorial supporters in his presidential ambition are Hemenway of Indiana and young Brandegee of Connecticut—which is, of itself, enough to "locate" them.

Will "the interests" nominate him as the Republican presidential candidate in 1908? The present plan of the Aldrich-

Ryan control of the merged machines of the two parties seems to be to nominate at the Democratic convention the most easily beaten of the Democratic presidential possibilities, and to put up as the Republican candidate some "safe and sane" man who belongs to them, or at least will not impede them. Possibly he will be Fairbanks. But the possibility seems remote. Indeed, by 1908, the people may become awake to the truth about the merged machinery of the parties.

Hale and Frye—to complete our survey of the Senate's leaders—have been for twenty-five years the senators from Maine. Sharp and painful is the contrast between Hale, opponent of militarism and made-in-England imperialism, and Hale, helper of "the interests," our only dangerous enemy. Indifference to the people and contempt for their rights as against the riches and social and political power of "the interests" saturate the atmosphere of the Senate. The rare occasional senator who proposes some timid measure of justice, or protests—with due regard for "senatorial courtesy"— against some measure of more than usual injustice, feels like an uncouth fellow thrusting coarse dress and harsh accents upon an elegant company of gentlemen. And many senators are, through long custom and gradual degeneration, as unconscious of the moral quality of their actions as are the great rascals of Wall Street when they make heavier the burdens of the masses, make deeper the sighs of poverty, by issuing floods of stocks and bonds that inflate prices and constrict wages.

Hale is one of the Senate's twenty-five millionaires; is worth five or more millions. Frye has a competence. But both are alike infected with the self-excusing idea that their friends of "the interests" are, to use President Baer's famous phrase, "the men to whom God in his infinite wisdom has given control of the property interests of the country." The railroads— that is, the exploiters of railroad stockholders and users— dominate New England politics. In Maine, as in New Hampshire and Vermont, it is the Boston and Maine. Thus Hale and

Frye have their senatorial seats from legislatures ruled by "the interests," and would lose those seats if they developed however shadowy symptoms of "demagoguery." Further, both have a not unnatural passion to be "influential in the party"—and how be influential there if out of harmony with the forces that finance and control its machine?

Only last spring (Cong. Record, May 14, pages 7011, 7012, etc.) Hale was celebrating his twenty-fifth anniversary of "merger" service by acting as suave, cynically polite floormanager against La Follette's effort to get sincerity and strength into the railway-rate bill. As for Frye, his chief public occupation since 1901 has been urging the ship-subsidy grab which Hanna (Cong. Record, June 5, 1900, page 7119) promised an influential group of "campaign contributors." As passed again by the "merged" Senate last winter, Frye's measure proposed a grant of nine millions a year for twenty years to already rich and prosperous ship-builders and ship-owners. We built last year eleven hundred and two merchant vessels, which was more than any other country built. The 1893 report of the commissioner of navigation shows that ships are built cheaper on the Great Lakes than on the Clyde or the Mersey. We sell to foreign consumers everything that goes into a ship. As both Aldrich and Cannon did not dare vote this one-hundred-and-eight-million-dollar grab on the eve of a doubtful election, Aldrich had his Senate pass it to stimulate campaign contributions.

Neither Hale nor Frye is in the Senate for the people. In the vital matter, the people *versus* the confiscators of their property, Hale sits for his millions well invested with "the interests," and Frye for his dear friends in politics and social life. Those rich friends, being comfortable and in possession of more than their share, wonder at discontent, call confiscation conservatism, and extol the virtue and piety of "stand-patism."

Except Martin of Virginia, who is Ryan's chief senatorial political lieutenant after Bailey of Texas, and who rivals Aldrich and Allison for subtlety and stealth, none of the

Southern senators owes his seat to *direct* railway dictation; on the other hand, no Southern senator, not even Tillman, nowadays defies "the interests," without a tremor—except as the politician of the party out of power is always permitted to pour out the "hot air" of futile ravings against vague monopolies, to make "political capital." Such is the result in the South—as in the North—of legislatures in large part, often almost entirely, composed of petty lawyers, on, or eager to get on, the pay-rolls of the "law departments" of the giant corporations, especially the railways.

As to Virginia's, or rather Ryan's, Martin, here is a compact summary of the truth about him, made by that sterling Virginian and stanch Democrat, William L. Royall, at Chester Hill, Virginia, on June 1, 1905:

"Gen. Fitzhugh Lee, the popular idol, whom ninety per cent. of the people of Virginia expected to be sent to the United States Senate, was defeated by Thomas S. Martin, *a man whose name had never been heard by five thousand people of Virginia.* Soon there were whisperings of bribery and corruption. The thing took definite shape in the form of charges in the press that the railroad companies of the state had raised a corruption fund of forty-five thousand dollars; that this had been sent into the negro counties, where the elections were what the ballot-box stuffers pleased to make them, to have representatives sent to the legislature who would elect a man to the Senate to be a tool of the railroads."

Mr. Royall went on to relate how the legislature was finally forced to appoint a committee to investigate; how that committee disregarded its legislative mandate, which had been sweepingly worded to placate the people; how it by formal resolution confined its inquiry, to quote the resolution itself, *"strictly to the conduct of the senatorial candidate"!* Of course Martin came off clear. And the report now is that Ryan purposes to have himself elected to succeed Daniel, Martin's colleague. The state of Washington and Jefferson!

Such are the leaders of the Senate. The character of a leadership stamps the character of the led. The character of the leaders and of the leadership of the Senate obviously cannot change until the Senate is swept clean of the men who select and follow those leaders.

Certainly, never was the Senate so beset as at its last session by the forces that make for publicity and therefore for patriotism. What was the actual result, as distinguished from the assertions of party organs and organs and agents of "the interests"? Did the senators, the leaders and the led, about face and serve the people? Did the leopard change his spots, the Ethiopian his skin?

HOW GOOD BILLS ARE NULLIFIED

As we have discovered, the main tests of treason are two: tariff legislation and railway legislation, because chiefly in those ways do "the interests" fatten upon us. The present tariff law has for the past six years been attacked fully as vigorously by Republicans as by Democrats. Mr. McKinley, the most extreme of protectionists, in the speech he made just before he was shot down, five years ago last September, exclaimed, "The time for exclusiveness has passed," and called for reciprocity treaties. Was anything done last winter and spring toward securing reciprocity treaties, or toward revising robbery out of the tariff? Not a thing. The word from "the interests" was "stand pat." "It will disturb our business," said they; and, as "our business" is robbery, it undoubtedly would. So Aldrich held the Senate—and Cannon the House—in line for "the interests."

Early in the session Senator Tillman introduced a bill to "prohibit corporations from making money contributions in connection with political campaigns" (Senate bill No. 4563). The campaign contribution formed and fosters the conditions under which the will of "the interests" has become "the policy of the party," conditions under which Aldrich, manager of the Republican national machine, and Ryan, chief financier of the Democratic national machine, can meet in a room in the Fifth Avenue Hotel or in the Hotel Gotham, New York city, on Sunday afternoons while Congress is in session, and— if they are not merely talking about the weather—decide what Congress shall *not* do; for that is the chief concern of "the interests," now that they have the best of the public lands and satisfactory tariff schedules.

What became of this bill to emancipate, partially at least, our politics from "the interests"? It was referred to the Senate's committee on privileges and elections, thence to a sub-committee composed of—Knox, Bailey, Foraker! When Tillman had shown that he did not propose to let the trio smother the bill, and when it became evident that the public was watching to see what became of it, Foraker reported it to the Senate; and on June 9th it passed by unanimous consent. A victory for the people! A complete vindication of the virtue of the Senate! But—not so fast! The "merger" applies to the House, remember—and in all vital matters Joe Cannon is the House, just as Aldrich is the Senate. The bill went to Joe Cannon. He put it in that one of his pockets which is labeled "House committee on the election of president, vice-president, and representatives in Congress." The people appealed and protested; but there it stayed. Joe and his House were "too busy" to assail the corruption that fills Senate and House with smooth agents and cowed or squirming subjects of "the interests" disguised as "the party."

But that is not all. There was the "Beveridge" meat-inspection bill. It passed the Senate practically as Beveridge wrote it. Apparently the master of the "merger" was going to permit Congress to do a little "pandering to public sentiment," at the expense of the beef barons, who of all the united yet divided family of "the interests" are the least beloved by their brethren. But each branch of "the interests" has its own special senators or congressmen or both. The beef trust's special friends are Senator Cullom and Joe Cannon and Jimmie Wadsworth, chairman of Joe Cannon's committee on agriculture. Cullom, as usual, worked underground. Cannon and Wadsworth, of necessity, worked, in large part, in the open. It is useless and would be tedious to trace the betrayal of the people step by step. The bill in its original form was inadequate but honest. As finally passed, Aldrich "reluctantly" accepting Cannon's amendments, it was an act of treachery to the people. Why? Let us see.

The original bill insured thorough inspection by providing that the inspectors be paid by the packers, at so much a head or carcass. Thus the Department of Agriculture, in getting a force of inspectors, would not have to rely upon a Congressional appropriation that might be inadequate, or might be withheld or cut down when the excitement died away and the people were lulled into security by the belief that Congress had safeguarded their interests. But upon the pretext that the people ought to pay, as they were the beneficiaries—this, when the beef trust would make millions out of the government guarantee—Cannon and Wadsworth made the thoroughness of the inspection dependent upon the adequacy of a fixed appropriation of three million dollars. The former appropriation, for the inspection which had permitted the beef trust to become a wholesale poisoner of the people, had been seven hundred and fifty thousand. With the former list of one hundred and fifty establishments to inspect thoroughly instead of carelessly; with an added list of one hundred widely scattered establishments to be looked after; with the lowest estimate of the cost of adequate inspection about six millions a year, the House—that is, Cannon—at first stood out for an appropriation of only one million dollars; stood again at two million dollars; and finally conceded to Mr. Roosevelt and Senator Beveridge three million dollars as the limit. And, obviously, less than adequate inspection is no inspection at all; is a lure to false security on the part of consumers.

Again, under the former law, our patriotic Congress had instituted, at the request of the beef trust seeking a foreign market, an inspection of meat for export; but it had excluded meat for American consumption! Under the original Beveridge

bill, the inspection labels had to be dated, so that the beef
trust could not relabel three- and four- and five-year-old cans
and furbish and "freshen" decaying meat and work it off as
good, new meat. With not an attempt to excuse or explain a
treason of release of the people to beef-trust rapacity, the
"merger" *voted down the dating of the inspection labels.* Why
did Mr. Roosevelt and Senator Beveridge finally yield? For
the same reasons that so often lead honest but firmly partisan
politicians to accept "compromises"—faint-hearted belief that
it is the "compromise" with corruption or nothing, and desire
for credit with the people of "doing something."

   The so-called Beveridge bill leaves the beef trust just where
it was, except that it *now has a government endorsement on
all its products.* The inspection cannot be thorough; there
is not a sufficient appropriation. It will be somewhat less
farcical, *for a time,* than it has been—and that is all. The Jim
Hill branch of "the interests" holds the beef-trust branch in
particular hatred, because it has made Jim Hill crawl at its
feet for business at its own rates. Thus it was that Jim Hill's
Nelson voiced the truth. Said he (Cong. Record, June 29th):

"The ordinary American consumers and the ordinary American
farmers have been left out of the question. Three objects have
been sought to be accomplished: first, to placate the packers; next,
to placate the men who raise the range cattle; and, third, to get a
good market for the packers abroad. The beef trust can now force
us to eat the canned goods, whether they were made yesterday
or are as old as Methuselah. I hope that in the future we may
be able to correct this legislation, but the senator (Beveridge)
will be a much grayer man than I am before he gets the upper
hand of the packers or the range cattlemen."

   Such is the truth about the "glorious victory of the
people" over the beef trust. The new law is long and its impressive phrases sound formidable. But its essence is in the
size of the appropriation and the omission of date upon
inspection labels.

   But that is not all. For seventeen years the people had

been trying to get a law that would check the operations of what is commonly known as the "poison trust." For seventeen years the Senate had refused to permit the "industry" to be molested. Finally, however, through official reports of the Department of Agriculture, the fact that *more than fifty per cent.* of the drugs and manufactured goods in cans and packages was adulterated became too notorious; deaths and violent illnesses from the products of the poison trust became too numerous. A campaign was coming on, and the people were in an ugly mood.

When the pure-food bill first entered last winter's Congress, it was an honest measure, modeled upon the laws that have long been efficient in Europe. The vital points for efficient regulation are two:

First. That the government shall be able to seize the poisonous or fraudulent goods wherever found, and to get at the person offering them for sale as well as their maker, so that the dealer will have an interest in protecting his customers.

Second. That all manufactured food and drug products shall conform to a definite standard of excellence, fixed by a permanent expert board. The manufacturers cannot then plead that they did not know they were adulterating, cannot bring hired chemists to swear that the adulterations in their goods are harmless.

What of the so-called pure-food law? What are its provisions at these vital points? As to dealers in poisonous foods and drugs, it says:

"No dealer shall be prosecuted when he can establish a guaranty signed by the wholesale jobber, manufacturer, or *other party* residing in the United States, from whom he purchases such articles, to the effect that the same are not adulterated or misbranded."

That is, the dealer need not concern himself at all about the goods he is handling. All he need do to protect himself is to get from somebody or other—any dummy put forward by manufacturer or jobber will do—a certificate that the goods are all right. The certificate does not even need the signature of a legally, responsible person. Dealers in stolen goods are not protected in this way; why should dealers in fraudulent and poisonous food be so protected?

As to the second point—the fixing of a standard—the law *makes no provision whatever for standards of purity for foods and drugs beyond vague phrases which can be picked to pieces by lawyers and by experts in the employ of the poison trust and testifying in behalf of members of the trust who have got into trouble.* The report of the House committee on interstate commerce which accompanied the original bill and explained its provisions says (page 4):

"It is, however, *essential* to the success and operation of any pure-food measure that standards of food products shall be arrived at, for the guidance of the officials charged with the administration of the law and often for the information of the courts."

And the report goes on to say that it is "therefore" provided in the bill that "the secretary of agriculture shall have a board of five experts," etc., etc. But the law as it stands does not contain this "essential"; *the Senate struck it out.* And so the administrators of the law and the courts have no guide. Under criminal statutes of long standing, it was impossible to indict as a common criminal a purveyor of disguised poisons. The new, the boasted, "pure food" law adds nothing to these statutes. In fact, it takes from them; the poisoner for profit is now subject merely to the light fines and possible light prison sentences provided by this law.

LEGISLATION THAT DOESN'T LEGISLATE

Why did Representative Mann and the others honestly desiring a real pure-food law accept this trick law, worse than no law at all? Partly because it does contain some good, though not important, provisions as to misbranding; chiefly for the same reasons that made Mr. Roosevelt and Mr. Beveridge call their meat-inspection defeat a victory—impetuous optimism, the desire to feel that they had "done something," the desire to get credit with the people for accomplishment, the oncoming Congressional campaign. The pure-food men did the shouting, but the poison trust got the victory, *even to refusing to permit Congress to compel the canning branch of the trust to use cans of honest sizes.* It is unfortunate that space limits prevent the reprinting here of the entire pure-food debate in both Senate and House. The people would be instructed—and shocked—by the astounding callousness of so many of their "representatives." *Not a single amendment of the original honest bill, beyond trivial corrections of grammar and clumsy phrase, was made with any other intent than to increase the license and immunity of the cheats and poisoners and to decrease the efficiency of the law.* The "safe and sane" legislators were anxious only that the line be drawn, as far as they dared draw it, on the side of the swindlers and poisoners for dividends; for the pockets of the plunderers, not the pockets of the people; for the safety of criminals, not the safety of American citizens and their families.

But that is not all. Senate bill No. 5133 forbade railways to keep train handlers at work more than sixteen hours at a stretch, and compelled at least ten hours for getting home, sleeping, and getting back to work. Since the long hours of railway workers are admittedly the chief reason why our railways kill more than ten thousand persons a year, injure more than eighty-four thousand, and put hundreds of thousands in jeopardy of narrowly averted accidents, such a proposal becomes simply a forbidding of wholesale murder. On June 26th Senator La Follette began his battle to compel the senators to go on record as for or against this bill. The obstruction tactics began with a motion by McCumber, of the "Jim Hill bunch," that the bill go over. There were no less than sixteen time-wasting roll-calls before the Senate, which was "too busy" to consider the safety of three-quarters of a billion annual American railway passengers, finally yielded to La Follette's persistence and took up the bill. The only "merger" men who fought openly were McCumber, Kean, Foraker, Gallinger, Carter, and Warren. The only arguments were the expense to the railways, and that Congress had no right to interfere with a man who might wish to work more than sixteen hours a day. The "merger" escaped an aye and no record vote by agreeing to vote finally upon the bill on Thursday, January 30th, next, at 3 p.m., "unless sooner disposed of." Senator La Follette let "senatorial courtesy" persuade him to consent to this. We shall see next January what happens to this bill, with the election over and the fate of the "merger" senators whose seats are at stake decided, and another election two long, crowded years away.

But that is not all; there was the railway rate legislation. Laws long on the statute-books, though just recently begun to be enforced, amply cover discriminations and rebates. The real demand of the people as to railways, the demand the "merger" Senate and House tried to deceive and quiet with a trick railway-rate law, centers about this fact:

The people are robbed by means of the railways through having to pay freight and passenger tolls based on extortionate dividends to subsidiary corporations organized for "milking" purposes, and on an over-capitalization of the railways themselves, amounting to about sixteen billion dollars—actual value, four billions; stocks and bonds, twenty billions.

This means directly and indirectly a heavy tax on every American family; a cut into your profits, your salary, your wages, your savings; poorer clothes for your family, fewer comforts and luxuries, greater hardships in hard times. To measure that tax, not merely the net earnings of the railways, about three-quarters of a billion a year, but the *gross* earnings, about two billion dollars, must be investigated. Also, like all indirect taxes, it wastes fully as much as it takes. How did the "merger" Senate meet, or rather dodge, that vital question? From February until June it discussed everything and anything, chiefly the Constitution, hours on hours, days on days. It spent *less than five minutes,* and that incidentally—a col-

loquy between Senators Beveridge and La Follette—in debate
upon the real issue. It discussed for weeks "broad" and "nar-
row" court reviews—a matter of concern to shippers only. What
was the object of those vast clouds of dust, raised by Aldrich's and Cannon's orators, assisted by the Bailey and Williams
"bunch"? To distract the attention of the President and the
country from the real issue.

That real issue lies buried under the typical trick-law
phrase of the new statute which says that rates must be *"just
and reasonable."* The "merged" Senate, for the obvious reason
of treachery to the people, refused to define what "just and
reasonable" means or to permit the Interstate Commerce Commission to gather the information upon which the justice and
reasonableness of rates could be determined by it and by the
courts. On May 14th, Senator La Follette introduced an
amendment to repair this vital error and to make the bill a
real measure instead of a pretentious fraud. His amendment
was that

"The Commission shall investigate and ascertain the fair value
of the property of every railroad engaged in interstate commerce.
. . . All final valuations (after the railways have been heard before
the Commission and before the courts) shall be *prima facie* evidence of the fair value of the railroad property (in fixing rates)."

The "merger" did not dare debate this proposal. Senator
Hale, for the "merger," moved to kill it. La Follette compelled
a call of the ayes and noes. The vote for this motion to relicense again "the interests" as they were relicensed by the
Cullom interstate commerce act of 1887 to cheat and quiet
the last great uprising against robbery by railroad manipula-
tors, comes as near being a poll of the "merger" as can be
got. Of course, the Democratic members of the "merger" are
missing, as they were not needed and so could be let off to
"make political capital" for the Democratic wing of the "merger." Here are the fifty senators who rallied round Aldrich:

Alger, Alee, Ankeny, Brandegee, Bulkeley, Burnham,

Carter, Clark of Wyoming, Crane, Cullom, Dick, Dillingham, Dryden, Flint, Foraker, Frye, Fulton, Gallinger, Hale, Hansborough, Hemenway, Hopkins, Kean, Kittredge, Knox, Lodge, Long, McCumber, McEnery, Millard, Nelson, Nixon, Penrose, Perkins, Piles, Platt, Scott, Sutherland, and Wetmore.

Paired senators for the "merger" were:

Allison, Spooner, Burton, Burrows, Clapp, Depew, Heyburn, Proctor, Smoot, and Warren.

Several senators were absent unpaired, so we have not here the full strength even of the Republican wing; and "merger" Lieutenant Elkins, attacked and up for reëlection in West Virginia, voted with La Follette. Still, the vote is a valuable index, though the full strength of the "merger" is more than seventy-five out of a possible ninety!

Does the law give the Commission any power at all in fixing rates? Charles A. Prouty, Vermont Republican and interstate commerce commissioner, giving an analysis of this law, lauded as a "glorious victory for the people," said ("Review of Reviews" for July, 1906) that the original bill, as passed by the House (the President's bill), gave the Commission the power to fix rates, but the Senate intervened. He added:

"Whether the bill as finally agreed upon confers this power can only be positively affirmed after the courts have passed upon that question. . . . Upon the decision of this question depends in large degree the effectiveness of the measure."

"No sudden or startling results of any kind will follow from this law," says he. And he says well; it is as "safe and sane," as thoroughly "mergered," as the Cullom act of 1887. The grant of power to fix rates is doubtful; and no basis is provided for fixing "just and reasonable rates." Such is the "victory for the people," the "vindication of the statesmanship and patriotism of the Senate." No wonder honest Senator Tillman could not be wheedled into signing the final conference report on this bill. No wonder President Baer of the Reading openly laughs at the law. What a travesty, to call such a cheat law!

"VICTORIES FOR THE PEOPLE"

But that is not all. The steel trust's Congressionally chartered canal connecting Lake Erie with the Ohio and Mississippi River systems (H.R. 14396) will be, as its chief senatorial spokesman, Knox, pointed out, of national importance, connecting as it does the Great Lakes with the Gulf of Mexico and, by way of the Panama Canal, with the Pacific. It was therefore of supreme importance that low tolls be guaranteed—which they could not be if the canal were burdened with water stocks and bonds. It was of equal importance *that Congress take advantage of the rare opportunity of a nationally chartered corporation to lay down the principle of just capitalization.*

According to the company's own experts, the cost of the canal could not well exceed fifty million dollars. Yet the Aldrich-Cannon Congress granted a charter permitting stocks and bonds of eight hundred thousand dollars a mile—about one hundred and fifty million dollars! La Follette proposed that the Interstate Commerce Commission be empowered to regulate the issues of stocks and bonds and so prevent stock and bond watering. Nelson of Minnesota conducted operations for the "merger." There was no debate—how could the "merger" debate such a plain proposal of patriotism and justice? He curtly moved to table the amendment. And it was tabled, and the people were betrayed by a vote like the one recorded above, except that to that black list must be added these names:

Benson, the new senator from Kansas, Burkett, Elkins, Warner.

On the final vote—on the bill itself—La Follette struck his flag and voted for it. Why? "Senatorial courtesy!" We must give La Follette full credit for courage and conscience in his gallant struggles in this and other vital matters, for his genuine accomplishment in forcing the Senate to order an investigation of the grain-elevator trust. Still, we must also note that in his very first winter he, on two signal occasions, bent before "senatorial courtesy," which is the "merger's" sleek contrivance for slathering treason with cant and for flattering virtue into silence or submission.

Such, then, are the laws that are hailed as the "great victories for the people." There were other similar acts of treachery to nation and people—acts of commission and acts of omission. We may not now go into them. Let us pass over them and the neutral laws—those routine measures of appropriations, foreign relations, and the like, which in the broad mean nothing one way or the other as to treason or patriotism. Let us close with a glance at the act which the "merger" has so confidently thrown to the farmers as a sop, as a proof that treason does not rule in the Capitol.

The impression has gone out—we can guess how—that the Standard Oil Company was bitterly opposed to free, denatured alcohol, because it meant that every farmer could make cheaply his own light, power, and fuel, and so would stop buying the Standard's high-priced product. Further, the cry from Washington—we can guess why—was that the final passing of the law was a great defeat for the Standard. The facts are these:

First. The new law forbids the making of denatured alcohol anywhere but "in a bonded warehouse specially designated or set aside for denaturing purposes only" and "in the presence and under the direction of an authorized government official."

Second. The Standard Oil Company cares nothing about the new fuel as a competitor of its gasoline, because the manufacture of denatured alcohol is difficult and as yet expensive, and it has a heat value one-third less than gasoline ("Electrical World," July 7, 1906).

Third. The Standard is rapidly buying up the distilleries, the only places where denatured alcohol can legally be made. There is a large but limited demand for the alcohol in certain manufacturing processes. The Standard will supply that demand in the Standard's familiar way.

So much for the one act at the last session of Congress which has been cited as a clear-cut, indisputable refutation of the charge that "the interests" rule the two party machines, with the people deceived and defrauded.

Such is the stealthy and treacherous Senate as at present constituted. And such it will continue to be until the people think, instead of shout, about politics; until they judge public men by what they do and are, not by what they say and pretend. However, the fact that the people are themselves responsible for their own betrayal does not mitigate contempt for their hypocritical and cowardly betrayers. A corrupt system *explains* a corrupt man; it does not *excuse* him. The stupidity or negligence of the householder in leaving the door unlocked does not lessen the crime of the thief.

APPENDIX A

The President's Response: Theodore Roosevelt on "The Man with the Muck-rake"

ON April 14, 1906, angered by the Foreword and first article of "The Treason of the Senate," President Theodore Roosevelt delivered a major address on "The Man with the Muck-rake," while dedicating the cornerstone of the House Office Building in Washington, D.C. Because, by implication, the President's speech was a criticism of David Graham Phillips's techniques and style, and because his speech stimulated a host of similar strictures, it is reprinted here (from the *New York Tribune*, April 15, 1906).

Over a century ago Washington laid the cornerstone of the Capitol in what was then little more than a tract of wooded wilderness here beside the Potomac. We now find it necessary to provide by great additional buildings for the business of the government. This growth in the need for the housing of the government is but a proof and example of the way in which the nation has grown and the sphere of action of the national government has grown. We now administer the affairs of a nation in which the extraordinary growth of

216

population has been outstripped by the growth of wealth and the growth in complex interests. The material problems that face us today are not such as they were in Washington's time, but the underlying facts of human nature are the same now as they were then. Under altered external form we war with the same tendencies toward evil that were evident in Washington's time, and are helped by the same tendencies for good. It is about some of these that I wish to say a word today.

In Bunyan's *Pilgrim's Progress* you may recall the description of the Man with the Muck-rake, the man who could look no way but downward, with the muck-rake in his hands; who was offered a celestial crown for his muck-rake, but who would neither look up nor regard the crown he was offered, but continued to rake to himself the filth of the floor.

In *Pilgrim's Progress* the Man with the Muck-rake is set forth as the example of him whose vision is fixed on carnal instead of on spiritual things. Yet he also typifies the man who in this life consistently refuses to see aught that is lofty, and fixes his eyes with solemn intentness only on that which is vile and debasing. Now, it is very necessary that we should not flinch from seeing what is vile and debasing. There is filth on the floor, and it must be scraped up with the muck-rake; and there are times and places where this service is the most needed of all the services that can be performed. But the man who never does anything else, who never thinks or speaks or writes save of his feats with the muck-rake, speedily becomes, not a help to society, not an incitement to good, but one of the most potent forces of evil.

There are in the body politic, economic and social, many and grave evils, and there is urgent necessity for the sternest war upon them. There should be relentless exposure of and attack upon every evil man, whether politician or businessman, every evil practice, whether in politics, in business or in social life. I hail as a benefactor every writer or speaker, every man who, on the platform or in book, magazine or newspaper, with merciless severity makes such attack, provided always that he in his turn remembers that the attack is of use only if it is absolutely truthful. The liar is no whit better than the thief, and if his mendacity takes the form of slander he may be worse than most thieves. It puts a premium upon knavery untruthfully to attack an honest man, or even with hysterical exaggeration to assail a bad man with untruth. An epidemic of indiscriminate assault upon character does not good but very great harm. The soul of every scoundrel is gladdened whenever an honest man is assailed, or even when a scoundrel is untruthfully assailed.

Now, it is easy to twist out of shape what I have just said, easy to affect to misunderstand it, and, if it is slurred over in repetition, not difficult really to misunderstand it. Some persons are sincerely incapable of understanding that to denounce mudslinging does not mean the indorsement of whitewashing; and both the interested individuals who need whitewashing and those others who practise mudslinging like to encourage such confusion of ideas. One of the chief counts against those who make indiscriminate assault upon men in business or men in public life is that they invite a reaction which is sure to tell powerfully in favor of the unscrupulous scoundrel who really ought to be attacked, who ought to be exposed, who ought, if possible, to be put in the penitentiary. If Aristides is praised overmuch as just, people get tired of hearing it; and overcensure of the unjust finally and from similar reasons results in their favor.

Any excess is almost sure to invite a reaction; and, unfortunately, the reaction, instead of taking the form of punishment of those guilty of the excess, is very apt to take the form either of punishment of the unoffending or of giving immunity, and even strength, to offenders. The effort to make financial or political profit out of the destruction of character can only result in public calamity. Gross and reckless assaults on character—whether on the stump or in newspaper, magazine or book—create a morbid and vicious public sentiment, and at the same time act as a profound deterrent to able men of normal sensitiveness and tend to prevent them from entering the public service at any price. As an instance in point, I may mention that one serious difficulty encountered in getting the right type of men to dig the Panama Canal is the certainty that they will be exposed, both without, and, I am sorry to say, sometimes within, Congress, to utterly reckless assaults on their character and capacity.

At the risk of repetition let me say again that my plea is, not for immunity to, but for the most unsparing exposure of, the politician who betrays his trust, of the big business-man who makes or spends his fortune in illegitimate or corrupt ways. There should be a resolute effort to hunt every such man out of the position he has disgraced. Expose the crime and hunt down the criminal; but remember that even in the case of crime, if it is attacked in sensational, lurid and untruthful fashion, the attack may do more damage to the public mind than the crime itself. It is because I feel that there should be no rest in the endless war against the forces of evil that I ask that the war be conducted with sanity as well as with resolution. The men with the muck-rakes are often indispensable to the well-being of society, but only if they know when to stop raking the muck, and to look upward to the celestial crown above them, to the crown of worthy endeavor. There are beautiful things above and round about them; and if they gradually grow to feel that the whole world is nothing but muck their power of usefulness is gone. If the whole picture is painted black there remains no hue whereby to single out the rascals for distinction from their fellows. Such painting finally induces a kind of moral color blindness; and people affected by it come to the conclusion that no man is really black and no man really white, but they are all gray. In other words, they neither believe in the truth of the attack nor in the honesty of the man who is attacked; they grow as suspicious of the accusation as of the offence; it becomes well-nigh hopeless to stir them either to wrath against wrongdoing or to enthusiasm for what is right; and such a mental attitude in the public gives hope to every knave, and is the despair of honest men.

To assail the great and admitted evils of our political and industrial life with such crude and sweeping generalizations as to include decent men in the general condemnation means the searing of the public conscience. There results a general attitude either of cynical belief in and indifference to public corruption or else of a distrustful inability to discriminate between the good and the bad. Either attitude is fraught with untold damage to the country as a whole. The fool who has not sense to discriminate between what is good and what is bad is well-nigh as dangerous as the man who does discriminate and yet chooses the bad. There is nothing more distressing to every good patriot, to every good American, than the hard, scoffing spirit which treats the allegation of dishonesty in a public man as a cause for laughter. Such laughter is worse than the crackling of thorns under a pot, for it denotes not merely the vacant mind, but the heart in which high emotions have been choked before they could grow to fruition.

There is any amount of good in the world, and there never was a time when loftier and more disinterested work for the betterment of mankind was being done than now. The forces that tend for evil are great and terrible, but the forces of truth and love and courage and honesty and generosity and sympathy are also stronger than ever before. It is a foolish and timid no less than a wicked thing to blink the fact that the forces of evil are strong, but it is even worse to fail to take into account the strength of the forces that tell for good. Hysterical sensationalism is the very poorest weapon wherewith to fight for lasting righteousness. The men who with stern sobriety and truth assail the many evils of our time, whether in the public press, or in magazines, or in books, are the leaders and allies of all engaged in the work for social and political betterment. But if they give good

reason for distrust of what they say, if they chill the ardor
of those who demand truth as a primary virtue, they thereby
betray the good cause and play into the hands of the very
men against whom they are nominally at war.

In his *Ecclesiastical Polity* that fine old Elizabethan
divine, Bishop Hooker, wrote:

"He that goeth about to persuade a multitude that they
are not so well governed as they ought to be, shall never
want attentive and favorable hearers; because they know the
manifold defects whereunto every kind of regimen is subject, but the secret lets and difficulties, which in public proceedings are innumerable and inevitable, they have not ordi-
narily the judgment to consider."

This truth should be kept constantly in mind by every
free people desiring to preserve the sanity and poise indispensable to the permanent success of self-government. Yet,
on the other hand, it is vital not to permit this spirit of
sanity and self-command to degenerate into mere mental
stagnation. Bad though a state of hysterical excitement is,
and evil though the results are which come from the violent
oscillations such excitement invariably produces, yet a sodden
acquiescence in evil is even worse. At this moment we are
passing through a period of great unrest—social, political and
industrial unrest. It is of the utmost importance for our
future that this should prove to be not the unrest of mere
rebelliousness against life, of mere dissatisfaction with the
inevitable inequality of conditions, but the unrest of a resolute and eager ambition to secure the betterment of the
individual and the nation. So far as this movement of agita-
tion throughout the country takes the form of a fierce discontent with evil, of a determination to punish the authors
of evil, whether in industry or politics, the feeling is to be
heartily welcomed as a sign of healthy life.

If, on the other hand, it turns into a mere crusade of
appetite against appetite, of a contest between the brutal
greed of the "have-nots" and the brutal greed of the "haves,"

then it has no significance for good, but only for evil. If it seeks to establish a line of cleavage, not along the line which divides good men from bad, but along that other line, running at right angles thereto, which divides those who are well off from those who are less well off, then it will be fraught with immeasurable harm to the body politic.

We can no more and no less afford to condone evil in the man of capital than evil in the man of no capital. The wealthy man who exults because there is a failure of justice in the effort to bring some trust magnate to an account for his misdeeds is as bad as, and no worse than, the so-called labor leader who clamorously strives to excite a foul class feeling on behalf of some other labor leader who is implicated in murder. One attitude is as bad as the other, and no worse; in each case the accused is entitled to exact justice; and in neither case is there need of action by others which can be construed into an expression of sympathy for crime.

It is a prime necessity that if the present unrest is to result in permanent good the emotion shall be translated into action, and that the action shall be marked by honesty, sanity and self-restraint. There is mighty little good in a mere spasm of reform. The reform that counts is that which comes through steady, continuous growth; violent emotionalism leads to exhaustion.

It is important to this people to grapple with the problems connected with the amassing of enormous fortunes, and the use of those fortunes, both corporate and individual, in business. We should discriminate in the sharpest way between fortunes well won and fortunes ill won; between those gained as an incident to performing great services to the community as a whole, and those gained in evil fashion by keeping just within the limits of mere law-honesty. Of course no amount of charity in spending such fortunes in any way compensates for misconduct in making them. As a matter of personal conviction, and without pretending to discuss the details or formulate the system, I feel that we shall ultimately have to consider the adoption of some such scheme as that of a progressive tax on all fortunes, beyond a certain amount, either given in life or devised or bequeathed upon death to any individual—a tax so framed as to put it out of the power of the owner of one of these enormous fortunes to hand on more than a certain amount to any one individual; the tax, of course, to be imposed by the national and not the state government. Such taxation should, of course, be aimed merely at the inheritance or transmission in their entirety of those fortunes swollen beyond all healthy limits.

Again, the national government must in some form exercise supervision over corporations engaged in interstate business—and all large corporations are engaged in interstate business—whether by license or otherwise, so as to permit us to deal with the far-reaching evils of over-capitalization. This year we are making a beginning in the direction of serious effort to settle some of these economic problems by the railway rate legislation. Such legislation, if so framed, as I am sure it will be, as to secure definite and tangible results, will amount to something of itself; and it will amount to a great deal more in so far as it is taken as a first step in the direction of a policy of superintendence and control over corporate wealth engaged in interstate commerce, this superintendence and control not to be exercised in a spirit of malevolence toward the men who have created the wealth, but with the firm purpose both to do justice to them and to see that they in their turn do justice to the public at large.

The first requisite in the public servants who are to deal in this shape with corporations, whether as legislators or as executives, is honesty. This honesty can be no respecter of persons. There can be no such thing as unilateral honesty. The danger is not really from corrupt corporations; it springs from the corruption itself, whether exercised for or against corporations.

The eighth commandment reads, "Thou shalt not steal." It does not read, "Thou shalt not steal from the rich man." It does not read, "Thou shalt not steal from the poor man." It reads simply and plainly, "Thou shalt not steal." No good whatever will come from that warped and mock morality which denounces the misdeeds of men of wealth and forgets the misdeeds practiced at their expense; which denounces bribery, but blinds itself to blackmail; which foams with rage if a corporation secures favors by improper methods, but merely leers with hideous mirth if the corporation is itself wronged. The only public servant who can be trusted honestly to protect the rights of the public against the misdeed of a corporation is that public man who will just as surely protect the corporation itself from wrongful aggression. If a public man is willing to yield to popular clamor and do wrong to the men of wealth or to rich corporations, it may be set down as certain that if the opportunity comes he will secretly and furtively do wrong to the public in the interest of a corporation.

But, in addition to honesty, we need sanity. No honesty will make a public man useful if that man is timid or foolish, if he is a hot-headed zealot or an impracticable visionary. As we strive for reform we find that it is not at all merely the case of a long uphill pull. On the contrary, there is almost as much of breeching work as of collar work; to depend only on traces means that there will soon be a runaway and an upset. The men of wealth who today are trying to prevent the regulation and control of their business in the interest of the public by the proper government authorities will not succeed, in my judgment, in checking the progress of the movement. But if they did succeed they would find that they had sown the wind and would surely reap the whirlwind, for they ultimately provoke the violent excesses which accompany a reform coming by convulsion instead of by steady and natural growth.

On the other hand, the wild preachers of unrest and discontent, the wild agitators against the entire existing order, the men who act crookedly, whether because of sinister design or from mere puzzleheadedness, the men who preach destruction without proposing any substitute for what they intend to destroy, or who propose a substitute which would be far worse than the existing evils—all these men are the most dangerous opponents of real reform. If they get their way they will lead the people into a deeper pit than any into which they could fall under the present system. If they fail to get their way they will still do incalculable harm by provoking the kind of reaction which in its revolt against the senseless evil of their teaching would enthrone more securely than ever the very evils which their misguided followers believe they are attacking.

More important than aught else is the development of the broadest sympathy of man for man. The welfare of the wage worker, the welfare of the tiller of the soil, upon these depend the welfare of the entire country; their good is not to be sought in pulling down others; but their good must be the prime object of all our statesmanship.

Materially, we must strive to secure a broader economic opportunity for all men, so that each shall have a better chance to show the stuff of which he is made. Spiritually and ethically we must strive to bring about clean living and right thinking. We appreciate that the things of the body are important; but we appreciate also that the things of the soul are immeasurably more important. The foundation stone of national life is, and ever must be, the high individual character of the average citizen.

APPENDIX B

The Senate's Response: Joseph W. Bailey
on "The Treason of the Senate"

ON June 27, 1906, Senator Joseph W. Bailey, Democrat from
Texas and acting minority leader, delivered on the Senate
floor a major criticism of "The Treason of the Senate." Because it was the only attempt by a Senator to controvert
Phillips's charges directly and specifically, and because it was
indicative of the Senate's approach to the questions raised by
Phillips, Bailey's speech is reprinted here in its entirety (from
the *Congressional Record*, 59th Congress, 1st Session, Vol. XL).

MR. BAILEY. Mr. President, to be misunderstood by some
good men and to be misrepresented by many bad men is a
penalty which every man must pay for actively participating
in the politics of this free Republic; and it would be worse
than a waste of time for any Senator to answer all of the
unfounded and malicious charges which may be circulated
against him. I am, moreover, inclined to believe that the rule
pursued by nearly all public men of making no answer to
any charge is the wiser one, because if some are answered
and others are left unanswered the very fact that an answer

has been made to some and not to others will be used as an evidence that the unanswered ones are true. For this reason an answer must be made to all or to none; and as any man would make himself ridiculous by asking the public to listen while he corrects every story which the ingenuity of personal and political malevolence may invent, the only safe rule is to trust an intelligent public to judge him by what he says and does without reference to what he is charged with having done or said. But the fact that the publication which contains the false and offensive matter to which I object is owned by a Member of Congress seems to take this case out of the general rule and to demand the answer which I am about to make.

I shall not deal with this as a matter personal to me, because it is of a kind which, if dealt with in that way, would require a different place. Indeed, if I considered it purely and only from a personal point of view, I would not regard it as worthy of any notice; for nothing which this magazine can say will injure me with my constituents or in the estimation of those with whom I have served in either House of Congress. But, Mr. President, I can not free myself from the belief that I owe it to the American people to show them what manner of men these are who are striving to destroy popular faith in the integrity of all public servants.

Several months ago the Cosmopolitan Magazine, which I am informed was up to that time a reputable publication, fell into financial difficulties, and was sold to WILLIAM R. HEARST. As I state this upon information and not upon my own knowledge, I think it proper to lay before the Senate the facts as they were furnished to me by a gentleman familiar with the transaction. In a letter to me upon the subject that gentleman says:

The proposition to sell being satisfactory to the creditors, negotiations were entered into with W. R. HEARST, who agreed to buy the magazine. HEARST was represented in the arrangement of the sale by one Carvalho.

The purchase price agreed on was $500,000. Instead of paying this sum in cash, HEARST organized a dummy corporation to take over this magazine, and called it the "International Magazine Company," he (HEARST) personally guaranteeing the bonds that were issued in settlement of the outstanding debts and over that of a sum up to the purchase price. The creditors and Walker accepted the bonds of this International Magazine Company at par. They are five-year bonds, drawing interest at the rate of 5 per cent, payable semiannually.

Immediately following this change of ownership this magazine announced a series of sensational articles entitled "The Treason of the Senate." As those articles were deliberately planned and widely advertised, the public had a right to expect that they would be written with scrupulous care and a due regard for truth and justice; but so far from meeting this reasonable expectation, they have been so manifestly designed to prejudice, rather than inform the public, that intelligent men have laid them aside in absolute disgust. Some readers of less intelligence, however, are inclined to believe them, and I have already heard of some shallow and inflammable minds who support them with the argument that if they were not true they would have been denied. For the sake of the men who desire to know the truth and who would not do even their political enemies an injustice, I have determined to expose the reckless mendacity of the man who writes these articles.

I do not, of course, feel at liberty to refer to what he has said about other Senators, because I must respect their determination to pass his attacks on them in silence, and I am therefore driven to the necessity of using the article in which he slanders me. But before proceeding with that, I feel myself warranted in saying a word about one who was grossly abused, and who was not here then, and who can never be here again to speak in his own defense. While Senator Gorman was confined to his home by the sickness which terminated in his death, he was made the object of a bitter arraignment and pursued even beyond the grave, for in his last article this writer renews his miserable aspersions upon the dead Senator.

It has been observed by every intelligent man who has read these articles that the basic charge which runs through them all is that Democratic and Republican Senators are acting together in a secret agreement, and the unsuspecting reader is asked to believe that this secret agreement is carried out behind closed doors and in committee rooms. It was necessary to impress this view upon the public in order to give the articles even an appearance of the truth, because if it had been said that the Democrats and Republicans cooperate in the open Senate, the CONGRESSIONAL RECORD would completely and overwhelmingly refute that charge. It was therefore necessary to first imbue the public mind with the belief that Senators acted one way in the secrecy of the committee room and another way in the open Senate. In accordance with this line of appeal to the suspicions of the people this writer has selected as a special instance to illustrate and establish that charge, the tariff act of 1894 commonly known as the "Wilson bill." He declares, and in order that there may be no mistake about it, I will read exactly what he says:

As usual, ALDRICH and GORMAN retired to their Finance Committee with the tariff bill—as the Senate was "Democratic," Gorman had taken the chairmanship of the committee and the leadership of the Senate that goes with it, and Aldrich had become nominal second in command. All the mischief, all the treachery that was put into that bill in the secrecy of that committee by those slippery twins will never be known; it is impossible for anyone not in on the secret to grasp the effect of the sly amendments slipped in here and there.

If the man who wrote that statement had sincerely desired to know the truth, he could have learned it with very little trouble; and if he had been seeking to enlighten those who read his articles, he would not have misled them with a statement like that. Whether he knows the facts and deliberately misstated them, or whether he merely pretended to know them when he did not, he is equally unworthy of belief.

Mr. President, when the Wilson bill was under consideration in the Senate, Senator Gorman was not the chairman of the Finance Committee. Indeed, sir, Senator Gorman was not even a member of that committee at that time, nor was he ever a member of it until within the last three years. What must fair-minded men think of a writer who charges that a Senator abused a position in the face of the official record which shows that he did not occupy the position which he is charged with having abused?

Every man who knows anything about tariff legislation knows perfectly well that for many years the practice has been that the majority members of the Committee on Ways and Means in the House of Representatives first make the tariff bill, and only submit it to the full committee after they have completed it. The minority is then permitted to read it and to criticise it; but they are not permitted to change it. The majority being responsible for the bill, make it to suit themselves and take their responsibility before the country. The same course of procedure is followed in the Senate, and neither Senator ALDRICH nor any other Republican Senator was permitted to even see the amendments to the Wilson tariff bill which were agreed upon by the Democratic majority until after they had finished their work. I do not complain that all men do not understand how tariff bills are made, because many good men have not taken the trouble to inform themselves in that respect; but when a man assumes to explain to the people how any particular bill was made he imposes upon himself the double duty of learning the truth and telling it.

Coming to the article in the last issue of this magazine, in which he assails my reputation and public services, he is guilty of even more vicious misrepresentations, if possible, than those he made about Senator Gorman. While he ought to have examined the official list of the Senate committees before attempting to name the chairman of the most important one, he may not have done so, and his misrepre-

sentation, though inexcusable, may not have been intentional. No such extenuation, however, can be offered for his
misrepresentation in respect to me, because he read the record
which he distinctly misrepresents in some particulars and deliberately suppresses in others. His first accusation against me
relates to a matter which was thoroughly investigated by the
very legislature which elected me to the Senate, and it was
shown to be so entirely unjust and absurd that the decent
men among my most implacable enemies in Texas no longer
discuss it. In order that the Senate and the country may understand how palpably and how grossly he has misrepresented
that episode, I must be pardoned while I briefly recall it.
In 1897 or 1898 a foreign corporation then transacting business in our State was convicted of violating that section of our
antitrust law which prohibits exclusive contracts, and its
permit was revoked. In the spring of 1900 that judgment
was affirmed by the Supreme Court of the United States, and
the officers of that corporation then sought to settle with the
State by offering to pay whatever penalty might be considered
a proper punishment, provided that they could continue their
business in Texas. I was asked to intercede in their behalf,
and, upon the distinct and positive assurance that the company
was an independent one and not controlled by any trust, I
advised our State officials to permit it, upon the payment of
a fine commensurate with its offense, to continue its business
in Texas.

The attorney-general, who was a college mate of mine
and a true man in every sense, submitted to me the judgment
of the court, and expressed the opinion that he could not,
under the terms of that judgment, consent to such a settle-
ment. After carefully examining the judgment I concurred
in his opinion, and advised that the only lawful course was
to dissolve the offending corporation and organize a new one,
but that advice was given upon the understanding that when
the new corporation came into the State it should obey our
laws. Immediately after that conversation I returned to Wash-

ington, and knew absolutely nothing further about the transaction until I read an attack upon the attorney-general in
respect to it, when immediately and without the slightest
hesitation I defended him, and avowed my responsibility by
stating what I had advised. As so often happens in the bitter-
ness of political strife, the circumstance was seized upon and
magnified in many ways, and it was charged that I had received a fee ranging from $50,000 to $500,000, according to
the imagination of the relater. Finally one man, who was more
reckless than the rest and who happened to be a member of
the Texas legislature, introduced a resolution directing an
inquiry into my connection with the case. Every friend of
mine in that legislature, with a single exception, would have
voted against that resolution except for my earnest insistence.
They contended—and they were right—that there was nothing
in the matter which called for an investigation. They pointed
out the fact that it was not contended that the matter was
connected in the remotest degree with the legislation of Congress, and could not therefore by any possibility involve my
official or personal integrity. To all of this my answer was
that if the resolution were defeated the lies would multiply and
some honest men would be misled into the belief that an inquiry would have revealed some misconduct on my part, and
at last my friends in the legislature yielded to my view of the
matter and voted for the investigation. A committee was appointed, consisting of four gentlemen who had supported me in
my race for the Senate and three who had supported my opponent. That committee unanimously reported to the legislature
exonerating me and our State officers from every shadow of an
imputation.

Mr. President, it was a case in which there could have been
no wrong. Had I chosen to accept employment in that case, I
had a perfect right to do so, and I desire the Senate to know
that I did not leave that question the subject of any doubt in
the minds of that legislature. I told the committee in no spirit
of defiance, but merely as a matter of proper self-respect, that

I had a right to do all that I was accused of doing; and I will read to the Senate what I said to that committee of the legislature. Here it is:

> I desire to have it understood in this connection that had I known that the Waters-Pierce Oil Company would be compelled to dissolve and resort to a legal reincorporation and that they would be pursued in the courts, I would not have hesitated one second about accepting employment from it and taking a fee, provided my labor as their attorney had not taken me from public duties in Washington.
>
> There could not have been the slightest question about my right to accept a fee to defend them in the courts so long as I believed that they were willing to obey our laws. There could not have been any possibility of their case coming before the body of which I was a member, and therefore neither my vote nor my official conduct could have influenced the decision of it, nor been influenced by their employment of me.
>
> I am a lawyer, and I sincerely hope that I will never be such a political coward as to fear to defend any man or any business when I think their rights are assailed unjustly or with unnecessary severity. Neither am I such a fool as to really want to keep a legitimate business out of the State, nor such a demagogue as to pretend that I do.

With that statement before them, the committee, in the first instance, and the legislature, in the second instance, unanimously exonerated me from any misconduct.

Mr. President, the first misstatement in this magazine article relates to this—no, not the first misstatement, but the first misstatement in it which refers to my public service, relates to this very question of the investigation before the legislature. The writer of this article says:

> McFall (. . . the member of the legislature who had introduced the resolution of inquiry . . .), however, on January 17, submitted an affidavit to the committee. He rehearsed the facts of the Waters-Pierce ejectment from the State and charged—
> "That by reason of BAILEY's influence and personal and political popularity and prestige, they (the Waters-Pierce Company) were enabled by a mere sham of dissolution and reincorporation to continue in business in Texas.

"That the said JOSEPH W. BAILEY did, on or about May 2, 1900, accompany H. C. Pierce, president of the Waters-Pierce Oil Company, to Waco for the purpose of holding a consultation with the county attorney of McLennan County, with a view of compromising said suits (the suits were for $105,000 in fines); that the proposition of compromise by said Pierce was $10,000 to the State in full of her claims and the payment of $3,500 to the county attorney as an extra fee for advising the compromise; and that the said BAILEY indorsed said proposition and urged its acceptance."

Mr. President, the Senate has observed that this magazine writer declares that statement to be an affidavit. But any man who has the curiosity to look into the matter will find on page 137 of the house journal of the legislature of Texas, under date of January 21, 1901, the statement from which this magazine quotation is made, and there is not a semblance of an oath to support it.

I attach no particular importance to whether the statement was sworn to or not, because my observation leads me to believe that any man who will tell a lie will swear to it if he thinks it is safe to do so; but I am amazed to learn that a man who pretends to write so carefully as this magazine writer would have us believe he does, not only prints a naked allegation and describes it as an affidavit, but then suppresses a statement in the same report which shows that the man who is said to have made the affidavit declared to the chairman of the committee from his sick bed that he did not know a single fact or circumstance to sustain even that weak charge.

When the man who introduced this resolution was summoned by the committee to appear and sustain his charge, he retired to his home and went to bed, and instead of coming to answer the committee he sent day after day a doctor's certificate that he was unable to come. The committee finally instructed its chairman to go to his home and ascertain whether or not he was really sick. If he were not sick, then they would bring him to the Capitol, and if he were sick and still not too sick to testify they would go to his house and take his statement under oath. In obedience to the committee's instruction, the chairman repaired to the residence of this witness, and here is what the witness told the chairman to say to the committee and what the committee embodied in its report:

> After the committee adjourned at noon on the 17th instant the chairman, the Hon. S. J. Hendrick, visited the Hon. D. A. McFall at the home of the latter, to ascertain how soon Mr. McFall would be able to appear before the committee and to testify, and the chairman reported to the full committee that Mr. McFall had requested him to say that it would be useless for the committee to prolong its session for the purpose of awaiting his evidence, because he could not swear to any fact or circumstance that would tend to establish the charges.

Mark you, Mr. President; the committee did not leave him to say whether he could swear to *any fact which would establish the charge,* but they put the question to him, as they had put it to other witnesses, if he knew any fact *or circumstance* which would *tend to establish the charge,* and his answer was that he did not. Yet this magazine writer incorporates the unsupported and unsworn statement of McFall in this article, and describes it as an "affidavit," concealing the fact that the same legislative record from which he took it contained the statement which I have just read in the hearing of the Senate.

This writer next declares, Mr. President, that there was a serious question in the legislature about my exoneration, and he says the final vote was 73 to 41. The final vote on the resolution, it is true, was 73 to 41, but stated in that way it is as misleading as a direct and positive falsehood would be. The truth about it is this: The committee made two reports, a majority report signed by six and a minority report signed by one. But both reports exonerated me and the State officials from all shadow of blame.

The difference was that the majority report, in addition to its exoneration of me, contained a resolution denouncing the liars—some of them were in that legislature—while the minority report, joining the majority in its exoneration of me, protested against the resolution denouncing the men who had calumniated me and the State officials. That was the only difference.

In the same report which this man read—I assume that he read it because he quotes from it, and if he did not read it he is that much more reckless in his work—he found this statement. After the majority report was submitted, they moved to substitute the minority, and on that motion the first vote was taken. Perhaps it is better that I should read the majority and the minority reports. I will not detain the Senate, of course, by reading the entire reports. The majority report concludes in this way:

Whereas the committee of the House of Representatives, appointed to investigate the charges against the Hon. J. W. BAILEY and certain State officials in connection with the readmission of the Waters-Pierce Oil Company into this State, have performed their duty; and

Whereas by the most diligent inquiry they have not been able to find a single fact or circumstance discreditable either to the Hon. J. W. BAILEY or to any State official, but, on the contrary, all of the evidence before said committee completely and overwhelmingly exonerates the Hon. J. W. BAILEY and all State officials from the charges of misconduct: Therefore, be it

Resolved by the house of representatives, That we denounce the malicious imputations and insinuations against the integrity of the Hon. J. W. BAILEY and our State officials as the most cruel, vindictive, and unfounded attack ever made upon the character of a faithful public servant in Texas.

The minority report begins as follows:

We, the minority of your committee appointed under the resolution introduced by the Hon. D. A. McFall, and adopted by the house on January 11, 1901, providing for the investigation of the facts relating to the dissolution and reincorporation of the Waters-Pierce Oil Company, its admission to do business in Texas, etc., agree to all the report of the majority, except wherein they recommend to the house the adoption of the proposed resolution.

There was absolutely no difference, Mr. President, between the majority and the minority upon the question of my exoneration. The only controversy was as to the denunciation of the men who had instigated the political assault. Upon the motion to substitute the minority for the majority report the vote stood 44 to 70. The minority report was thus rejected, and the vote came upon the adoption of the majority report. The gentlemen who voted against it were the same gentlemen, with one exception, who had already voted for the minority report. I want to read to the Senate some reasons which were given by gentlemen who supported the minority report:

We vote for the minority report of the BAILEY investigating committee for the reason that we believe that it as fully exonerates Mr. BAILEY and any State officials as does the majority report, and casts no insinuations on the motives of any citizen of Texas who may have criticised the readmission of the Waters-Pierce Oil Company into Texas to do business, and who have questioned the propriety of Mr. BAILEY's connection therewith. . . .

There were statements by other members of the legislature to the same effect, and so it is that when this writer says there was a serious division in the legislature of Texas over my exoneration he deliberately attempts to deceive the public.

He says:

BAILEY was elected Senator on the same day.

But he omits to say that I received 137 votes in that legislature, while only 6 were cast against me, and he omits also to say that after six years, during which this matter has been discussed until decent men have become disgusted with it, my next election to the Senate is as certain and will be as unanimous as the first.

But he says that all of this has happened because we have a political machine in Texas. He presumes upon the ignorance of the people who may read this article as to political conditions in Texas. It is the one Commonwealth of the Union in which a political machine has never yet been constructed, and in which a political machine could never endure. And amongst all the men who have taken part in the politics of that great State, no one is more exempt from the charge of being a machine candidate than I was then or than I am now.

Mr. President, I never in my life organized a committee to promote my election to any office. No man ever contributed a dollar to secure either my nomination or my election. More than that, when I was a candidate for the Senate I appealed directly to the people. My demand was that in every county my candidacy and that of my opponent should be submitted to a direct vote in the primary, and that course prevailed in nearly every county. I canvassed that State for one month— as I now recall it, exactly one month—and I spent in that race for the Senate less than one month's salary.

I happen to remember it well. When I learned that my opponent had withdrawn I was at the depot in the town of Smithville, and my friends were congratulating me upon the cessation of the contest. One man said it would save me a great deal of work and a good deal of money. Another gentleman who stood by said it would save me a good deal of work, but it would not save me any money, because I was one of the kind that do not spend money in elections. After some little banter between the two, this friend asked me how much I had spent. I said that I left Washington with exactly one month's salary; and to settle their dispute I examined my book and found that I still had a $20 bill left with some change in my pocket. Less than one month's salary in a Senatorial contest during which I canvassed the State for an entire month!

Mr. President, I was five times elected to the House of Representatives; I have been once elected to the Senate; and I have spent less money in all those elections than the man who owns this magazine spent, perhaps, in a single ward when he was a candidate for mayor in the city of New York. His sworn return shows, according to the papers, that he spent over $60,000 in that contest. That is forty times as much as I ever spent in politics in all my life, and yet he talks about my machine and corrupt political methods. It is a matter of great satisfaction to me to say that there could be no surer way of inviting defeat in the State of Texas than for a man to use his money or to organize his machine.

Mr. President, if I needed any help in Texas this article would have contributed it. It so happens that every time it touches any question which relates to that State it is so obviously incorrect that even if what else it said about me had been true the people of Texas would not believe it, because, knowing that everything was false about which they possessed personal knowledge, they would naturally conclude that everything else was false.

The next specification which this magazine writer makes against me is entitled "The Indian Territory grab." Here is its first sentence:

Last April, when a huge Indian Territory coal, timber, and oil grab was on its stealthy way through the traitor Senate, under the auspices of the "merger," and under cover of fake railway-rate bill excitement, it was LA FOLLETTE, a new Senator from far-away Wisconsin, who exposed it.

Before the distinguished Senator from Wisconsin became a member of the Senate I had gone before the Committee on Indian Affairs and had urged that these mineral lands still belonging to the Indians should be reserved from sale and consecrated to the education of the children in that country. I said the same to the Senator from Wisconsin.

I do not sanction the statement that the provision which the Indian Affairs Committee brought into the Senate was a steal. I think that provision was supported by men as honest as the Senator from Wisconsin or I, but I do believe that it was an unwise disposition of those lands, and therefore I resisted it and throughout the contest over it I was cooperating with the Senator from Wisconsin. If he stopped a steal, I helped him, and I ask the Senator from Wisconsin to rise in his place and say whether or not we cooperated in that matter.

Mr. LA FOLLETTE. Mr. President, I take great pleasure in saying that I conferred with the Senator from Texas (Mr. BAILEY) before I offered any amendment or took part in any discussion in opposition to the sale or the disposal in any manner of the coal lands in the Indian Territory, and that I received from him valuable suggestions, advice, and cooperation in whatever I did or undertook to do with respect to those lands.

Mr. BAILEY. Mr. President, that is precisely the manly statement which I would expect from the Senator. We thoroughly agreed not only upon that, but upon other matters, to which I now desire to call the attention of the Senate.

Further on in this same paragraph this writer says:

And the amendment, which made it possible for home seekers to buy Indian lands, but impossible for corrupt corporations to grab them, was killed on a point of order.

Here, again, I was cooperating with the Senator from Wisconsin. The only difference between him and me was that he wanted those lands disposed of under the supervision of the Secretary of the Interior, in whose wisdom, I will say, he has more confidence than I have. I do not doubt the honesty of the Secretary of the Interior. If I had ever doubted it, he has done all that is necessary to remove that doubt. But I have always found that he was looking more after the Indians in the Indian Territory than the white population there. Perhaps that was his duty as Secretary of the Interior. But for years I have acted upon the theory that that was a white man's country, and that the law designed to preserve the Indian would tie the hands and retard the progress of the white man. That was the only difference between the Senator from Wisconsin and myself.

The difference between me and other Senators who insisted upon the point of order and opposed the amendment was, and only was, that they felt that if the restriction on alienation was continued the value of the land would greatly enhance, the benefit of which the Indian would obtain. My difference with them was simply this: That the lands would enhance in value enormously, but the Indian would not get the benefit of it, because in the meantime others would use and occupy it at a nominal rent; and believing that the Indian would not get the benefit in the end, I advocated the immediate sale of those lands, so that the present tenants in the Indian Territory might purchase it and become home owners. If any Senator or any citizen chooses to examine the CONGRESSIONAL RECORD of the 27th and 28th of April he will find that for two hours I stood on the floor of the Senate and plead for the privilege of those tenants there to buy this land now, and I warned the Senate that if these restrictions on its alienation were continued, the land would so greatly enhance in price that when the Indians could sell it a poor man would be unable to buy it. That was the argument I made from beginning to end.

Again, Mr. President, this writer says, under the caption of "Indian Territory grab":

> On the other hand, the CONGRESSIONAL RECORD so full of surprises for the careful reader, reveals that BAILEY has been, in his fourteen years at Washington, one of the chief introducers of Indian Territory railway and land bills—bills granting rights of way to railways, bills renewing, extending, and broadening charters.

He then proceeds to give a list of the bills of that character which I have introduced. It would not be singular if I had introduced more bills affecting the Indian Territory than any other Senator or Member. I live within 7 miles of the border line between the Indian Territory and Texas. That Territory has no Representative or Delegate in Congress. It has no Senator in this body. If bills are introduced permitting its development, Senators and Representatives from other states must introduce them. And yet, Mr. President, I was always careful about introducing any bill relating to the Indian Territory, and the RECORD shows what this magazine conceals, that I introduced every bill it enumerates, with a single exception, by request, and they were marked "by request," thus disavowing all responsibility for it. When a citizen of my State sends me a bill and asks me to introduce it, if I have time to examine it and it commends itself to my judgment, I introduce it on my own responsibility. But if I do not have the time to examine it, or if after examining it I do not approve it, I do as every other careful Senator and Representative does—I mark it "by request."

Mr. President, the only bill in this list which I did not introduce by request was for the Gainesville, McAlester and St. Louis Railroad. That was a corporation organized by the most reputable business men in the town where I live, for the purpose of building a railroad from my home to the coal fields of the Indian Territory. I know every man connected with it, and I was so thoroughly and heartily in sympathy with the project that I would have been one of the incorporators except for the fact that being a member of Congress it was necessary for me to obtain the charter, and for that reason I was unwilling to have even a nominal connection with it. Can any man believe that a sound-minded Senator or Representative would refuse to introduce a bill which allowed his own people to build a railroad that would bring cheap fuel to his neighbors? Fuel is an important item in the prairie country of northern Texas, and a Representative who would not have proposed a proper bill enabling his neighbors and his constituents to lighten their fuel cost would have been recreant to their best interests and to his plain duty.

Again, this man says:

All the measures introduced by BAILEY looked well enough; no doubt many of them were harmless enough in and of themselves; no doubt many of them might have been most beneficent if properly investigated and freed of all sly looting schemes.

In this article he testifies to the integrity and efficiency of the Secretary of the Interior, and perhaps it will console him to know that every one of those bills was referred to the Interior Department before it was even reported favorably by any committee, and if they were not properly "freed from looting schemes" the fault lies with the Secretary of the Interior, to whom the writer gives a certificate of high character. The Secretary of the Interior is one of the few men whom he praises, and that moves me to suspect that the Secretary of the Interior is one of the few men who do not stand in the way of somebody's ambition.

The next charge against me is that I spent some of the present session in discussing "the fake railroad rate bill." I will not insult the intelligence of the American people by answering that grave charge. It is rather a high compliment to me that after five months of diligent quest they have found no more serious charges than these. They have raked the gutters from Houston, Tex., to New York, coming by way of Lexington, Ky., and not forgetting the horse-training stables there, and the end of it is a feeble attempt to infer some wrong.

He makes another charge. He says I was opposed to the pure-food bill, and here is the way he testifies to my constituents that I was right:

The Gorman, or the so-called "Democratic" gang reaches the same end of protecting the plutocracy by the way so long used by and for the antebellum slavocracy.

That is a mild appeal to the dead prejudices of the North; but it will affect nobody except some one who is so simple-minded as to believe what he finds in the Cosmopolitan Magazine. This writer then adds:

The Constitution must be *strictly* interpreted; the rights of the States must not be violated!

And he puts an exclamation mark there, as if to evidence his abhorrence of such a doctrine. Mr. President, whether it was used by what he calls the "slavocracy" or not, I cheerfully range myself upon the side of the men who believe in a strict construction of the Constitution and in a sound defense of the doctrine of States rights, and I welcome him, as I welcome every man, to make all the capital against me he can out of that circumstance.

It will surprise some people to know that this is the sum of all that was said about my public career or in reference to my political connection in an article which for five long months has been advertised as a coming sensation. He says some other things about my business and professional career to which I make no reply. He says that I practice law successfully, in that I make money. If he will ask my clients, he will also find that I have practiced law successfully in the way of protecting their interests. If that is a crime, it is time the country should know it. Mr. President, I despise those public men who think they must remain poor in order to be considered honest. I am not one of them. If my constituents want a man who is willing to go to the poorhouse in his old age in order to stay in the Senate during his middle age, they will have to find another Senator. I intend to make every dollar that I can honestly make, without neglecting or interfering with my public duty; and there is no other man in this country who would not do the same, if he has sense enough to keep a churchyard.

I have been in Congress fourteen years, and the man does not live who can put his finger upon a speech or vote that I have ever made or cast in the interest of my clients and against the interest of my constituents.

This man says himself—I dislike a little to call him as a witness, but surely he will not be deemed a witness partial in my favor—beginning the very second paragraph of his article:

Of course, in the House, in the Senate, and on the stump, BAILEY has spoken as strenuously for people and country as any other politician.

No man would be willing to say in the presence of men who know the truth that I have ever spoken one way and voted another. There is the record. It is an open book, four-teen years long, and not a single instance can be found where I have spoken and voted differently.

This man says I speak for country and people. As I vote like I speak, then I must vote for country and people. And yet though I have spoken for country and people and voted for country and people, he asks the men in whose service I work day and night to believe that I have betrayed their interests.

Mr. President, perhaps I owe the Senate and the country an apology for having dignified this screed by noticing it in the Senate. I have done it against the advice of nearly all my friends, but I have done it under a solemn sense of obligation to the public.

I want to say this: It may have been somewhat barbaric, but I believe in the old civilization, under which when a man slandered you you had a right to call him to answer for it. But I recognize that I live in another civilization, which does not permit that course. I want also to say to the country that the very fact that these attacks are permitted to pass unchal-lenged encourages men to make them. They misstate the record. They suppress the truth. Why? Because they feel that the men whom they attack will sit silent under their misrepresentations.

But, Mr. President, it is reassuring, even when we think of this, to remember that they constitute only a small per cent of the magazines and newspapers of the land. As in every neighborhood we find men and women who are banished for their evil habits from decent association, so in the midst of the splendid publications striving to enlighten, uplift, and glorify mankind, we must not despair when we find such as this. They can no more corrupt the mind of the American people than the degenerate amongst men and women can de-grade society.

Even in my most resentful mood against papers and publications like this I have never seen the time when I would abridge the just freedom of the press. I believe that the light ought to beat fiercely on every man who occupies a high position, but in God's name let it be the white light of truth without the taint of yellow in it.

These men do harm, almost unmeasured harm; but they do it in another way, and that other way is this: They slander the upright, and therefore when reputable publications accuse the treacherous the public are incredulous about the charge. No men have ever done the rascals a greater service than those who try to make the people believe that all men are rascals. That creed can never find acceptance in this land, and the only effect of such teaching is that at last the pendulum swings back to the other extreme, and the people conclude that nobody is half as bad as they are painted.

Such publications as this ought to be scourged by decent magazine writers from the company of well-behaved men and women. They ought to be outlawed, as it were, in a literary sense, and left to suffer under the contempt, into which they unjustly sought to bring honest men.

Mr. President, there is one other matter which I wanted to call to the attention of the Senate, but I have almost overlooked it. The day after this article appeared in the magazine, to which Mr. HEARST's name is not attached, there appeared an editorial in the Evening Journal, to which Mr. HEARST's name is attached. It is a double column of mendacity and malice, and yet the only direct averment against my public service is that I have voted to give away the public lands to corporations; and he says that in the face of the RECORD, which shows that I never voted to give an acre of public land to any corporation in my life.

This article is not altogether political; it is a little commercial. Listen to this: And remembering that Mr. HEARST owns the magazine, for whose bonds he stands a guarantor to the extent of $500,000, we can easily understand what interest he has in its financial prosperity. So he tells his readers through his paper:

We believe that a majority of our leading citizens will read Mr. Phillips's entire article for their own information, and we urge them to purchase the July Cosmopolitan and do so.

There is some thrift mixed with a little politics. HEARST's magazine prints a slander against a man, and then HEARST's newspaper advises those who read it to buy the magazine; and this editorial not only appeared in his New York publication, but it appeared in his Chicago one as well.

Mr. President, it is a great temptation for me to say what I think about these people, but that would offend the dignity and propriety of the Senate, and I forbear. (*Applause in the galleries.*)

INDEX